BREAKING THE CHAINS
OF THE
ANCIENT WARRIOR

Tests of Wisdom for Young Martial Artists

by

Dr. Terrence Webster-Doyle

Martial Arts for Peace Association
Atrium Society
Middlebury, Vermont, USA

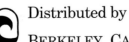 Distributed by NORTH ATLANTIC BOOKS
BERKELEY, CALIFORNIA

Martial Arts for Peace Association
c/o Atrium Society
P.O. Box 816
Middlebury, VT 05753, USA

Cover Design:	*Robert Howard*
Production Coordinator:	*Thomas Funk*
Creative Consultant:	*Jean Webster-Doyle*

Library of Congress Cataloging-in-Publication Data

Webster-Doyle, Terrence
Breaking the chains of the ancient warrior: tests of wisdom for young martial artists /
by Terrence Webster-Doyle
p. cm. — (Martial arts for peace ; 5)
SUMMARY: *Inspirational stories for martial arts students presenting tests of wisdom involving attributes including honor, strength, humility, peaceful conflict resolution, and love.*
Each test contributes to character development.
Audience: For grades 4-9.

ISBN 0-942941-32-2 (pb)
ISBN 0-942941-33-0 (hb)
1. Martial arts—Juvenile fiction.   I. Title. II. Series.
PZ7.W4378Br 1992   [Fic]
QBI94-831
Library of Congress catalog card number: 92-073958

Atrium publications are available at discount for bulk purchases or educational use. Contact Special Sales Director, Atrium Society, (800) 848-6021.

Printed in Hong Kong

Dedication

This book is dedicated to all the young Martial Artists of the world. You are the next generation. It is up to you to learn strength of character from your teachers. Learn to be kind, gentle, brave, and respectful. And, most of all, learn to be intelligent, for intelligence is what is needed to understand and break the chains of the Ancient Warriors.

This book is also dedicated to Sensei John "O."—a friend and colleague who knows that young people need to be taught *values* through the martial arts.

TABLE OF CONTENTS

Foreword by Linda Lee Cadwell
Mastering the Martial Arts Code of Conduct

TESTS OF WISDOM

Breaking the Chains: *The Test of Respect*
Hall of Battle: *The Test of Bravery*
Way of the Golden Dragon: *The Test of Selflessness*
Curse of the Ancient Warrior: *The Test of Honor*
Mind Like Moon: *The Test of Unity*
Gordian Knot: *The Test of Spirit*
Games Martial Arts Masters Play: *The Test of Trust*
Gift of the Moon: *The Test of Charity*
Attacking Nothingness: *The Test of Compassion*
Defeating the Enemy Without Fighting: *The Test of Understanding*
Unbroken Flame of Attention: *The Test of Harmony*
War of the Rose: *The Test of Strength*
Quest for Peace: *The Test of Order*
Fighting the Paper Tiger: *The Test of Focus*
Way of the Sword: *The Test of Excellence*
Beginner's Mind: *The Test of Wisdom*
Faceless Face: *The Test of Purity*
Face of the Enemy: *The Test of Humility*
Bell Ringing in the Empty Sky: *The Test of Love*

To the Young Reader
To the Adult Reader
Questions for Understanding

FOREWORD
Linda Lee Cadwell

Dear Student—

When Bruce Lee began writing articles in the 1960s about his way of martial arts, he was regarded with great skepticism. Thousands of years of martial arts tradition had preceded this young upstart who dared to write,

The classical man is just a bundle of routine, ideas and tradition.
When he acts, he is translating every living moment in terms of the old.

Bruce was branded a non-conformist, a rebel, an iconoclast and a heretic. But over the years, as more of his writings were released, it became clear that he was a thinker beyond his time. Now, 21 years after his death, many of his ideas, both technical and philosophical, are quoted as the source of modern teaching.

Similarly, Dr. Terrence Webster-Doyle dares to break with tradition by telling young people that to live in a peaceful world they must learn to use their intelligence to break the bonds of fear, hate and violence. This is not the usual message delivered in the martial arts studio. A few years ago I heard a story jovially related by a 10th-degree martial arts master about how he was traveling with a group of his students on an airplane. Another passenger was reading a newspaper that the teacher wanted to read. He joked that he told his student to "punch the guy's lights out" and grab the paper. The teacher and the students were so proud of their macho prowess.

Unfortunately this is the prevailing attitude in many martial arts studios. Contrast this story with the evolution of Bruce Lee's life as a martial artist. Bruce began learning Wing Chun Gung Fu in Hong Kong at the age of 13. His goal was to be the best fighter on the streets of Hong Kong, which he achieved in short order. When he came to the United States, Bruce branched out into the study of philosophy and psychology, both Western and Eastern, ancient and modern. Almost by coincidence he began to teach gung fu to a small group of students. He was involved in some physical confrontations, usually with someone who wanted to challenge the new kid on the block. He was always victorious, and his confidence in his combative skills increased. He began to realize that it was not necessary for him to accept confrontations in order to "prove" he could beat someone up.

5

Bruce used his intelligence to become aware of human interactions, and he enjoyed the challenge of employing his psychological self-defense skills to avoid use of violence. One time, for instance, Bruce was having lunch with a business associate and the waiter was inexcusably rude. Bruce just laughed it off and went on with his conversation. The friend was incensed and asked Bruce why, if he was such an expert, didn't he put that guy in his place. Bruce replied that when he woke up that morning it was a beautiful day and he felt great about what he had to do that day, and that there was no way he was going to lower himself to let an obnoxious waiter ruin his day. The episode was over, it was still a great day and the businessman was so impressed he has been retelling that story for 20 years.

Bruce's development from a Hong Kong kid with an attitude to a highly-evolved, self-aware man did not happen overnight. Possessed by the never-ending desire to learn, Bruce was able to focus in-depth on his effort to enhance his knowledge. He exerted maximum energy, whether physically training or reading from his vast library. There was never a wasted day in Bruce Lee's life.

It takes great courage of conviction to know that the way one leads one's life can forever change the lives of others. This is the essential art of being a teacher. At the time of his death in 1973, he was better known for his screen roles and martial arts skills, but at the very heart of his being, Bruce Lee was a teacher.

Bruce's first and best student was himself. Formal education was only the first stop in his pursuit of knowledge. "Self-knowledge is the basis of life as a human being," was one of his basic beliefs. Bruce felt that his life was a constant process of evolving toward self-actualization. His vehicle for discovering his self-awareness was the martial arts. For Bruce, the study of martial arts was truly a "way of life." When I was a student of Bruce's and especially during the years we were married, I observed that he was able to weave the physicality, the philosophy and the psychology of martial arts into all aspects of his life, and that a life of great harmony and balance could be built upon the foundation of the martial arts.

The books of Dr. Terrence Webster-Doyle are the first attempt I have seen to explain to young people and adults the concept of martial arts as a peaceful, non-violent "way of life" and to give students the tools to accomplish that goal. Too often the study of martial arts is thought of solely as the learning of combative techniques for the purpose of physically conquering another human being. With physical skills as a base, the martial artist develops the confidence to use psychological and sociological self-defense skills which enable him or her to deal with the fears and challenges of everyday life. This is what Dr. Webster-Doyle terms resolving conflict peacefully through nonviolent alternatives.

Another incident in Bruce's life illustrates the successful use of nonviolence. In 1973 in Hong Kong Bruce was making the movie, "Enter The Dragon." One day there were several hundred extras on the set who represented the fighters in the tournament. During a break, a bunch of these extras were talking and joking with Bruce when one of them got brave and started taunting Bruce, calling him a paper tiger, a fake, just a movie star. He challenged Bruce to a fight. It was a ticklish situation because it would look bad to all these martial arts extras if their hero backed down, and they all wanted to see if could fight in real life like he did in the movies. The success of the filming depended on Bruce's response, for surely if Bruce appeared cowardly or incompetent, the extras would turn and leave.

Bruce invited the challenger to come down from the wall where he was perched and just "play" a little bit, get warmed up, so to speak. The brave, but foolish, young man was treated to a brief demonstration of sparring with Bruce blocking and striking with hands and feet blazing, employing foot sweeps and other decisive moves which showed the fellow what was in store, but without hurting him. After a minute or two of this interplay, Bruce asked the guy if he was ready, but as fast as he could he was back on the wall cheering with the rest of the group.

Bruce had successfully defused the situation, the filming could commence, the troops were ready to follow their leader. Bruce knew that if he had defeated that extra in an actual fight, there would just be more challenges to follow. The important lesson illustrated by this story is that it was necessary for Bruce to have all his tools ready in his backpack—he had all his physical skills available for his use, and he had his psychological tools at hand to finesse the situation so that no one got hurt, everyone's self-respect was intact, good humor was maintained and the project could continue. And all those tools Bruce carried around in his mythical backpack were created by his intelligence. "Any dummy can get in a fight," he used to say, "it takes a smart guy to stay out of one."

We don't have to look further than our newspapers and television to know the world is overrun with violence. The attitude that war and cruelty have been going on since time began is the chain that binds us to the Ancient Warrior. The

7

enemy is ritualistic thinking that limits and narrows our vision. As Dr. Webster-Doyle tells us in his writing, rituals can create a framework that imprisons us and blocks awareness of what is really happening. In today's world, the tradition that imprisons us all is sadly a tradition of violence; from the heinous acts of one individual upon another to the global tensions that threaten daily to erupt, human history has conditioned us to accept violence as a means to resolve conflict.

Bruce Lee's interpretation of breaking the influence of conditioning is to gain understanding of self. The goal of Dr. Webster-Doyle's programs is to give young people the physical training that engenders confidence *not* to react in a confrontational manner, while teaching them to understand the roots of conflict within themselves, so that they may become influential in creating peace.

Even a small stone dropped into a pond creates ripples that travel far. Each student that reads Dr. Webster-Doyle's book is fertile ground to absorb the seeds of thought that are planted within these pages. I cannot stress enough how important these lessons are for the development of individuals at peace with themselves, for harmonious relationships, for respect between nations, and tolerance between cultures. Please study the tests with care and prepared to be enlightened.

Peace and Happiness,
Linda Lee Cadwell

MASTERING THE MARTIAL ARTS CODE OF CONDUCT

Dear Student—

Respect is the heart of the Martial Arts. It means being polite, courteous, and well-mannered. Being respectful is acting like a gentleman or gentlewoman. It is learning to get along with your family and friends, acting towards them in an honorable and thoughtful way. This is the Martial Arts Code of Conduct. It is what the Martial Arts are supposed to teach you so you can live peacefully. Martial Arts is much more than mere self-defense or a sport. It helps you to understand yourself and life. The real lesson to learn in Martial Arts is respect.

These words may seem "old fashioned" to you today, but they were the foundation on which the Martial Arts were built. Without respect, without being polite and well-mannered, the Martial Arts become mere fighting and can only create more conflict. The fundamental intent of all Martial Arts is to *end* conflict, to bring about peace by understanding what prevents peace. In order to have peaceful relationships, one needs to show respect, even for those who might do you harm. It is only through respect that you can learn about yourself and others, and begin to learn what Martial Arts are really about.

But there is a deeper respect than mere politeness and just being well-mannered. There are many people who are well-mannered, yet still create tremendous conflict because they have not been educated to understand the deeper feelings and thoughts in themselves.

For thousands of years, we human beings have inherited a tribal, warrior past that has come from fear and continues to create fear—and great conflict. It is the understanding of this warlike attitude, the Ancient Warrior, that needs the greatest respect, the most attention, for respect is being attentive, being aware of what is going on around you. This respect creates courage and strength. This respect develops your character. Your character is how well you act, especially in the face of fears and the hurts of life. Character is also called "spirit." If you feel weak and cannot face life's fears and hurts, then your character or spirit is not strong. If you look fear in the face or confront your hurt, your character or spirit is strong.

Life is a challenge, a test of courage and skill. You will need to develop your character or spirit to meet the ups and downs of life. But, even more importantly, as a true Martial Artist, you will need to develop a very strong character, a brave spirit to face the Ancient Warrior within you and in the world.

That is what this series of tests is about—to give you that strength of character to understand and "defeat the enemy without fighting." The enemy is what creates the warrior; the greatest enemy is fear because it is what keeps the Ancient Warrior alive. The greatest test in being a Martial Artist is to conquer fear. When fear dies, the Ancient Warrior will be defeated.

Are you ready for the tests of character? Can you face the Ancient Warrior with respect and learn from your encounters? Respect creates attention; attention brings about learning and in learning, intelligence will flower. It is this flowering, this awakening of intelligence, that will conquer fear and break the chains of the Ancient Warrior and the hold it has had on us for thousands of years.

With care,

Terrence Webster-Doyle

Dr. Terrence Webster-Doyle

RESPECT

*Respect is the act of intelligence that breaks
the chains of the Ancient Warrior.*

BREAKING THE CHAINS

The Test of Respect

"Let me tell you the story of the shadow," the Teacher said, stroking his white beard. The students sat upright in the old practice hall. The creaking of the trees in the night wind with the crackling of the fire somehow made the room both eerie and cozy. Shadows of the students played on the wall, enlivened by the fire in the large, stone fireplace. A screech owl cried, sending shivers down the back of each student. The Teacher leaned forward, his bright eyes ablaze, a neatly frayed Martial Arts uniform cloaking his massive body...

"Do you understand the meaning of the shadow?"

The students leaned forward in anticipation.

"Let me tell you its tale. There was a man so disturbed by his own shadow and so displeased with his own footprints he made up his mind to get rid of them both. The method he came up with was to run away from them. So he got up and ran. But every time he put his foot down, there was another print. And his shadow kept up with him without the slightest difficulty. He thought perhaps he was not running fast enough. So he ran faster and faster, without stopping, until he finally dropped dead. He failed to realize that if he merely stepped into the shade, his shadow would vanish. And if he stopped moving and sat down, there would be no more footsteps.

"Students," the white-bearded Teacher went on, "each of us has a shadow, and we all leave footprints in time. We are inheritors from our ancestors. Human beings have been violent creatures for thousands of years, fighting each other in endless wars. We have inherited this violence from our warrior past; we are the children of the Ancient Warrior. We are still violent, war-like creatures who fear the dark side. Violence stalks us like our shadows; it is inseparable from us. We only pretend we have gone beyond our primitive past. But, like our shadow and our own footprints, we cannot run away from the violence which is part of who we are.

"Dear students, the most important intent of the Martial Arts is to free us from this warrior shadow, break the chains of the past, and allow us to emerge as new human beings who have understood this immense problem and gone beyond it."

The flames of the fire played softly and silently on the figures in that large, old room. The polished wooden floor beneath them was hard and well-worn from years of practice.

"Our challenge as Martial Artists is to become new 'warriors,' Martial Artists for peace, Martial Artists with courage and understanding, seekers of truth. Most people see the Martial Arts as training in violence. Unfortunately, Martial Arts have too often been promoted and practiced solely as a means of physical self-defense—and not as a complete endeavor, incorporating the physical, mental, and spiritual.

"Your challenge here is to explore and uncover what this shadow is, how the Ancient Warrior in us can be met and understood, and to become free of these chains from the past which hold us in bondage, keep us in darkness, conflict, fear, and violence. Together we will explore this Ancient Warrior shadow in each of us; for to understand and go beyond conflict, the inheritance of our warrior past, is the ultimate purpose of studying the Martial Arts. Through this study, we examine the 'martial' in ourselves, our attitude that through war we can bring

about peace, a destructive attitude which has been passed from generation to generation, carrying with it tremendous suffering and sorrow. Can you see the importance of why we study the Martial Arts? Oh, dear students, begin to see this and you will begin to break the chains of the past and become free to live healthier, happier lives."

The students listened intently to their Master Teacher, for they realized he was speaking of something very important. They had come to this school from all over the world, sent by their Teachers and parents to study with Master Teachers who know and teach the real meaning of the Martial Arts. They had all been carefully selected to spend this time together. Many had applied, but only the serious were eligible. This was a great privilege, not to be taken for granted.

"You have been specially chosen to be here at the International Martial Arts for Peace Camp," the Master Teacher said forcefully. "Make good use of this time. We will be putting you through a series of challenging character developing tests you will need to meet and 'defeat' the Ancient Warrior. If you pass the tests before you, you will return to your schools world-wide, able to teach others about the Ancient Warrior—that which creates such tremendous violence and war. You will be ambassadors of peace, Martial Arts Educators for peace dedicated to understanding what creates conflict in human relationships and what it means to free oneself from the past. This is a serious undertaking, students. One that is very real. We are not playing games here! From this moment on, you will be constantly tested to see if you can meet the challenge. This is a trial of your strength and intelligence. It will be hard both physically and mentally. Remember, the most important weapon you have is not your fist nor your feet, but your brain—for to understand and defeat the Ancient Warrior, you will need to be very alert, aware, focused."

The moon shone through the window, softly pouring its light across the floor. The wind ceased and the fire grew dim.

"You will find out what it means to be a real Martial Artist who has cultivated fine qualities of character, such as honor, bravery, spirit, humility, and—most of all—intelligence and respect. For intelligence is the ability to understand yourself in relationship to others—and the Ancient Warrior, who reacts from fear and rage. Respect is the quality of mind which cares for oneself and others. Being respectful, one does not harshly judge the Ancient Warrior, but, rather, out of intelligence, one greets the Ancient Warrior as a teacher, someone we can learn from. Note we do not need to fear the wrath of the Ancient Warrior, for the Ancient Warrior is us. The Ancient Warrior is to be respected. He is not our enemy. Our judgment creates the 'enemy.' Fear is the 'enemy.' The chains of this dilemma have been handed down for thousands of years, from generation to generation. You, the new generation of Martial Artists, will learn to break these inherited chains. Being here is an opportunity to learn what the right use of the Martial Arts can do to end conflict, that which prevents peace.

"But first, it is time to sleep—to gain strength for the weeks to come, for the tests about to begin," the Master Teacher concluded, looking intently at each student.

BRAVERY

Bravery is not in fighting,
but in understanding the fighter within.

HALL OF BATTLE
The Test of Bravery

Great swords, helmets and metal battle armor dented from clashes
with the enemy.... Huge axes with thick handles wrapped in dark,
sweat-stained leather bindings.... Helmets adorned with animal
horns.... A heavy, spiked ball attached by a chain to a long, iron
shaft which could be swung with murderous speed to mutilate the
foe.... Arrows with sharp-tipped heads, and long bows.... Chain mail
to protect the body from metal weapons.... Long spears to be thrown
or carried when leading a charge against intruders.... A hall of
weapons and ancient armaments, the primitive warriors' tools of the
trade, a host of primitive killing machines....

The students, clothed only in their heavy, white cotton Martial
Arts outfits, stood in awe of this array of battle gear. A tunnel had led to
this musty battle hall.

"I wonder what you are thinking, students," one of the Master
Teachers said, breaking the silence.

"I cannot understand why anyone would want to use these weapons against another," one of the senior students replied.

"You can see, students, we have a long and bloody history of war.
Since the beginning of time, human beings have fought, killed, or were
killed. This was the way of most people on the earth. But there have
also been those opposed to war. There was once a temple in a distant,
foreign land where Martial Artists trained for peace. Those people were
dedicated to understanding why there was violence in the world and
gathered together in the remote hills beyond a small village to live,
work, and train together. Your school is like that temple of so long ago.
We are attempting to find out why we are so violent and war-like. This

18

is our task.

"Your tests begin today. You will be challenged in many areas of understanding, both mentally and physically. Some of you may not make it through this trial. I hope most of you will. It will take a seriousness that perhaps you've never experienced before. You are young people, but you will be expected to act in a mature way. Every day from now on, you will be experiencing profound challenges—challenges which will disturb you, awakening you to the urgency of life. Most people are asleep because they have taken the path of comfort and material gain. But that path is a trap. There will be many such temptations to beguile you. You must stay alert!

"The warriors of ancient times represent the biggest trap of all, that of letting fear take charge of your life. Out of fear comes the need to defend, and the need to defend creates warriors and war. Ancient warriors were thought to be very brave in their time. They fought great battles and won—and lost. Millions upon millions of lives were devastated even though battles were won. There are no winners in war. Everyone loses. You will need to understand how such warriors are created so you don't fall into the trap and join them. Bravery for them was found in fighting. Now, true bravery is seen as the ability to face that shadow of the warrior within yourself, to begin to awaken intelligence so the darkness of the past dies away in a flame of understanding. Perhaps you are too young to fully understand my words, but by the end of our time together, when you have completed all the tests, you will understand much better."

The students continued to walk through that great battle hall, past the implements of war and destruction which sent shivers of fear through their bones.

"Watch how you respond to what you see. The beginning of intelligence is in understanding yourself. The first step is the last step. It is only now that matters. Stay with the now even though the ghosts of the past will come to haunt you," the Master Teacher said knowingly.

They walked slowly, following the Teacher's voice, looking at the various weapons of the Ancient Warrior. The hall was getting narrower and darker as they progressed towards some unknown destination. The sun which had once bathed them in warmth, had long ago been left behind. In this deep, dark hall, the students felt depression and loneliness.

Deeper and deeper they went into that great hall, beyond the last display of ancient weapons, down into what seemed like a bottomless pit. There were only small lanterns to show the way. Three of the Master Teachers escorted the students, holding the small beacons of light. For what seemed like an eternity, this small band of people, clad in Martial Arts uniforms and padded sandals, traveled to the depths of the hall. As they moved along, they began to feel as if other people were in that dark tunnel with them. Were they being followed? Occasionally, a student or two would look back into the blackness to see if anyone was there. The students felt the hair on the back of their necks stand up when there was suddenly a cold breeze, as if from a huge door shutting behind them.

No one spoke. The only sound was of their footsteps on the stone floor. The only sight was of their shadows on the cold, wet, stone walls, created by the light from the lanterns. Their fear felt like some slimy, snake-like creature slithering up their spines. It gripped them by the back of their necks. They were straining to see ahead when suddenly everything went totally, absolutely black. There was no light at all!

They all stopped dead in their tracks. No one spoke lest he or she evoke that great demon they feared was in their midst. Surrounded by that complete blackness, that cold, stone tomb, each one felt strangers were among them—as if their group had doubled in size. Each felt as if an unknown person or entity were by his or her side, following behind closely. The impulse to scream or run was stifled by a low groaning. The students' legs felt like cement; their hearts were pumping so hard, they could hear the blood rushing in their ears. The groaning became more audible and turned into a great, sorrowful wail. It grew and grew until it filled the darkness and overwhelmed them. When the groaning overtook them, the fear disappeared. There was only an immense feeling of terrible grief, as if millions of souls were mourning. A tremendous sadness came at them from all sides. They were completely immersed in that terrible, soulful wail. They felt the wail came from both inside and outside of themselves. Were the other entities in that black hall reaching out to them, across time and beyond the wall of life and death? They all suddenly understood what was happening. They were totally blind in that utter darkness, a darkness so great that all time and movement came to a complete halt. They were at the end of the tunnel with no recognition of what was up or down, left or right, in or out. In that total awful darkness, the pitiful cries came to an end as abruptly as they had started.

There was now a cleansing feeling coursing throughout their whole beings, a cleansing so profound they had a sensation of being nothing and yet everything. As light as mountain-thin air, they began to regain a sense of themselves in time and space. They felt they had been reborn, freed of a burden of the past.

"Move forward and don't look back!" a voice suddenly called out from the nothingness. They all, as one, moved forward and slightly upward. They couldn't see anything, and yet they seemed to know what to do intuitively, as if they had been there before—many, many times before. As they moved, they began to see a very dim glow far out in front of them. The glow grew in intensity with each step towards it. Now, quickly, they came upon a magnificent light. The late afternoon sun shone as birds flew against the stark, blue sky, flecked with clean, white clouds. The fresh, fresh air!

"You have just met your shadows. You have greeted the Ancient Warrior! You now know real bravery. The trial has begun!" the Chief Instructor said with a voice filled with energy and life.

SELFLESSNESS

In the Art of Listening, one goes beyond oneself—
and in this movement, conflict ends.

WAY OF THE GOLDEN DRAGON
The Test of Selflessness

"There is an ancient riddle people believed would give them tremendous power and spirit if understood. Understanding the riddle would free them from fear, the Great Darkness causing so much suffering and pain," the Master Teacher said with authority. She pointed to the painting on the wall of the practice area. The painting was of a brilliant, golden dragon, its claws protruding outward in defense against a giant eagle swooping down upon it.

"Martial Artists of old were taught the Way of the Golden Dragon, a powerful secret which could not only be used for self-defense, but, more importantly, for healing and self-understanding. You will be shown this Way of the Golden Dragon, for you will need it to pass the Test of Selflessness." This was all she said.

For the next two weeks, the students vigorously practiced their Martial Arts forms. All styles were represented. Some forms imitated animals and came from China; other styles, less circular, were defined by angular, straight-line movements derived from Korean, Okinawan, and Japanese forms; some used throwing and locking techniques with very little blocking, punching, striking, or kicking. Day after day, the students were drilled in these many forms by Master Teachers. Not a word was mentioned about the Way of the Golden Dragon. Then the day came.

The students lined up outside the practice hall on the edge of the forest. The woods, dark and thick with tall pine trees, were so dense in parts the sun was almost blocked out. It was late afternoon, approaching evening. There would be no moon that night.

"Students, I want to introduce you to the Way of the Golden Dragon. To learn this way takes a lifetime, and yet it takes no time at all. Tonight you will be tested again. Your test is to enter the Way of the Golden Dragon and from there, enter the Gauntlet, over in the woods beyond," the Teacher said with a hushed reverence.

The students looked at the woods and wondered what lay beyond. They had been told not to enter the woods before this day. There had been stories about the woods and the Gauntlet. It was said no one survives the Gauntlet unless he or she can enter the Way of the Golden Dragon. But the students had been told by others that such stories were merely spread in fun to frighten new students. Yet in the back of their minds, the students weren't really sure if the stories were merely legends—or perhaps half-truths. Anything might happen.

"Expect the unexpected," the Teacher spoke sharply. "If you expect the unexpected, you will be prepared for what would otherwise surprise you. But if you are not expecting the unexpected, you may be caught asleep on your feet."

The students were questioned continually, challenged by the Teachers to think quickly and understand clearly what at first seemed like nonsensical statements or questions. This was called Mental Freestyle and it kept the students mentally and physically alert to the many dangerous pitfalls of the Ancient Warrior, dangers which could lead to being caught in the past, chained to the wrath produced by fear and defensiveness.

"Stop, look, and listen. Sit quietly and let the Golden Dragon come to you. Let it fill you with its power and clarity of mind. Listen and you will hear it without any sound. Learn the Art of Listening and you will know the Golden Dragon," the Teacher directed. The students sat on the ground and closed their eyes. "Listen to the silence," she spoke softly. "Hear the wind waves in the tree tops, the birds moving from branch to branch calling their mates. Listen to just what is here and *don't look back!* By looking back you will be caught in the prison of time, locked in the past. Let the past come and go, in and out, just like the river flowing, ever renewing itself, reflecting what is there but not holding on to any image."

The students listened carefully, as they had been instructed to do at the start and end of each practice session. They sat quietly, with eyes opened, observing the scene around them. The sun was setting in the west over the tops of tall hills behind the forest. Darkness was approaching on the swift wings of night. The early evening stars began to shimmer like sparkling, jeweled diamonds in the heavens. The students sat there for an endless moment and felt the earth move, the heat of the ground lifting upwards like invisible smoke rising to the endless sky and beyond. As the light of day surrendered itself to night, the heat subsided while the birds disappeared into nocturnal, secret hiding places. All sense of self vanished, and with it, all fear.

Silently there came a new awareness of a presence before them. An enormous creature of the night lay in the woods, a predator on all fours, lurking in the dark recesses of a cave. Their primal instincts became alerted. Pupils dilated, hearts beat faster, blood rushed to arms and legs. They knew now what they had to face in the Gauntlet, in the depths of that primeval forest. The predator was present; it was in them and in those woods. The Wrath of the Ancient Warrior was ready to meet them as they entered.

Night was now fully upon them as they moved forward to the edge of the forest, each student wearing a black uniform for night practice. Silhouetted figures moved among tall, dark trees under an endless black sky. The Gauntlet had begun; the test of selflessness was underway. "If you are captured, the test is over. Beware of what lurks within the Gauntlet," were the last words they heard.

They saw a large, black figure dart between the trees before them. Having been trained as Martial Artists, they instinctively knew what to do. The students spread out, moving stealthily among the trees, being careful to place each foot gently on the ground so as not to create any noise that could give away their position. Suddenly, one of the students quickly rolled to his left to avoid a trap. The cunning device was designed to catch your foot and hold it fast by a clamp, unhurt. The students were ready for the many traps in the Gauntlet. Without realizing it, they had been training for this for weeks.

The forest closed in around them like a cloaked shadow enveloping each student in darkness. One could sense the trees and branches. One could smell the pine sap and earth. Above, a sprinkling of stars dimly lit the tree tops. The students moved forward. Suddenly, there was a scream, a high-pitched shriek chilling their very bones. Had someone been captured? One of the older students had moved off to the north and was coming around a tall pine tree when a large, black figure came rushing forward, wielding a long, thin object in the air. The student instinctively lifted her arm to fend off the oncoming strike from the shinai (a bamboo "sword"). The *shinai* caught her on the wrist with a stinging, but harmless, whack! She quickly brought her right arm and hand up and over the outstretched hands of the attacker, and turned them sharply to the left, while twisting her body in the same direction. The attacker dropped the *shinai* and rolled a few feet to the right. Jumping up instantly, the attacker charged forward in a combat position. The student moved swiftly to meet the attack, grabbing both of her opponent's hands. While pivoting full turn, she threw the attacker, who again jumped swiftly upright, grabbing the student by her uniform. In turn, clutching the attacker's uniform, the student rolled backward, placing her feet on her opponent's midsection and pushing upward. The momentum thrust the attacker over and past her by a few feet. Having let go of her grasp, the student was up in a flash to grab the attacker's collar and—with arm under neck—hold her opponent in a vise-like grip. When the attacker slapped his own thigh with a free hand, she let go. The attacker scrambled into the woods. The student had not been captured!

Just a few dozen yards to the left of this attack, one of the students was standing completely still. There before him, in the dark, he could make out two human forms—bodies, faces, and heads covered in black, with just the slightest glint of intense eyes staring out. The student moved quickly to place one of the trees at his back. The two silent assailants moved stealthily towards him, one going to the left, the other to the right. As the two figures reached the student on either side, they attacked, only to run into each other through the emptiness left behind by the student! The two black-clad attackers looked around, blinking in surprise at the disappearance of their victim. There was only silence and the night. The assailants slowly circled the thick tree, finding no one. The student was gone, or so it seemed, when—without warning—the student was upon them from above, knocking the two assailants to the ground, pinning each with arm locks. Like the first attacker, the two assailants slapped their thighs with their free hands and the student let them go to disappear back into the forest night.

As the night wore on, it became so dark it was virtually impossible to see anything beyond an arm's reach. The students sensed that more traps and attacks lay ahead, and became increasingly nervous because the couldn't see. They remembered their Teacher telling them about the Golden Dragon. "Just close your eyes, feel the darkness with your spirit. Feel the night air on your cheek, sense the subtle odors, the minute sounds. Welcome the dark, invite any fear to come forward. Greet it without any resistance. Move as the wind; let the natural way move you. Give in and feel life move in you. This energy you feel is life-giving; it heals the mind, body, and spirit. It is there all the time. It is the Way of the Golden Dragon. Now, when you are in the dark forest, in the Gauntlet, let this force arise. It will show you the way of acting naturally. In this, you will see without seeing, hear without hearing, feel without feeling, know without knowing. Enter the Way of the Golden Dragon and you will emerge from the Gauntlet without being captured. You will be invisible to anyone who tries to attack or trap you. Fear, which is yourself, is what gives you away. Enter the Way of the Golden Dragon and you will be gone. Emptiness cannot be trapped; nothingness cannot be captured."

The students, as if one body, could hear their Teacher. Each stood still with eyes closed, and felt the wonder of the silence, the magnificent forest, the earth below, and the endless night sky above. From this silence there arose a sensation, a feeling, an awareness that was neither man-made nor imagined. The brain had come to a still point. Time had ceased and there was nothing—and everything. A light of a different source was beginning to illuminate the darkness, allowing them to

"see" through the coal-black night. A moonless, star-speckled silent night. A soft, golden, lightless light guided them as they moved forward through the Gauntlet without leaving a trace—not shadows nor footsteps—as if the forest swallowed up their trail. Without effort, the students became the Golden Dragon and emerged through the forest, eluding capture. The test was over. The Gauntlet was behind them.

HONOR

Honor is not fame or glory, but respect
for yourself and others.

CURSE OF THE ANCIENT WARRIOR
The Test of Honor

"No matter what you do, how hard you try, struggle, or fight, you cannot get away from the Ancient Warrior within you. To resist is futile!" The Master Teacher addressed the students in the early morning sun. The lake at the bottom of the hill shimmered with reflections of snow-capped mountains. Birds flew overhead without disturbing the delicate quality of the untouched morning.

"Do you see this wicker tube I hold in my hand? Each of you has been given one to remind you of this lesson. If you should break it by trying too hard to understand how it works, you will fail the test." In their palms lay a "Chinese Finger Puzzle," a multi-colored tube about five inches long and wide enough for one's forefinger to fit in each end.

"Insert your forefingers into each end of the tube, like so. The challenge now is to free your fingers. But, as you can see, your fingers become caught. If you pull too hard, you will break the puzzle and thereby lose. You must remove your fingers easily, without effort, without trying. Logically, one may think the only way out of the trap is to pull one's fingers out the same way they went in. But that will prove to be unsuccessful. However, there is something that will free you effortlessly: understanding how the puzzle works. When you figure it out, you will see its simplicity. First, you see the old way does not work. Then you discover that by simply pushing your fingers towards each other, the tension is released—and with a slight grasp of the tube's edges with the thumbs, one can easily keep the openings wide enough to remove the two forefingers easily."

The students played with their Chinese Finger Puzzles, putting them on, trying to pull them off, and then, without effort, releasing the tension and removing the puzzle with their thumbs.

"The Ancient Warrior within you is like this Chinese Finger Puzzle. The harder you try to escape, the greater the tension created. You're trapped. If you try too hard, you could break. This is the Curse of the Ancient Warrior; it is difficult to get away from it without destroying yourself or others. But if you remember the lesson of the Chinese Finger Puzzle and approach the Ancient Warrior in you with this awareness, then you will be able to be free—not through trying or effort, but through understanding the hold it has over you. Understanding will set you free. But you cannot condemn the Ancient Warrior. Judgment only makes it worse. You must honor it!"

"But, Sir," said one of the older students in surprise, "how can we honor that which we know is destructive?"

"Today you will meet the Ancient Warrior again, but not at night. In full daylight, we will evoke the Curse of the Ancient Warrior; we will meet the terrible wrath right here."

The Master Instructor stopped talking and lined the students up for warm-ups and stretching exercises, led by an Assistant Instructor. After thirty minutes, the students were asked to sit around the outdoor fighting area, measuring fifteen feet by fifteen feet. Three Apprentice Instructors who lived at the school approached the younger students. These older students were training year-round to become one day Assistants to the Master Teachers. Each hoped to become a full instructor—then, possibly, a Master Teacher. They lived and breathed the Martial Arts.

Two Apprentice Instructors sat across from the new group of novices; the third stepped up to the edge of the fighting area. The Master Teacher signaled to his Assistant in the middle of the floor. The Assistant pointed to a younger, novice student, and then, at one of the Apprentices. They both came forward. Cautiously, the younger student approached the fighting area to meet the older Apprentice. There was an air of intensity and danger. The Assistant motioned for them to face each other. They bowed towards one another, to the Assistant, and finally, to the Master Teacher sitting a short distance away. Without a word being said, freestyle—a contest of skill in self-defense—was about to begin. No contact was allowed, except for blocks, sweeps, holds, and locks. If one of the contestants were trapped in a hold or lock, all he or she had to do was slap his or her leg to signal for his release when the discomfort became too great. Punches, strikes, and kicks were always pulled just short of their intended targets, so the students could practice full power techniques with absolute safety.

"Begin," commanded the Assistant Instructor. Slowly, the two students moved around each other. Then, with lightening speed, the older student lashed out a footsweep, catching the younger student unaware and sending him to the ground. The older student swiftly moved on top to execute a painful arm lock. The younger student slapped his leg to signal release of the hold, but the older student kept the pressure tight, hurting the arm even more. The student again slapped his leg, but to no avail. In defense, he reached out and grabbed his opponent by the hair and pulled. The older student released his grip and jumped to his feet. The younger student got quickly up, visibly shaken by this lack of proper conduct on the part of the older student, but before he could regain his composure, the Apprentice shot out a sidekick, catching the younger in the midsection, knocking the air out of him. The older student came in with a reverse punch to the face which the younger student narrowly avoided. The older student kept up the attack relentlessly, once knocking the younger student out of the ring. Unhurt, but dazed, the younger fought back again and again to protect himself from the onslaught of this older, stronger student. The Assistant Instructor did nothing to stop the fight, neither did the Master Teacher.

When the fight had first begun, the younger student was nervous but still in control. Now, he felt himself losing control. A slow-creeping, dark feeling made its way into his consciousness; a slow-burning anger began to smolder. The rage grew like a demon in his skull until he finally lost control. Holding back tears, the younger student started screaming at the larger, stronger student. His eyes blazed with fury, hurt, and fear. The Apprentice came at him again with a flurry of punches and kicks, sweeping the legs out from under him. The Apprentice again pinned him face down, the novice struggling in vain to get free.

"Stop!" commanded the Assistant Instructor. Finally it was over, with the younger face down, unharmed, but in rage and shock. He jumped to his feet to face his older opponent, eyes glaring with revenge.

"Come here, student," the Master Teacher called to the enraged novice.

The younger boy did as he was told and stood shaking, eyes ablaze, in front of his Teacher.

"Meet the Ancient Warrior," the older man said as he motioned to his Assistant. The assistant pulled out a hand mirror and turned it toward the novice, enabling him to see his own reflection. The boy looked at the face staring out at him and saw an Ancient Warrior's face. The eyes looking back were warrior's eyes. For a moment, the boy stood looking at what he could not recognize as himself, but did know as something he had felt in himself, today and before. Frozen for an unending moment, he understood what his Teachers were telling him. He was seeing himself through the eyes of the warrior within. The Wrath of the Ancient Warrior!

"Can you honor what you see? Can you respect the Ancient Warrior within?" he heard his Teacher ask.

He began to see a change in the face looking back at him—his face, the timeless face of all humanity, the face of fear, anger, rage. The eyes slowly softened and the Ancient Warrior's wrath subsided. Now, he began to see a face with thousands of years of suffering, a face lined with the sorrow of ages, a face scarred by millions of battles. As he felt that immense sorrow and tremendous suffering, he could honor himself and all humankind. He did not condemn what he was witnessing. In that moment free of judgement, the face receded and a new face took its place—one of youthful spirit looking innocently out to him, full of curiosity and wonder. And then, it was over, gone. The Assistant put the mirror away.

"Thank you for taking and passing the Test of Honor," the Master Teacher said gently. In his Teacher's eyes, the boy saw great respect and honor for his new understanding of the Ancient Warrior within.

UNITY

*Unity is wholeness, that which is not divided
and hence, not in conflict.*

MIND LIKE MOON
The Test of Unity

The school's cat slumbered quietly in the corner, seemingly unaware of the small, gray, field mouse scurrying across the floor. The mouse, sensing danger, stopped and sniffed the air with its tiny, red nose, thin whiskers vibrating. Fifteen feet from the sleeping cat, the mouse sat motionless a few yards from its hole and safety. The students silently watched this life or death journey. Without any warning, from what appeared to be a dead sleep, the cat leapt forward with grace and stunning agility to capture its prey. But the mouse had a little measure of safety and scampered into its hole, just as the cat landed an inch behind it.

"Did you observe that trial, that test of life and death? A serious affair—like our lives—except the dangers are not as obvious to us as they are to the mouse," the Master Teacher whispered so as not to disturb nature unfolding.

That night there was a glorious full moon which shone brightly on the water's mirrored surface. Students descended the hill to the lake with their Teachers. Looking towards the horizon, they could see moon rays evenly blanketing the land. An owl flew silently over the water's edge and into the forest beyond. The only sound was footsteps.

"Sit here," one of the Master Teachers said in hushed tones. "Just observe and listen. This is your test. There are no answers. There is nothing to say."

The students sat together, yet apart. The moon had risen even

43

higher in the sky, turning from a butter-orange to a creamy yellow the higher it went. There was no limit to the sky. The earth felt huge: a giant, round mass journeying through the galaxies like a wandering monk in search of the end of time.

They were bathed by moonlight and immersed in the lake, mountains, stars, and sky. There was no separation; all division between them fell away. There was no remembrance of what had gone before, no hoping for what was to come. They stayed there until the moon was high in the heavens.

SPIRIT

Spirit is that energy needed to cut through the confusion of self-made illusions.

GORDIAN KNOT

The Test of Spirit

Dawn was just about to appear, filling that indiscernible moment between night and day when birds begin their daily hunt for food. The students looked towards a long, sloping meadow.

The eldest Master Teacher strode across the open yard, stopping in front of a row of three straw-bundled posts. He knelt down in front of one post and placed a sword on the ground in front of him. He sat quietly for a few minutes. The students watched him intently, not sure of what to expect. As the sun's first ray's broke forth, heralding the new day, the Master Teacher leaned forward, grasped the sword handle with his right hand and the sword sheath with his left. With a sudden, swift, spirited movement, he drew the sword from its case and stood upright, cutting through all three hay-bundled posts in three fluid, effortless motions. In a moment, he was sitting on the ground again. He ceremoniously resheathed the bright, steel sword and closed his eyes. The bundled bunches of hay lay neatly halved. The Master Teacher bowed deeply, his forehead touching the earth. He then got up with agile dignity and retraced his steps to the long wooden building behind the students.

The students had witnessed movements only a Master of the Sword would attempt. The sword is sharp and the movements quick. Students and Apprentices were warned not to practice this dangerous feat.

Later in the morning the students met with an Assistant Instructor to face their newest test—the test of their spirit.

"If you hesitate, you may hurt yourself, perhaps even breaking your hand," the Assistant Instructor stated firmly. "This is not a game. It is a serious endeavor. It is not some sort of side-show or circus feat to dazzle and impress. Breaking is a means by which you can test your spirit. Spirit is giving your full attention with great passion, energy, and boldness. Spirit is being resolute of mind, feeling that fire in you which brings out your fearlessness. Break without fear. See it already broken in your mind and it will be so. All that is left is to do it! But if you think of failure or try to analyze how to achieve it, you will fail to break the board properly. You may be able to break it by brute force. Anyone can do that. But to have what you break fall away as naturally as snow from a branch is indeed something to experience!"

Each student, in turn, attempted to break the boards with various punches, strikes, and kicks. Most boards broke, but a few did not, causing some minor bruises.

"You lack spirit!" the Master Teacher reprimanded. "You hit at the board as if with a sledge hammer. You are using brute force. You do not just let it break. See it in your mind. Then, let it break. Just naturally extend you hand out as if you are swatting away an annoying fly. The movement is a natural one, not one of willpower. You cannot pass this test if you do not relax."

The broken wood was collected and taken to the firewood box for kindling. The students gathered around their Master Teachers as one began speaking. "Students, sword cutting and board breaking represent slicing through the mind's clutter, its entanglement of thoughts. Thoughts can tie the mind up in knots, creating disorder and chaos, clouding vision and preventing clarity. A knotted mind creates turmoil in the world. A mind agitated by thoughts from the past, thoughts evoking feelings of fear or wrath, can create great harm and violence among people. Trying to analyze the confusion, the conflicting thoughts, can paralyze you. You cannot think your way out of thinking; thinking cannot resolve the chaos thinking itself is creating. So, what can you do when thoughts and feelings of past confusion arise? What happens when the wrath of the Ancient Warrior floods the brain, disorienting you?"

The students listened to the words of their Teacher, at the same time observing their minds and their many passing reactions. Listening and observing, in a heightened state of attention, the students could truly learn—not the learning that is carried over into memory as knowledge, but learning that is in the moment, learning that sees and acts simultaneously in ending inward confusion and conflict.

"Cut the knot! Break the chains! Focus like a razor, a white beam of light! Feel spirit rising in you! Spirit cuts through and 'kills' confusion instantly. If confusion should raise its head again, the light of focus can end it completely. Should you meet the Ancient Warrior on the road, 'slay' it with your sword of truth and understanding—for it is only a ghost, nothing to be afraid of.

"And, if you see another's confusion, or sense danger in another before it is manifested—before the other is even aware of it in him or herself—you can end it at its root," the Teacher said emphatically.

"Now practice your breaking with great spirit. Act cleanly, break cleanly. Let the board fall away without effort. And when you meet the Ancient Warrior, you will end the battle before it begins."

TRUST

Trust is not unquestioning obedience,
but rather the capacity for seeing and
acting on that which is true and real.

GAMES MARTIAL ARTS MASTERS PLAY
The Test of Trust

The long Ceremonial Hall was alight with dozens of flickering candles. At the end of this long room was a large, low, black, wooden altar. On the altar was a statue of a half-human/half-animal creature with numerous arms in dance-like gestures. Beside it were two large bronze bowls, and a vase with flowers. On the floor near the altar was a large brass gong engraved in an unknown script, encircled by an intriguing design of animal figures with a large dragon in its center. The room had a heavy, sweet odor from the many burning sticks of incense in the bowl on the altar. Behind, on the wall, was an ominous picture of the Chief Instructor's Master Teacher with the inscription, "Great Enlightened Heavenly Teacher." The floor was bare except for round, black cushions placed in long rows. The only light came from an oval window high on the wall, casting a light on the altar and out along the floor.

An Apprentice Instructor led the students in and told them to follow what she did without question. The students had never experienced such a place before. They were hushed by the awesome spectacle. They sat down on the cushions in the typical Martial Arts, knees-tucked-under position, in wonder at this mysterious occasion.

After sitting for a while in silence, they heard a door open to the side. Not looking in the direction of the noise, they kept their focus on the altar. In a moment, a small, old man with a long, white beard appeared and knelt down in front of the altar. They couldn't recognize the man because the area was dark and he had his back to them. The old man was dressed in a white Martial Arts top with a flowing, white, gown-like "skirt." The figure began to chant in language they had never heard before. At times he bowed low to the altar. Then, he turned to the brass gong, still with his back to the students, and struck it once. The sound echoed through the room. Again and again, he hit the gong. The loud brass clashing in the old hall reverberated until the walls seemed to shake.

Slowly, the old man in the white robe moved towards the altar and knelt again within arm's reach of several objects too far away for the students to see clearly. With his back still to the students, he resumed chanting. With his right hand, he began to wave a whip-like device. With his left, he gestured towards the large picture of the "Great Enlightened Heavenly Teacher." The Apprentice Instructor motioned to the students to bow. Each time they were to bow, the Apprentice raised her hand. The students bowed and bowed as they had been told to do without question. The small, old, bearded man in white now began to talk to the picture in a voice filled with passion and reverence.

"Oh, Great Enlightened Heavenly Teacher, please hear me. I evoke your memory, your spirit. Come to us from the ages. You are our Spiritual Master, oh, Divine One! We pay you homage and obedience. We worship you as our Deity!" His voice raised to an emotional pitch with each invocation.

The students sat in awe of this spectacle. They became aware of a strange, powerful energy in their bodies. The influence of the large, old hall, the candles, the strange smelling incense, the mysterious looking altar, the chanting voice methodically droning on, the clashing of the gong, and the cryptic gestures of the magical looking old man in flowing white clothes...their heads swam in it all. Their senses were overcome with so many sensations. They felt special, holy, as if they were elite warriors chosen for the work of the Great Enlightened Heavenly Teacher.

"Oh, students," said the old man with his back to them. "You are the chosen ones, the ones to follow in His footsteps! You are the powerful elite, the warriors of His will! We are a brotherhood; a bond has been created for us by His recognition, His divine selection. You are the inheritors of His Masterhood." The old man's voice crackled with controlled excitement.

The feeling in the room was immense; the energy created by the experience was ecstatic and overwhelming. All felt lost in the moment, carried away by the zeal produced by the combination of elements.

"And students, you must remember one thing, and only one thing," the old man shouted. "You must obey, follow the authority of the Masters *without question!*"

He swiftly turned to face the mesmerized group of students. For a moment, everyone sat completely still, stunned by what they saw. They blinked and some even rubbed their eyes. It couldn't be so! Even in the light of the candles, the face was recognizable. The school's gardener sat before them with a large smile on his face. He began to laugh—first a small, polite laugh, soon growing to a belly laugh with tears streaming down his face.

The students were confused and shaken. What was the school's gardener doing dressed in these special clothes and why was he laughing? No one knew what to say. From the side door, two figures came into the room, two Chief Instructors. The older man sat to the right of

the gardener in white, and the woman Chief Instructor sat to his left. They were both smiling.

The woman spoke first. "Students, are you aware of yourself right at this moment? It is important to see what you are doing," she said firmly. "We have tricked you. This has been another test. We have been playing a game, a very dangerous game, one which can hypnotize, creating false images for you to worship. Do you understand what I am saying?"

One of the students in the front spoke up hesitantly. "Excuse me, Teachers, but what is the gardener doing dressed like that?"

"Do you mean all of this—the altar, the incense, the robes—are just part of an act?" another student asked, mystified.

"Students, you are so vulnerable, so susceptible to what we adults tell you, especially adults who look and act like great authorities. It is all too easy for you to fall into our web, our hypnotic trance. We felt we needed to test you on this weakness we all possess. When we are young, we trust adults around us to show us what is right and true so we can live intelligent, happy lives, free from conflict and sorrow. But, unfortunately, there are many people in the world who want to take advantage of you, to condition you through strange rituals, foreign words, and experiences, so you will be manipulated to do what these people want you to do: to follow them unquestioningly, to give them your money, your obedience, and even your life. The main point of this test was to show you how easy it is to impress and hypnotize you."

"I'm afraid I believed it for a moment. What scares me is that I enjoyed it. Well, enjoy is not the right word. I just felt a strange desire in me that was very, very pleasurable, as if something in me needed that feeling. It's hard to explain," a student commented. "I still feel dazed by the experience and shaken up too."

"We have certain rituals at this school. The Martial Arts all have rituals. Students bow to their Teachers, to their school, and to each other. These rituals create a structure. Like a house, ritual creates the framework. But, beware! Ritual can imprison you and catch you up in a maze of convoluted mind games where you think you are the center of it all," the Master Teacher warned earnestly.

"Sir, what should we be aware of? How can bowing create a prison?" a student asked.

"Young lady, you see only the surface of things. You see bowing and you follow dutifully, like a good student. But, how far will you go before you question? Questioning breaks the influence of conditioning. Questioning exercises your brain, your intelligence. Questioning, if you don't immediately respond with what you think might be the correct answer, can lead to awareness and the observance of what is really happening."

"But you are our Teachers; you know what is right and good for us," said one of the younger students. "We trust you."

"We are your Teachers, but we are not your authorities. There is a difference. I hope you can understand what I say. I will try to explain this as easily and simply as possible," the Teacher responded affection-ately.

"We see that young people are intelligent, but are like tiny seeds which have not yet been put into the ground. Our job is to plant the seeds and water them, to nourish them until they are strong enough to grow and survive on their own. Then they, too, will bear fruit and plant their own seeds to be nourished. This is the way of things. Birth, death, and rebirth—the natural cycle goes on.

"That little, individual seed has in it the potential for infinite life. It contains the germ of life itself—the seemingly endless cycle of nature. That little seed is intelligence, life force, life energy, with the might to push a slight, fragile blade of grass through stone. It is tremendously powerful! You are that seed; each one of us is. So, we have to be careful how we care for the seed that we are. If we think the seed does not have the ability to grow from its own power, then we may destroy it by trying to grow it in artificial ways.

"As Martial Arts Teachers, we nourish the growing student. Helping a young person to understand what is right and good is a serious and important job, perhaps the most important work a human being can do. Your parents are your teachers, too, of course. We who teach the Martial Arts, along with your parents and school teachers, need to work together as a team to help you to be intelligent, capable, happy human beings. It is our job to show you the many traps in the world, the pitfalls you can fall into because the world is so full of challenges. Life is a serious but exciting adventure, and there are many tests you need to prepare for. Here at this school, we are trying to prepare you for the test of life itself, for the many trials you encounter each day. The greatest test is that of understanding and resolving conflict peacefully. This is our main intent here. We will help you understand how conflict is created so you will not become its victims. So many people fail the tests of life because they don't have the right education. People think education is learning history, mathematics, and how to read and write. But that type of learning is only one small part of education. Learning about how to get along with other people is the most vital part.

"I know that perhaps all of this may be too much for you to understand right now. Just remember you can live a healthy, happy life and that the Martial Arts, if taught in the right way, can help you. And that is why we are all together at this school."

"I think I understand some of what you say," said an older student. "I can see how violent the world is, and I think what you are saying is that we can understand violence because we have created it—by the way we think and act. But there is much to learn."

"Don't worry, you will understand all we are teaching you if you really want. It takes work! You must be willing to listen and actively participate by questioning to find out what is true and what is not. We Teachers are not here to tell you what to think, what is true, or to demand that you obey us without question. We want you to question what we tell you, for in questioning, you are practicing 'Mental Freestyle,' as we call it. You are exercising that muscle between your ears," the Teacher responded. "But beware, students—there are many traps along the way. Be alert, question, listen! Don't accept what someone tells you as true without finding out for yourself. For even if your Teachers know what is right and good for you, how do you know? Trust your intelligence, for intelligence will tell you what is true. Intelligence is a small seed within you. That seed needs to be nurtured to be able to grow into full bloom."

The students came up to the "altar" invented by their Teachers, to look at all the "stage props" used to hypnotize them. The picture of the "Great Enlightened Heavenly Teacher" was actually a picture of the school's cook in disguise. After that day, the students were more aware of how easily they could be influenced and began to see how this could happen anywhere. They also began to see the terrible danger when people become too hypnotized or fall asleep.

CHARITY

Love and do as you will,
for in love there is intelligence.

GIFT OF THE MOON
The Test of Charity

The moon hung above them in the clear, night sky. "This moon is called the Dragon Grasping the Pearl," the Teacher said softly.

The students looked up at the quarter moon. Its lower right side was brightly lit while the rest remained hazy. Indeed, it looked like a finely translucent pearl, resting in a crescent-shaped claw. Near the moon shone the evening star. Such a lovely sight! The rest of the sky was dotted with fainter stars millions of light-years away.

"I want to tell you a story about a giving man, a man of charity. He passed a great test without ever knowing it was a test. The story goes like this..." The Teacher leaned forward with his chin resting on his hands. The students were sitting on the ground around him under the night sky. The trees looked like fingers pointing up towards the heavens. What a wonderful mystery life is under the stars!

"Teshu, a Martial Arts Master, lived a very humble and simple life in a small, mountain hut near a burgeoning city. He spent the days practicing his forms and writing a book, gardening and swimming in the mountain stream pools. He had a good, untroubled life.

"One evening, a thief came to the hut to rob Teshu, but found there was nothing to steal. Teshu had only a few belongings.

"Teshu had been out on a walk and when he returned, he caught the thief in his hut. Realizing the thief was a sad and very poor man,

Teshu said to him, 'You have come a long way to see me, and you should not return empty-handed. Please take my clothes as a gift.'

"The thief was bewildered. He took the clothes, bowed, and left.

"Teshu sat, clothed only in his undershorts, watching the moon. 'Poor Man,' he thought to himself, *I wish I could have given him this beautiful moon.*'"

COMPASSION

Sharing the sorrow of another because you, too, feel the pain—
in that there is compassion.

ATTACKING NOTHINGNESS
The Test of Compassion

"What is one of the greatest tests of all, Teacher?" a student asked one bright morning.

"I know of one test which meant a great deal to me. It is a story of a great teacher, a Teacher of mine, just after a war had ended. This teacher had not supported the war because she was strongly against killing. She felt there must be more intelligent and humane ways to resolve conflict—without using violence. In her search, she had dedicated her life to the practice of the Martial Arts.

"One day, she was walking through a small town on her way home when a large, drunken man came crashing out of a house. My Teacher heard cries for help from a woman and a small child huddled inside. The drunken man held a sword and was cursing and challenging anyone near him. There was a small crowd of people who had gathered upon hearing the commotion. The drunken man looked desperate and dangerous. His clothes were ripped and soiled with vomit.

"Cries continued to come from inside the house. People watching this spectacle were frightened. No one seemed prepared to help. The dirty man charged drunkenly at the crowd, sending people fleeing for cover. The drunk then turned to look at my Teacher, who was standing quietly by the side of the road, looking attentively at the huge man.

"'Whatta ya looking at?' he half-shouted, half-mumbled as he

glared at my Teacher.

"'Nothing,' my Teacher calmly responded with a friendly smile.

"The screams from the house were getting worse. Perhaps one or both of the people inside had been hurt. The crowd cautiously gathered again, but kept a safer distance from the menacing drunken man.

"He spat out drunken slurs. He made a threatening lurch forward, brandishing his long, sharp, warrior's sword at my Teacher. But, she stood still, not moving back from the man's hostile advance.

"'Sounds like someone is hurt in there,' my Teacher said, pointing to the house.

"'Yeah, so what! Them is my wife and kid and I can do with them as I please. You gonna do something 'bout it?' The man stepped forward again, moving closer to my Teacher.

"'Looks like you are hurt,' my Teacher said gently, pointing to the large gash on his arm.

"'No one can help me now. I'm a warrior. I have been trained to kill. I just came home from the war,' the big man said with an unexpected quietness, responding to the lack of fear from my Teacher.

"The big man stopped still, the menacing sword hanging loosely in his meaty hand. Blood was dripping down his arm onto the ground, leaving reddish-brown spots on the road.

"'I've been at war, I've been at war, and there are bodies all over the place. They just kept on coming and we couldn't stop them. They just kept on coming and coming,' he said, swaying from side-to-side as if a giant tree ready to fall.

"My Teacher was a great Martial Artist. She could defend herself against the most highly trained people. A drunk, even with a sword, was no match for her. And yet she stood there talking with this sad stranger on a dusty road.

"'You know, I am married and have a daughter. Do you have a son or daughter? My family lives in the next town and I am traveling there to meet them. My husband is a wonderful person. He loves us very much and we love him. And my daughter! She is so beautiful and smart. She is now in school and I am so proud of her,' my Teacher went on happily as the man stood there listening, transfixed by the story he was hearing.

"'Yeah, I am married, and I have a girl, too. They are in there,' the big man said, gesturing with his free hand towards the house. 'I must have really frightened them. I kinda went crazy. I just see the enemy everywhere. I can't stop the fighting,' he responded to my Teacher.

"'It's okay. There is nothing to worry about. It's all over now. You can stop fighting,' my Teacher said kindly with tears in her eyes.

"The big man looked through his drunken haze at my Teacher and could see my Teacher's tears. He wiped his nose with his bloody arm and slumped down to the ground in a crumpled heap. He began sobbing and sobbing, emitting a terrible cry.

"My Teacher walked over to him and put her hand on the man's shoulder and said, 'It's all right, it's all right. Let it go.'

"The big man's body convulsed with spasms of sobs. The crowd watched in silence.

"My Teacher gently grasped the sword the big man was clutching.

71

Sensing that his only weapon was being taken from him, he tried to rise and strike my Teacher, but before he could get up, she had removed the sword and tossed it aside. The big man reeled drunkenly and fell into my Teacher's arms, still sobbing.

"My Teacher sat down on the ground with the man and held him in her arms, rocking the drunk while he cried. After a period, he became quiet. Gently laying him down on the ground, my Teacher entered the house of this man to find his wife and young daughter cowering behind a large table.

"'Please, don't be afraid. I will not hurt you. Your husband is all right now. Do you understand? It was the war, the war,' my Teacher said sadly. She led the shaking woman and girl out into the street to where the big man lay. 'He needs your help now. You have to be strong. No matter what he has done in the past, you must forgive him and love him. Only in this way will he heal those terrible wounds. Do you understand?' my Teacher asked gently, looking first into the eyes of the woman, and then those of the small girl.

"'He will not hurt you. He is defeated. The war is over for him. Now help him.'

"The woman looked deeply into my Teacher's eyes to gain strength. The woman became quiet and pulled her child close to her for reassurance. She nodded to my Teacher, then knelt down next to her tragic, broken husband. The young girl, following her mother, did likewise. They both reached out and put their hands on his massive back. The woman began to wipe the blood from his arm and forehead with her scarf. The man quietly cried, his huge body jerking with subsiding sobs.

"Weak and shaken, the woman turned to my Teacher. Her eyes met my Teacher's eyes and she could see love. It was this unjudgemental love that healed the broken warrior and saved his family from more sorrow and suffering. To me, this is the most wonderful test of all—the test of compassion, of love.

UNDERSTANDING

We are what we think we are—
in understanding that, there is freedom.

DEFEATING THE ENEMY WITHOUT FIGHTING
The Test of Understanding

"What does this mean, students?" the Teacher asked, pointing to the writing on the board.

We are what we think.

All that we are arises from our thoughts.

With our thoughts, we make the world.

"You need to be challenged both physically *and* mentally if you are to be free of the chains of the Ancient Warrior, free of the inherited fear and violence creating such tremendous suffering in the world. You are challenged physically in self-defense Freestyle; you are challenged mentally in Mental Freestyle. Your mind is your greatest weapon. In order to cut through confusion and chaos, your mind needs to be like a very sharp sword—a sword of truth and understanding—not a physical sword which hurts and destroys. The chains of the past will weigh you down unless you act quickly and think. Be alert, awake!" the Teacher said with urgency in his voice.

One of the students spoke up, "I think this means our thoughts signify who we are...what we think is what we do."

"It means we have been conditioned to think certain thoughts and to act in certain ways. Like being brainwashed," another student responded energetically.

"We are responsible for what goes on in the world because we

create action by our thoughts. Violence and terrible wars are created by how we think and act. This comes from being chained to our past, chained to the Way of the Ancient Warrior. The chain is the conditioning we've inherited. It's like a disease everyone has, and when you come into the world as a small child, you get the disease and become sick like all the people around you. But, you don't have to get sick if you can understand what is happening," one of the senior students added.

"I can see you are beginning to learn the lesson well. Are you starting to see why we are here? How important Martial Arts training can be? How it can help you understand and go beyond conflict, both within yourself and within the world?" the Teacher asked his students.

"How does thinking make the world?" the Teacher continued. "How does it create conflict? Thought can create illusions and we can get caught in make-believe worlds. We have to look for what is true or false in our thinking and in what thought has created. This is by far the greatest challenge for the Martial Artist—understanding how thought creates conflict through the illusions it weaves."

"Thought creates the illusion that a certain belief is right and more important than other beliefs. This divides people, separates them, and creates conflict," an Apprentice Instructor spoke out.

"We create an enemy in our minds, and this in turn creates physical conflict," said a young student.

"How?" the Teacher questioned.

"An enemy is like a frightening monster in a nightmare. It's only a dream, but we think it's real while we're dreaming it."

"Let's go into this for a moment," the Teacher continued. "Can anyone tell me how this works? How we create the enemy? Go slowly and carefully."

"Well, I can see that if you are attacked by a large, black dog, for example, that dog becomes your enemy, a real physical threat, so you need to defend yourself. Now, what if you see another large, black dog a few days later, but it isn't the same dog. You automatically react to this dog in a self-protective way because it reminds you of the one who bit you. So, you think this dog is your enemy, too, when it really isn't," the senior Apprentice Instructor commented. "We react to certain people in a similar way. Suppose you've been told a type of person or group of people are a threat to you. This type of thinking originated in the days of cave people, when men and women had to gather together as tribes to protect themselves from wild animals and other groups of people who were a threat to their survival."

"Go on," the Teacher encouraged.

"Well, it seems to me that what we've done is to carry on that tribal way of life when it isn't even necessary anymore...or to our benefit. We still think of other groups or tribes as a threat to our survival. So, a particular enemy is created in the minds of a whole people. Like the dog who bit you, you carry that memory and apply it to the next black dog you see, and your fear eventually gets passed on to your children. A fear gets passed to the next generation, and that generation passes it down to the next. We have finally inherited what you call the 'Ancient Warrior.' The Ancient Warrior was created from the need to protect oneself and one's group or tribe from the 'other'—the 'enemy'—who was, at one time, an actual physical threat to my, or our, survival. But, that was a long time ago. And, yet, we are still reacting to certain groups or tribes in the same way—as if it were then. Does this make sense?" the senior Apprentice Instructor questioned.

"Yes, it does. That was a clear example of how thinking from the past can get carried over to the present to continue the conflict. This has gone on for centuries. The intelligent Martial Artist understands how thinking functions and how destructive thinking gets carried over from the past, continuing to create conflict in the world. We need to understand *we are the world, and the world is us*—it is all one and the same thing. *We* create the world by how we think and act! If we can see the truth of this simple fact, then we can be free of the destructive, tribal, divisive thinking and acting which creates enemies and warriors. Dear students, please look at this for yourself. Some of you may be too young to grasp all of this, but keep at it and you will understand. Just remember to watch your thoughts; be aware of how they can bring the past into the present and create conflict. Start with simple examples in your own lives—like when you think of something you really want but cannot have, how such a thought creates conflict. Then look at the other examples. As you keep looking, *if* you are serious and truly want to find out, you will begin to see how thinking has created enemies, warriors, and war. It's all in our minds, like the monsters in our nightmares. Our challenge is to wake up from the dream! This is our greatest test, the test of understanding *how we create conflict* by the way we think and act. Students, the test has just begun!"

HARMONY

In harmony there is no actor acting—no "me" doing.

UNBROKEN FLAME OF ATTENTION
The Test of Harmony

The arrow flew swiftly through the crisp, thin air and landed dead center in the target. The twang of the bow, the swift flight of the wooden, steel-tipped shaft spiraling silently towards its goal, then the dull thud of its landing—those were the only sounds to be heard. All had happened so easily, so effortlessly. The Master Teacher sat down on the ground and closed his eyes, in the same position he had taken before shooting the arrow on this moonless, pitch-black night. They had all seen it for themselves when they approached the target. Dead center! The arrow was imbedded deeply into the target's inner-most circle. They stared at it in silent awe. From where he had stood, he could not have seen the target in the dark.

"How can someone hit a target at this distance and enter the bull's-eye without seeing the target?" another Teacher asked the next day. "You are going to find out, for this is your next test," she continued with energy.

The students were all issued bows and quivers of arrows. The early morning fog was lifting off the archery field as they took up their places next to each other in a long line, facing targets a short way off. These targets were much closer to the shooter than the targets used by the Apprentice Instructors and Teachers.

In turn, each student notched the arrow, pulled the taut bowstring, and let the arrow fly. Arrows showered down to the earth, sprinkling the long, green lawn with wooden sticks. Only a few came close to the targets. Again, they all fired in order; again, the wooden shafts, propelled through the air, landed haphazardly around the target areas. This ritual of archery went on for over an hour. A few finally hit the oversized targets. Hard as they could try, no one seemed able to hit the center of the target as had their Master Teacher the night before. He had hit the bull's-eye from a much greater distance than they were now shooting from, with a smaller target, and at night without any moonlight! The students had been the same distance from the target that night, yet none of them could see it in the darkness of the night.

Practice was over for the day. Their Instructors made no comment as the students packed up their bows and arrows. The next day, after an early workout in Freestyle, a swim in the lake, followed by breakfast and an hour tending the organic garden, the students assembled again at the archery field. There was an obvious and extreme change in the arrangement of targets. The oversized targets with large circles had been moved closer than their former positions and placed within five feet of the shooting area.

"Line up, take your bows, and notch your first and only arrow for today," the Teacher directed without emotion.

The confused students did as they were told. They were asked to suspend questioning during this day's practice, and to observe non-judgmentally. The students lined up and took their ready positions. On command, they notched their bows with the wooden arrows. In turn, each shot an arrow into the target just a few feet away. When all had finished, the Teacher congratulated them.

"Very good, students. You have each hit the bull's-eye. That was the intention, was it not?"

The students looked confused. Indeed each had hit the bull's-eye. There was no way anyone could miss at that distance! The arrow was almost touching the target as each student readied to fire. Missing the center was almost impossible. The Instructor ended the lesson for the day.

The following morning, the students were again taken out to the archery field. Today there was a different arrangement, though, for all the large targets had been removed.

"Now, students, I want each of you to hit the bull's-eye today. In order to pass this test, you must do so. Do you understand?" the Instructor inquired.

"No, Sir, I don't," one of the students responded. "There are no targets. How can we hit the bull's-eye?"

"Do you need glasses, students? Can't you see the targets out there?" the Instructor yelled back, as he strode away from them down the archery field. Reaching a spot much farther away than the first day's practice targets, he called out to them, "Do you see the targets now that I am pointing them out to you, or are you still blind?"

The students were even more confused. They looked at their Instructor standing between two trees, one on either side of the long and narrow field. He was gesturing to something they could not see.

"Can you still not see it?" he repeated. "Well then, come here if you are so blind."

The students walked forward in unison towards their Instructor. As they drew closer, they still could not see what he was pointing to. The Instructor kept shaking his head in disbelief.

When they came within a few yards of the Instructor, they could finally make out a thin string tied between the two trees. On closer inspection, they saw sewing needles suspended from the thread in a single row.

"Now, this is your target and the test is to hit the bull's-eye—to

thread the eye of the needle with your arrows," the Teacher said in all seriousness.

The students looked even more dumbfounded at this impossible command. How could an arrow fit through the eye of an ordinary sewing needle? They couldn't even hit an oversized target at normal placement, much less hit a needle's eye at this great distance!

"Please, no questions now! Just do as I ask," the Teacher said simply.

The students went back to their starting positions, took up their bows, and notched their arrows. On command, each of them, in turn, shot their arrows at the unseen targets so far away. Arrows cascaded through the air, landing in the general vicinity of the invisible targets.

"Try harder, try harder," the Instructor implored of them. "You must hit the needle's eye; it is imperative you try as hard as you can. This is the test!"

All morning, the students tried. Then, after lunch, they tried and tried and tried again. Late into the day, they continued shooting arrows towards the targets until they were exhausted. They went to bed early that night after supper, dreaming of bows and arrows, of hitting the target, of arrows magically piercing the eyes of hanging needles. The next morning the students woke up refreshed, ready to take up the archery test again. Today, the old targets were back in their original places. The students lined up and assumed their positions.

"Today, you will learn about the unbroken flame of attention, of harmony, of being one with the bow and arrow and target," the Teacher said upon greeting them in the early morning. The dew was still on the grass and leaves of the trees. The bright, clear sunshine glistened on the small beads of water, sending out tiny, sparkling reflections. The birds were quiet. The sky was brilliant blue and cloudless. There was a newness, a freshness about this moment.

"I want each of you to pick up the cloth by your feet and tie it around your head as a blindfold so you cannot see," the Teacher stated.

On the ground next to the arrow stands were dark, narrow pieces of cloth. Each student picked up a strip and carefully tied it around his or her head and over both eyes.

"Now, I want you to listen carefully to what I say during this time. I want you to forget the bull's-eye, forget where the arrow is supposed to go, forget there is any target or purpose to archery at all. All you need to do is draw the bow and when the string reaches a certain point which you will feel, *just let it fall*—like ripe fruit from a tree."

They had listened carefully. Slowly, each drew the bowstring until it reached a point where it could no longer be held. The string burst from their fingers and they heard the "twang" of the string as the arrow shot into the unknown. As they felt for their next arrow, one by one, the students began to remember their collective dream. They could see and feel the arrows flying through the air and magically piercing the eyes of the needles. Again and again, they relived the magic of their dreamed archery contest. As they shot their arrows in the darkness of their blindfolds, they listened carefully to their Instructor as he talked them through their lesson, their test.

"*You* get in your way. Don't focus on anything except what is actually happening now. Feel the strain of your muscles as you pull the bowstring; feel the tension at the moment before the arrow releases. Draw the bow with your spirit, effortlessly, naturally. You have it within you, like the Way of the Golden Dragon. This does not depend on strength, but rather on presence of mind, on the vitality and inner awareness with which you shoot. 'It' shoots! 'It' hits! Bow, arrow, and person become one in harmony. There is no division, no separation. Let the arrow fall like snow from the branch."

For a timeless period, the students let arrows fly. After a while, there was a new sensation pervading them and infusing each with a sense of lightness and transparency. The arrow notched itself, the bow lifted itself, and the wooden, steel-tipped shaft let itself go, winging its way into the unknown, as if it was nothing at all. And, so it was—nothing at all. The test was underway; the test was forgotten! It was over when it began.

STRENGTH

When you are that which you observe—
when the flower's blossoming blossoms you—
in that there is strength without limitation.

WAR OF THE ROSE
The Test of Strength

"Throw him, throw him!" the Master Instructor said, urging the boy on. "Use your hips, move with the throw; don't just stand there like a stone Buddha. Lift, using the natural way. Don't force it. You're not throwing around sacks of cement. Use leverage. Move at the point of ease. Create that small movement, pivot that small circle, then put your whole being into it. Move with your breath. Mind...breath...body. Hear what your breath is saying. Move with your breath."

After over two hours of instruction, the students sat down to cool off.

"You all try so hard, but have little strength. The harder you try, the weaker you are. *You* are defeating yourself! Do you understand?" The Master Teacher looked intensely at each student, his eyes directly meeting theirs.

"Perhaps a story might give you an insight into what I am saying. A long time ago, a man named Carlos lived in a small village halfway between two great cities. Carlos was a kind and gentle young man. He was also physically strong. He practiced the Martial Arts, studying many different forms. Carlos had come to this country to study these Arts, for his life and only love was his practice. He lived for the Martial Arts. One day, as he was walking northward to one of the great cities, he met a band of rough men on the road. They were surrounding a powerfully built, yet smaller and older man. The older man stood calmly in the middle of this group of thugs as they encircled him and called him names.

"'Come on, old man. Show us how strong you are,' taunted one of the thugs.

"'Yeah, weak one, show us your skill. You are supposed to be a great Martial Arts Master. To me, you look like an ordinary man,' said another.

"The older man did look ordinary, but only to the untrained eye. His clothes were ordinary; his looks were ordinary. But there was something about him that, to Carlos, was indeed extraordinary. It was something very subtle in the way he stood there, dignified and upright, looking at the thugs and yet, not looking at anyone at all. He seemed as if he were in a dreamlike state. His eyelids were half-closed and his arms were relaxed by his sides. He stood with his sandaled feet slightly apart, while he waited motionlessly. He said nothing.

"'Hey, old man, you gonna fight us? Can you take us all on? Why so quiet? What do you have to say before you get your beating?' one of the boisterous thugs called out, egging him on.

"Carlos watched the older man intently from a distance as the thugs closed in on him. One grabbed the older man around his neck from behind and held him with a choke hold. For a moment, they all froze. Carlos noticed the older man had turned his head to the side, so his chin was tucked down to his chest and fitted into the fold of the younger man's bent arm. With one hand, the older man lightly grasped the choking hand of the thug. The thug pulled very hard on the older man, even lifting him up off the ground. It looked like the older man was defeated, perhaps even choking to death. Carlos was about to intervene when the older man made a quick movement and suddenly stood behind the thug, holding his arm up and pressing it into his back. The younger man screamed out in pain, 'You're breaking it! Let go! Ow, you're breaking my arm!'

91

"At that moment, another thug leapt towards the older man. Using the captured thug as a shield, the older man ran the two younger men into each other with a sickening thud. The charging thug fell backward with his partner on top. Stunned, the two just lay there. Then, another two thugs attacked, but the older man was ready. He ducked down under the closer one and lifted himself up at just the right point, catching the first oncoming man under his midsection, hurling him through the air to crash into the second charging thug. The two collided in mid-air and landed in a heap near the first pair of defeated men.

"The last two thugs yelled and charged. The older man stepped deftly to one side with the agility of a young deer and caught the two oncoming attackers by the arms. He swung them around in one direction, suddenly reversed to the other, and swept them both off their feet, leaving them to crash to the ground. Applying a joint lock on both the men's arms, he held them fast until they shouted out in pain.

"'Let go, you're killing me,' said one in extreme agony. 'I give up.'

"He let go of the two men. After a few minutes, they were all on their feet, only slightly hurt, but stunned by what had happened. Quietly, they sulked off to nurse their pride and bruises.

"Carlos stood transfixed. The older man brushed himself off lightly and picked up the bundle he had lain aside at the start of the fight. He started to move down the road. Carlos, realizing this man was surely a great Martial Arts Master, ran after him. When he came up to the older man, Carlos knelt on the ground and bowed.

"'Please, Teacher, I want to be your student. Teach me your strength. I will do whatever you say,' Carlos cried out.

"The old man took no notice of Carlos and kept on walking. Carlos was very stubborn so he kept up with the older man and threw himself

92

on the ground again, asking to be taught. Once more, the older man simply ignored Carlos. They neared the outskirts of the great city. The agile old man quickly turned a corner. As Carlos ran and turned the same corner, the older man stood waiting for him.

"'So you want to be taught, to be shown the secret of strength. How much will you give me to know this?' he asked curiously.

"Carlos stopped in his tracks, caught off-guard by this sudden turn of events.

"'I will give you anything you want, Teacher,' Carlos said earnestly.

"'Come to my house tomorrow and I will show you my secret. But, only if you can defeat me.'

"Shocked, Carlos was about to say that defeating such a great Martial Artist would be impossible, when the older man went off.

"'Where do you live?' Carlos called after the older man.

"'Just ask, and you will find me. Until tomorrow morning.'

"The next morning, Carlos went back to the very spot where he had left the old man and asked a group of women talking in the road where the great Martial Arts Master lived. They pointed to a small hut on the top of the hill.

"Carlos walked up the steep, dirt road. There he saw a small but well-kept hut. In the backyard, he could see the Teacher practicing Martial Arts moves—slow, rhythmic movements. Carlos watched the older man in awe. *'How can I defeat a man such as this?'* he thought to himself. *'He is truly a great Master of the Martial Arts. I can see he is very powerful. His movements show tremendous strength. I cannot beat such a man! He is much too strong. His actions come from a pure mind.*

Such a man can never be defeated.'

"Bowing low, Carlos announced himself.

"'Greetings, great Teacher. I am here as you asked.'

"'Good, let's go then. Attack me. Ask no questions,' the older man cried out. 'We have no time to discuss. Attack!'

"Carlos was temporarily stunned by this urgent demand. Before he could recover, the older man charged forward and grabbed Carlos by the collar and, turning quickly to the side, sent him flying through the air. Carlos landed in a pile of hay at the end of the small yard. Unhurt, he quickly leapt to his feet. His Martial Arts training was automatic. When the older man charged again, Carlos was ready. But to no avail, for the older man dodged Carlos' attack and rolled away, while at the same time, swept the young man's feet out from under him. Carlos again jumped up and tried in vain to stop the older man. Again and again he failed. Finally, the older man grabbed him from behind, applying the same choke hold the first thug had used in his attack on the older man the previous day. Carlos felt the Teacher's strong arm around his neck, pressing tightly, keeping him from breathing. Just before Carlos blacked out, the older man let go and adeptly stepped in front of Carlos, looking him straight in the eyes.

"'You fool, you defeated yourself. You could have defeated me, but you let yourself lose before you even started,' the old man shouted at Carlos.

"'Do you still want to know where my great strength comes from?' the old man inquired, looking intently into Carlos' eyes.

"Half-choking, his eyes watering, Carlos nodded.

"'Then come back at midnight and I will show you,' the older man said emphatically. The Teacher turned quickly on his heels and, grabbing a walking stick, strode rapidly out of the yard and up and over the hill.

"Carlos stood for quite a while, trying to regain his breath. The older man had attacked him many times, but had never hurt him.

"That night, exactly at midnight, Carlos approached the Teacher's house. He found him sitting quietly in the backyard under the light of the full moon.

"'Sit here,' the Teacher said, pointing to the right of where he himself sat. Carlos took his place next to the older man, on a small mat which had been set there for him.

"'What do you see, young man?' the Teacher asked after a few minutes, breaking the silence.

"'Flowers,' Carlos said. For, in front of them both was a lovely garden of red roses illuminated by the bright moonlight.

"'Do you see the very large one in front, separated from the rest? We will watch this rose until morning. By then you will know the secret of my strength.' The older man spoke softly in hushed tones. He said nothing else. They sat in silence.

"For hours the two sat there watching the lone rose in the garden. At first, Carlos was curious at what everything meant. Then after a time, he began to get restless. His legs started to ache and his back hurt from sitting for so long. His mind began to wander and he wanted only to leave. He thought about home and how nice it would be in his comfortable bed, sleeping on soft, downy cushions. He was annoyed at sitting there looking at this simple flower. He felt foolish and angry, staring at this rose, the rose staring back at him. It seemed as if the rose was at war with him, trying to defeat him, to break down his will, to sap him of his strength. It seemed to be a battle of wills, a staring match.

95

"The night became very quiet. Even the crickets had gone to sleep. There was nothing except stars above and the moon casting a soft, pale, white light on the scene below. The two men sat. The Teacher never moved. Carlos was exhausted. Hour after hour the long night crept on.

"Carlos kept looking at the rose, the moonlight gently lighting the flower. The anger had passed and he felt calmer now. Finally, he could sense the slightest lifting of darkness. Slowly and delicately, the night gave way to day. The moon receded and the sun inched up in the eastern sky. Faint rays of sunlight spread their fiery color across the horizon.

"Carlos watched the rose in the new light. He could see its petals. He could feel them opening in the early morning dawn. He could smell the odor arising from the flower. He could sense the growth of its roots in the soil. He could almost hear the rose blooming. His eyes became the rose; his ears, his mouth, his fingers, his whole being became the rose. And, in being that rose, there came a growing strength, a tremendous sense of energy flooding his senses. It grew upwards from his spine and downwards from his spine. It went up to the sky and down into the ground. The sky and earth were the rose. An energy was growing inside him. The rose was everything—and yet it was only a lone rose in a garden of roses.

"The old man spoke for the first time that night, breaking the silence which had enveloped them both. 'Can you defeat me now, student?'

"Out of that silence an insight was born. *I am defeated only by myself,*' he heard himself thinking.

"Carlos looked at the older man, his Teacher, and smiled.

"'There is no need to, for we are that,' Carlos said, pointing at the rose in the garden."

* * *

"Understand the story of the war of the rose and you will understand where great strength comes from. Be the rose, dear students. Forget thoughts of winning or losing. You will defeat yourself by comparing yourself to another. You will lose your strength by thinking another is more powerful than you," the Teacher said, bringing the group of young Martial Artists back into the present moment. "Do you understand the story? If you say you do, you do not!"

The students began their chores of tending the flower gardens, weeding between the plants, watering seedlings so they could grow and blossom—as they had done every year, year after year.

ORDER

Can knowledge create order?
Or, does knowledge create more disorder?

QUEST FOR PEACE
The Test of Order

Each student had his or her own particular chore to complete the cleaning of the practice hall in an orderly fashion. Cleaning the hall and the school as a whole was a respectable activity. To be chosen for the harder tasks was an honor, for this meant you were giving your attention to the tasks at hand—your chores were done with care.

After their chores, the students were called together by one of the Master Teachers.

"Today I am going to ask you a question no one will be able to respond to correctly," the Master Teacher said with twinkling eyes.

"The question is, 'What creates order?' or 'How do we bring about order?'"

The students' hands went up immediately, waving to be chosen to give their answers.

"Order is created by putting everything in its proper place."

"Order is brought about by thinking right thoughts."

"We bring it about by having good relationships with people."

"We create order by understanding disorder."

"You learn well, students. All of your answers are quite right, but they are all wrong. No one has responded correctly to my question," the Teacher said with some annoyance.

"I don't understand, Teacher. You say we all gave you right answers, and yet did not answer the question correctly. What is the correct answer?" a senior student inquired.

"I will ask it again, 'What is order?'"

The students sat quietly this time, hesitant to answer the question. One small, young boy raised his hand and the Teacher acknowledged him. The boy pointed to the library of books in the corner of the practice hall, books which were valued and well taken care of. Every day, one of the students would put them in perfect order. The students and Teacher all turned to look where the young boy was pointing.

"Good, he understands!" the Teacher exclaimed.

Then, the same boy, sitting on the floor among his fellow students, attempted to move the people around him into a straight line. The students, somewhat baffled by this young boy's silent urgings, reluctantly moved as he pulled and tugged at them.

"Good, he understands," the Teacher exclaimed again. "Can you see what he is doing? When asked, 'What is order?' he sat silently when most hurried to give *explanations* of order, answers you had memorized. When asked again, 'What is order?' you fell silent and he pointed to the order of the books in the library. He gave us an *example* of order. Then he started to create order by getting the rest of you to line up in a straight and orderly fashion. By this, he gave us an *experience* of order. Do you understand the difference?

"Now, I want each of you to respond to the question again, but without any words. You must answer through silence. Now, 'What is order?'" the Teacher questioned once again.

The students looked at each other, then got up slowly and began to mill around the room. One of the students went over to the books and arranged them with great precision. Two students went over to the entrance where the others had left their shoes and began to put them in more careful order. A few students went to the dressing areas and began to straighten up the clothes. All around the school, students were creating experiences of order.

"Now come back and line up quickly, in one straight line," the Teacher commanded suddenly.

The students stopped what they were doing and ran to line up. There was some shoving and jostling to get to the head of the line. A few stragglers tried to push into the already formed line, but the other students were reluctant to let them in.

"What happened to that order just now?" the Teacher asked sharply. "You seemed to understand how to bring about order. You were fast to demonstrate that knowledge, but when asked to line up, your order fell apart. Why?"

"We forgot," said one of the students.

"You forgot? That means order is just a thought regarding what you should do. Order is an 'ideal.' But, is order only a thought or an ideal? Is order only what we have been told it is? Our brains have been conditioned to come up with answers for everything. We are very clever. But, to *do* order, to *experience* it, cannot come about through a learned answer. Answers are knowledge, something you know and have been taught. Memorized knowledge is necessary to answer correctly when someone asks you a question about mathematics or science. But, when someone asks you about order, what does the brain immediately do? It comes up with an *explanation* of order. But, is the explanation order itself? Is knowledge order? Let's put it another way. Can an explanation or knowledge of order bring about order? Or does knowledge in this case create disorder? Go into it slowly, for this is very important in under-

standing what it means to break the chains of the Ancient Warrior," the Teacher urged.

"Someone tells you order is, for example, peace of mind, or having good relationships with people, or putting everything in its right place. The brain memorizes that explanation and then, because it 'knows' or has 'knowledge' about order, it thinks it has created order. But all the brain has done is form a concept, a thought, an explanation of order. Do you see this? It is actually quite elementary if you look at it simply," the Teacher continued.

"So someone asks, 'What is order?' and what happens? The brain immediately searches for the answer, the explanation from its great or small resources of knowledge. Your hands go up and you want to be the first to give the correct answer. You have been trained to do this, and under certain circumstances, it may be the correct thing to do. If I ask you, 'What is 2 + 2?' you would tell me the answer is four. This is correct knowledge, an *explanation* answering the question correctly. You may also demonstrate 2 + 2 by taking four stones and putting two together in two separate piles. This would be giving an *example* of 2 + 2. And, if I ask you about order—what creates order or how to bring it about—you give me a well thought-out answer, an explanation. *Does this explanation, this knowledge stored in the brain, actually create order?*

"Order is essential in understanding why there is so much violence and suffering in the world. If you want to understand and be free of the chains of the Ancient Warrior, you must understand the differences among an explanation, an example, and an experience. The first is telling, the second is showing, and the last is doing. It is the *doing* of it—not because you *should* create order, but because it makes sense. Order creates beauty, clarity of mind and body. It comes from *seeing*, from *insight*, and not from any command to be orderly.

"If you only know the explanation, the knowledge—as so many people do—then you will create disorder, more violence, and continue warring. The Ancient Warrior lives in knowledge carried over from the past. Knowledge won't end knowledge carried over from our violent history. *Insight* is needed to break the chains of knowledge by *seeing* the bondage. Knowledge of our bondage only adds to more knowledge and creates the illusion of understanding.

"Dear students, this may sound complex. It is, but you *can* understand if you give your full attention to it. All you need to do is look at your own brain. It is how this brain functions, or malfunctions, that needs to be understood. *We* create our own problems. *We* have created the wrath the Ancient Warrior feeds on. And we continue to carry on this problem from generation to generation. Order is necessary, not only as an explanation, but as something which occurs naturally, out of insight, sensitivity, intelligence, out of understandingwhat creates disorder. Understanding that which *prevents* order brings about order! The mind needs to create order to prepare itself for that which is beyond thought and time—to enter into the essence of the flower, the silence of nothingness. This is the essential work of the Martial Arts: to bring about order so we are free of the chains binding us to our violent past. Understand this and you will truly master these wonderful Arts. And your quest for peace, for ending the Ancient Warrior in you, will blossom in that newly discovered order."

"Now, look to your right, to your left. See the disorder, but without judging it. Don't say that the disorder you see is bad or wrong. *Just see it!* Be aware of it and in that nonjudgemental awareness watch, observe how your mind naturally creates order and beauty. Through that observation—through perceiving without thinking about it—the brain freely and effortlessly ends the disorder.

FOCUS

In that quality of attention when there is focus,
there is no room for fear to enter.

FIGHTING THE PAPER TIGER
The Test of Focus

"Teacher, how many boards can you break?" asked one of the students.

"Why, I can't break any," answered the Teacher with a kind smile.

"But, Teacher," the surprised student responded, "how can you be a Master of the Martial Arts if you cannot break boards?"

"You tell me, dear students," said the Teacher, "how many boards have attacked you lately?"

The class, including both the Teacher and the inquisitive student, laughed heartily.

All morning, and after a light lunch, the students had been practicing the basics of punching and striking. They were using punching boards, thickly wrapped pads on top of shoulder-height, wooden shafts imbedded into the ground. The students would practice their punches and strikes on these matted boards to test their focus, their ability to concentrate the mind and body at one point and release that energy on the target just beyond the surface of the contact point. They had developed great power using these matted boards and felt more confidence in their physical skills.

"You are not strong until you can defeat the Paper Tiger," the Teacher called out during the lesson.

"Perhaps you can break boards, bricks, stones, and probably your bones practicing like this. But, this is not the ultimate test of focus. Sit down and I will demonstrate focus." The students sat in a semicircle around their Teacher. Birds hopped about pecking the earth for any little food they could find. A woodpecker's intense hammering on a nearby tree distracted the students for a moment.

"Have you ever watched a woodpecker?" the Teacher asked, responding to the moment.

"The bird has great energy because it is not distracted. It is single-minded. But, this doesn't mean it is not aware of everything around it. Focus doesn't mean solely concentrating on one single thing. Focus is total. And because it is, that is where the energy lies—the energy to wholly master a Martial Arts technique. When you focus in Freestyle, do you see only the eyes of your opponent or do you see his or her total body, the physical and even spiritual being? Can you also be aware of the cricket in the grass near you or the bird flying above, or feel the warm sunlight on your back and the cool breeze on your face? That is focus. It includes everything and yet, that everything is also, at the same time, concentrated to a single point—like the woodpecker."

The Teacher sat silently for a few minutes to let the lesson sink in, and also to allow the students time to listen carefully to the woodpecker's focused, urgent, and compelling activity.

"Now, let's fight the Paper Tiger!" the Teacher said with energy. "I will show you how to really focus!"

The Teacher hung a thin piece of white rice paper from two delicate pieces of string, loosely tied to a tree branch at shoulder-height. Closing his eyes, he moved into an upright, combat stance. His body was completely relaxed, but remained strong. His hands were poised in front of him, one high, one low. His feet were apart, his legs bent slightly at the knees. He slowly opened his eyes and then, with the quickness of a cobra, he struck out at the paper. The paper moved ever so slightly, as if a breeze had just kissed it.

"There, it is done!" the Teacher exclaimed.

The students sat politely with confused expressions on their faces. Nothing had happened except that their Teacher had quickly struck at the paper. But the paper still hung suspended from the branch by strings.

"But, sir, what is so great about hitting a piece of paper?! It didn't even fall down. At least when you break a board, you can see the two halves and thereby know your strength," one student said politely.

"Come up here, student," the Teacher motioned, "and see for yourself."

The student did as he was asked and looked carefully at the rice paper. What he saw astounded him. Right in the center, like a snake bite, were two finger-sized holes.

"Can you see the holes now? Perhaps you should all come up and look," the Teacher said.

"How did you do that? Is it easy? It looked like nothing at all!" students cried out in excitement.

"Would you like to try?" the Teacher asked.

"Yes, Teacher, we would like to fight the Paper Tiger," they responded, one and all.

"Tonight, meet me in the field behind the practice hall."

The students hurried through the day, completing their daily chores, fixing meals, and finishing their assigned readings. At nine o'clock, they met in the dark behind the hall. The moon was still somewhat full, so there was enough light to see. Their Teacher stood waiting with an Assistant.

Facing them was a row of brightly lit candles on top of round, wood pilings at shoulder-height. The scene looked lovely in the night—such beautiful, natural order.

"Now, line up in a row behind the candles, just like you did with the matted punching boards," the Teacher said softly in the night air. The Teacher stood watching the candles for a moment. They flickered gently. He placed himself in front of one of the candles in the same combat position he had adopted earlier that afternoon, when he had stood in front of the hanging paper target. He again closed his eyes and remained quiet for a few moments. He slowly opened his eyes, and, as quick as a king cobra's strike, lashed out at the candle. The light suddenly went out. He went down the whole row of lighted candles, performing the same technique. Candle after candle was extinguished with the Teacher's snake-like attacks. At the end, he once again closed his eyes. On opening them, he said to the students watching him, "Now it is your turn." He motioned to his Assistant to relight the candles.

Each student, in turn, moved into position in front of the candles. On command, each took focus, trying to punch out the candle flame. No one could. Some even punched the candle off its wooden piling. This was the only way any of the candles went out!

"You are trying to break boards," the Teacher observed. "The flame is not a board. A board is hard, fixed, and unmoving. The flame dances and jumps about with life. It is fluid, alive, and soft. You cannot extinguish it by trying to break it like you would a board. You are too willful, too full of your own strength and pride! You think you are strong and can defeat this simple candle flame, perhaps even defeat the Paper Tiger too, just because an old man like me can do it easily. You are too proud! Am I correct?" he asked the students. They looked down at the

ground, ashamed of themselves.

"Just as I thought. Oh, you young people, you think you know it all. So full of yourselves! But to tell you the truth, I, too, was like you once. See these bashed knuckles? I, too, thought I was strong, but the stone I was so sure I could break was much stronger," he laughed. "Don't worry, you will learn, despite your youth and pride."

For a long while, they practiced punching at the candle. Occasionally, when a flame would die, there were jokes made about a gust of wind or blowing out birthday candles.

"Let me demonstrate this again. Watch carefully. You know when I say, 'Be careful,' I mean take care, be attentive, be aware."

The Teacher, again and again, put out the candles with almost no effort at all.

"You see I do not try hard, but can put the candle's light out. Yet, you try very hard and the candle still stays lit. What is the difference?" the Teacher asked.

"We are trying too hard, Teacher," a student responded.

"So, what will you do? Let me tell you the secret. It's in the pull back, when your hand comes back to you. It is not in the outward motion of the punch or strike; in the pulling back, the flame is also pulled back and goes out. Therefore, you have to be very loose, calm, at ease. Like a whip. You see that a whip is limp, loose, but with a flick of your wrist, it will lash out and crack. It has strength in its ability to be flexible.

The students were then handed thin, wet towels. "Now, snap these towels like a whip, but sideways—not overhanded as you would do with a real whip." The Teacher demonstrated the movement with dexterity.

The students practiced snapping the wet towels until they moved like whips cracking the cool, night air.

"Now, drop your towel and snap at the candle flame."

The students, one by one, snapped their hands in a backfisted motion towards the flame, pulling their hands back faster than when their hands went towards the candle. Again and again, they tried until they could finally manage to get a flame to go out.

"Good, you are learning focus. You are learning the real strength you will need to defeat the Paper Tiger.

For about a week, this daily ritual of the candle flame continued, until the night of the test. They arrived early, at dusk, just after dinner. Instead of the candles, a row of small sheets of rice paper were suspended from string between two trees.

"You feel nice and contented after dinner, relaxed," the Teacher observed.

"Now, line up in front of the Paper Tigers and do as I ask. Hold your hand up in front of you with your first two fingers outstretched like the fangs of a snake. When I say, strike out—but not 'at' the paper. Rather, try to grab it with your two snake fingers."

The students lined up and were about to strike out when the Teacher asked them to close their eyes.

"In your mind's eye, see the holes already there. See your hand moving like a snake back into its coiled position. The act is done before you start. As with the flame, get out of the way and let the whip do the work."

On the teacher's command, the students struck out at the hanging paper. At first, the paper flew away from them. Some sheets were even ripped off the string. But, eventually, the students could actually rip the paper, if only in a crude fashion.

"This takes great practice, but you will learn to do it eventually. There is really no great secret. First, you must understand you are trying too hard, trying to break paper as if it is a rigid board. That kind of power is not the power you seek. This power will come from being relaxed, from knowing how to strike. Understanding real focus can eventually defeat the Paper Tiger. Focus is awareness, and awareness is also needed to defeat the Ancient Warrior. If you fight the Ancient Warrior in the same way as you try to break boards, *you* will break; *you* will be defeated. But, if you know the Ancient Warrior and its ways, then you have a chance to defeat it as you will understand what it takes to win."

"Everything we are doing here is towards this end of understanding the Ancient Warrior, the chains that bind us to a violent heritage. We are testing you so you can develop the qualities necessary to defeat the Warrior, not by force or brutality, as were the ways in the past, but by intelligence and understanding. The quality of being focused is an important test you will need to pass in order to qualify as a new warrior—a warrior of peace, a warrior of the Spirit that can end the conflict of our ancestors."

EXCELLENCE

Skill in action is excellence in living.

WAY OF THE SWORD
The Test of Excellence

The reading assignment for the evening told of a young man, in times long ago, who wished to study the Martial Art of Swordsmanship under the teaching of a great Master Swordsman. His only desire was to learn a discipline which could teach him excellence, not to master a Martial Art for hurting others. He believed the Martial Arts to be a spiritual endeavor and a way to understand the violence in the world. He knew the intent of all properly taught Martial Arts was to end conflict, not to contribute to it.

He traveled a far distance to meet this great Master. Upon arrival, the young man asked if he could study the Way of the Sword with the Master. But, as was the tradition in that time, he was not allowed to begin study of the Martial Arts immediately. He was assigned chores in the household, serving the Master Teacher and the senior students. The first teaching he received was in the Art of the Tea Ceremony, a very detailed ritual requiring concentration and inner peace. He studied this Art for over three years, but never received any lessons in swordsmanship. His main duty was to serve tea to the Master, which he did with great skill, respect, and peace of mind.

One day, the young man, now a skilled tea server, was sent to the nearby village to purchase some supplies. As he was walking down the crowded street, he accidentally bumped into a large, older man, who, as it turned out, was a Master Swordsman of great skill. This swordsman had a bad temper and showed his anger easily, but was nonetheless respected for his ability with the sword.

The young man immediately apologized for his clumsiness and

begged for forgiveness. The Master Swordsman told the young tea server his apology was not accepted, and demanded the tea server meet him the next day at noon to fight. The tea server ran back to the school and, filled with fear, told his Master what had happened.

The tea server explained the incident to his Teacher, saying that he didn't want to fight but was afraid this angry Master Swordsman would seek him out and kill him. The young man thought it best to meet the Swordsman so as not to bring harm to the school.

The Master Swordsman listened to his young student with much affection. "You are a good tea server; you know the Ceremony very well. When you serve me, I can see you are focused and have peace of mind. Each of your actions is simple and clear. Your body and mind are in harmony. Tomorrow when you meet this Swordsman, think not of fighting him; think only of serving tea as you serve me. If you do this, you will be unharmed."

The young tea server was unsure of his Master's advice, but knew him to be very wise. And, as the young tea server felt confident in his skill of serving tea, he knew that because of this training, his mind was calm and strong.

The next day, the young tea server traveled to town and met the angry Master Swordsman. He did not let the boldness and sheer strength of the Master Swordsman bother him, but rather, concentrated on the ritual he knew so well, feeling the inner peace of his perfected skill.

The two men faced each other and knelt down. The young man placed the sword given to him by his side. The Master Swordsman, looking fiercely at the tea server, also put his sword down. For a moment, both of them sat quietly, eyes downcast, focusing on their breath. The young tea server thought of nothing but serving his Master tea.

Each opened their eyes and quickly drew their swords, pointing the tips towards the other's throat. A small crowd had gathered to witness this event. They were all transfixed by the two fighters, each remaining so still. The Master Swordsman stared at his opponent with a terrible anger. The young tea server saw only himself offering a cup of tea to his own Master Teacher, holding the sword perfectly still in a gesture of love and respect.

For several minutes, the two men faced each other in this way. The tea servant kept his eyes focused and held his sword with remarkable poise. The Master Swordsman, on seeing the steadiness and peace of mind of the younger man, became confused and forgot his anger. The sword of the Master began to waver.

After fifteen minutes, not a thing had changed except the sword of the Master Teacher was shaking even more. The tea server, with his eyes still focused, held the sword tip pointing at his opponent's neck extremely still; he did not waver and was in complete control of himself.

The Master Swordsman could no longer stand facing one so focused and calm. He placed his sword back in its sheath and bowed low to the tea server. "You are truly a great Master of the Sword. I am defeated by your presence. I have never observed such calmness and peace of mind. Against such control, I have no chance," the Master Swordsman stated with great reverence and humility.

The young tea server returned to his school and told his Teacher what had occurred. "You have not had one lesson in Swordsmanship, but you are already an accomplished Master; you have done what others do not. You have mastered excellence, and in doing so, you have mastered yourself."

WISDOM

Wisdom is in seeing the illusions the mind create in its quest for freedom.

BEGINNER'S MIND
The Test of Wisdom

Three students were sitting cross-legged on the hillside overlooking a wide, long valley. The sun behind them bathed everything in the golden, late afternoon light. Lofty, lazy puffs of clouds hung suspended in a bright, blue sky. A gentle breeze cooled the backs of the sitting students. Birds flew from tree to tree; silence abounded.

The students sat quite still with their hands folded gently in their laps. Their eyes looked down at the ground. They were oblivious to the beauty around them. Nothing distracted their intended objective. They breathed in a controlled, precise manner. They seemed asleep, yet were indeed conscious—but not awake.

The Teacher approached them from behind. He stopped for a few moments and keenly observed the three students. He picked up two good-sized rocks from the ground and began to rub them together, creating an irritating, grinding sound. At first, the noise of the two rocks being rubbed together did not seem to bother the three students, but after a while, they could no longer keep their silence.

"Excuse me, Sir, but what are you doing?" asked one of the three students, trying to keep the sound of annoyance out of her voice.

"I am rubbing stones together to make a mirror," the Teacher called back, continuing to grind the two stones together.

"You cannot create a mirror by rubbing two stones together," the student responded politely, but with irritation.

"Neither can you attain enlightenment by sitting cross-legged," responded the Teacher with a smile.

"But, Sir, this meditation was handed down to us from our Teacher's Teacher's Teacher; it comes from the time of the Enlightened One from the Orient. Our style can be traced back to the original monastery where the Martial Arts began. Sitting meditation is our heritage; it calms the small mind so the Big Mind can enter. Through sitting, one will obtain Enlightenment, freedom from the prison of illusionary thought, free from the Warrior's past," the student replied proudly.

"Dear students, what is it you are trying to get free of?"

"We are freeing ourselves from ourselves—our desires, our past which chains us to the present," one of the students answered.

"How can *you* free *yourself*? This is like trying to lift yourself up by your own bootstraps! *You* are the chains...*you* are the past...*you* are the Ancient Warrior. Trying to get rid of the chains of the past is futile, because the *you* who is trying to free yourself from the *past* is one and the same thing. It's like trying to divide yourself up into two people—the past person who is not wanted and the present person who is trying to dismiss the past person. Like a house of mirrors, it is a trick of the mind.

"We are so greedy. We think we can get everything. Money, fame, position, power, and the most desired achievement of all—Enlightenment, that pure state of being, free from suffering and pain. But trying to free ourselves by some mechanical practice such as sitting only creates the illusion of freedom and brings more annoyance, pain and conflict."

"But, Sir, this tradition has been ongoing for thousands of years. It is the way of the ancient Martial Arts Masters," the student replied in a shocked tone.

"What makes you think that simply because something has been

126

going on for thousands of years it is right? And why do you unquestioningly accept the authority of the 'Masters of old'? How do you know they were right? If you accept the authority of the past because it sounds impressive, because it is very old, then you become a blind follower and will create more suffering. Find out for yourself what is true! In finding out through questioning, you will become alert, intelligent. It is this intelligence, this questioning, which will understand the chains of the past, the Warrior, and will end it. Not through sitting, but through your being alive, awake, and sensitive, will you achieve this. The intelligent Martial Artist has respect for his or her Teachers and elders but does not blindly follow their psychological authority, no matter how old their style, no matter how far back their Teacher's lineage goes. It doesn't matter if you have any heritage. What's important is to look for yourself now at this immense problem of conflict in human relationships—how we are chained to the past, the Warrior, and the mentality of war. A Martial Art can give you physical skill and a deep inward confidence so you do not automatically react to a threat by fighting or running away. It can also bring you to a point of psychological understanding of how the human brain has been conditioned to accept fighting and war as an honorable solution to solving the problems of relationship."

"Excuse me for being rude, but who are *you* to say that? Who are you to tell us what to do? How do you know? Isn't that just your opinion?" one of the students challenged, offended by the Teacher's words.

"I appreciate your boldness in questioning me. This is just what we are encouraging you to do. But we are also asking you to *listen* and find out for yourselves if what we say is true. I am not asking you to accept what I tell you; however, I am asking you to take it into consideration, to see if there is truth in it. For if you find out what I have said to be the truth, then it is not my truth—it is a truth anyone can see. Therefore, I don't have to tell you what to do or not do. You will know.

Do you understand?"

"What you say is a shock to us because we believe in our Teachers and their absolute authority. In our school, we repeat the sayings of the Masters, but now I wonder about this. I've never questioned it before; no one pointed out this was something to question. I have just accepted what was considered to be true. We repeat the school slogan each day at the start of practice, but now I wonder if this is just another habit which dulls the brain and puts us to sleep," one of the students responded thoughtfully.

"Looking at life anew is called 'Beginner's Mind.' Such a mind is 'pure' and sees life with freshness and vitality; like a child's mind, it is innocent and curious. An alert, active, and alive mind questions the authority of thepast and sees through illusions. This 'Beginner's Mind' is not habitual or mechanical. It does not fall asleep under the weight and authority of the past or of the 'Great Masters,' no matter how glorious that past may sound or how important those Teachers seem. But be very careful. Don't fall in love with the words 'Beginner's Mind' either! If you do, then you have again fallen into the trap, because words have then taken on the power and illusion of authority. You might think, *I am obtaining 'Beginner's Mind,'* and be caught up by the same old game of trying to get to an imagined state of freedom. Watch, be alert, and question. Now—how will you know if what I am saying is true or not?"

PURITY

One is rendered empty in the face of the eternal mystery of life.

FACELESS FACE
The Test of Purity

"Tonight you will face Death, and depending on how you respond, you will either die or become the Ancient Warrior forever," the Teacher said gravely.

The students looked puzzled. The practice hall was alive with candles, orange flames dancing on the ends of thick, rounded, wax columns. The trees creaked, and the eerie howling wind sent shivers down the spines of the students as they sat in the late evening's shadows.

Silently, they were led into the night. The wind whipped at their uniforms, pushing them ahead into the darkness. They followed the trail down towards the lake and then back up along the hillside to the mountain beyond. Two Teachers led the way with lanterns, and two brought up the rear.

"Watch where you are going," one Teacher called back.

They climbed higher and higher to reach the top of the magnificent mountain overlooking the lake. They had traveled this route before, but only in daylight. With the sun upon them, they could see the total expanse of the lake, to an even larger lake beyond. Surrounding both bodies of water were low hills covered with trees. The lake closest to them was dotted with small islands, some of which the students had visited by boat. It was such a breathtaking view in daylight. Their school and the land surrounding it could easily be seen from the highest point.

But tonight it was very dark. The cool night air blew hard as they struggled up the rocky trail leading to the mountaintop and the ledge overlooking the lakes.

It was difficult to sense time passing, or anything familiar, as they walked in complete darkness. The only beacons were the swaying lanterns held by their Teachers—just enough light to see where they were going, but not enough to see anything else. They felt they were leaving the comfort of the known and entering an unfamiliar land. They were also thinking nervously about what their Teacher had said at the start of this journey; were they to meet Death and the Ancient Warrior? However, they knew no real harm would come to them. Their Teachers often spoke in riddles and made strange statements that the students could not decipher at first, but usually came to understand after a test such as this.

The lead Teacher called out, "We're almost there. Put out your lanterns. Everyone grab the person's hand behind you and form a chain. Move forward slowly, and don't lose your partner's hand or you will be lost." Tentatively feeling their way up the last few yards to the top, the students inched their way forward into the unknown.

They felt the hard surface of rock underneath them and, as a group, moved carefully out onto the large ledge atop the mountain.

"Now let go of your partner's hand and sit down," the Teacher requested in a barely audible whisper.

They all sat on the ledge above the lakes and their school. Only a faint outline of the lake was seen in the night.

"Now look up and meet Death! But don't look back. If you do, you will be lost forever in the eternal chain of Ancient Warriors!" the Teacher spoke with sudden urgency.

Each student looked upward and beheld the sky filled with millions of stars! The concern they had felt at being on the ledge in dark-

ness vanished in that moment of awe and great wonder. It was as if they were gone and there was only the black night and crystalline stars in the limitless universe. Unknowingly, they sat there for a timeless period.

The next thing they were aware of was being back at the school, sitting comfortably in front of a roaring fire.

Their Teacher spoke as if for the first time. "You met Death, and died to the known, that which was you—all the petty worries and fears we live with constantly. In that moment of wonder, 'you' died, and in dying, the unknown was born. In the unknown, the past cannot enter. In the unknown, the Ancient Warrior is completely nonexistent. When 'you' die, the Ancient Warrior dies, because they are one and the same. You cannot try to get rid of the Ancient Warrior through any means. Death comes only when the mind understands what prevents Death—or by being temporarily overwhelmed with the beauty and wonder of nature itself, like you were tonight. But, be careful, you cannot capture the experience of 'Death,' the unknown. That is greed and will create only more conflict and suffering.

"When there is something so great and incomprehensible as nature, then the chattering brain shuts down in awe of that. Do you know how far those stars are from earth? The distance is measured in 'light years,' the time it takes light to travel in one year. In one second, light travels *186,000 miles*. And in one *year*, light will travel almost *six trillion miles!* The galaxy in which we live is about *100,000 light years* across. Can you imagine that distance? Our galaxy has a few hundred billion stars, including our sun. There are galaxies of stars which range in distance from two million light years to perhaps *over ten billion* light years. This is what we are!

"And, who am I?" the Teacher continued. "I am filled with the

134

known, the past, endless self-centered thoughts making up 'me.' Can 'I' die to the known, the chains of the past, and live free in the now, in the glory of the endless moment? Or, is this just some romantic nonsense?

"Dear students, see what prevents you from entering the unknown; see what holds you in chains. Who are you? What was your face before you were born, your faceless face? Discover that and there is purity of mind, a purity untouched by the known, the past, the Ancient Warrior. A pure mind is one which has understood and gone beyond its limitations. Purity is the ending of time, the ending of 'you.'"

The stars glimmered above the silent earth. There was nothing.

HUMILITY

Goodness comes when "I" am not there.

FACE OF THE ENEMY
The Test of Humility

The school bell sounded; the ring permeated and filled the space between—and there was only that. Morning dawned and a new day was upon them. There was no need to carry over the past.

"I want you to draw the Ancient Warrior, the Enemy, the shadow," the Teacher requested.

With paper and colored pencils, the students silently drew that which instantly came to mind. After ten minutes, the Teacher instructed them to bring their drawings to completion.

"Show me your drawings," the Teacher said with curiosity.

Drawings of demonic beasts and strange fighting creatures, evil-looking monsters in battle gear, wielding giant, bloody swords and axes, brutish, hairy warriors with piercing murderous eyes, and ghoulish, graveyard ghosts filled the pages.

"My, you have such vivid imaginations," the Teacher commented, somewhat amused. "Is this what you fear, or is this only an image of what frightens you? Do you see the difference? Can an image hurt you or can a drawing of a warrior attack you? So what are we afraid of—a real warrior or an imagined picture of a warrior?

"Now draw the image most people have of what they think a Martial Artist is. Don't censor yourself. Think like they do, and just let that image come out on paper."

After ten minutes, papers were presented. Again, there were

drawings of brutish, monstrous beasts, but this time, clad in Martial Arts outfits. Some looked like cave people; some looked like modern villains and terrorists. Some were pictured as 'good guys' killing 'bad guys.'

"Is this what the Martial Arts are, or merely what many people think they are?" the Teacher asked.

"Now think about what you've drawn and see that these pictures originated in your brain, formed by what you've been told or seen enacted. Can you see that these images are not real...that they're not accurate representations of the actual?

"A drawing of the Enemy—the Ancient Warrior—is only that: a drawing. What is there to fear in a piece of paper with some pencil scribblings? Unfortunately, the image of a Martial Artist as a violent, beast-like warrior is the one many people have. But, that is not what we practice here or what a real Martial Artist is.

"Let me approach this from another direction. Do you know what it would feel like if you *really* got hit with a full-power punch or kick? This is not make-believe. Make-believe people get hit, kicked, and shot, but don't seem to get hurt.

"Physical self-defense skills are taught in the Martial Arts to give you the confidence *not* to fight. But we must realize the danger of fighting and how real the danger is. Unfortunately, we live most of the time in illusions, captured by images of what life is, or what it could be.

"Here at this school, self-defense skills are taught as an Art, a physical representation of the primary force of nature within us. This physical Art allows us to bring about a feeling of great energy and power. Not power to hurt, but, rather, power to feel in its raw form— like thunder and lightning. We can so easily fall asleep and not *feel* life.

The Art of the Martial Arts wakes us up! And, in this, there is great beauty.

"Students, we have little time left together here at this school before you return home. You have come from around the world and will leave here as 'Peace Ambassadors.' Yet there is so much more to learn. You have just begun to discover the potential of these incredible Arts. Just remember the Martial Arts, *if* taught properly, can help you to understand and resolve conflict *before* it even becomes conflict—both individually and globally.

"Unfortunately, many people who train in the Martial Arts only acknowledge the physical aspect. They think studying physical self-defense skills alone will help them resolve conflict. This can become a brutal attitude, one which *creates* conflict by carrying on the 'eye for an eye,' 'might is right,' Ancient Warrior's code. This attitude *must* be questioned! Otherwise, the general public will turn away from the Martial Arts because they are tired of violence, tired of seeing people—especially children—being conditioned as 'trained killers' and 'thugs.'

"Many young people like yourselves are impressed with the physical side of the Martial Arts. They see demonstrations of mysterious and miraculous feats of strength and agility and want to attain that. But this is not the essence of the Martial Arts. Why are you so easily impressed with gymnastics tricks? These feats are not special or superhuman. Some would like you to think so, but such people are clever tricksters and magicians who wish to mystify you with their superficial skills.

"So many Martial Artists train physically, but lack real confidence and strength because they study the physical by itself and ignore the more important, mental side. The ability to defend against a physical attack is of limited value. Understanding conflict does not require

physical techniques, and physical techniques cannot end conflict peacefully or intelligently. Physical defense deals with the problem *after* it has become one. What we are doing here is learning to understand and deal with a problem *before* it turns into conflict. In this way, we prevent the birth of conflict at the root or cause. Physical skills only attempt to end conflict after there is danger and threats to physical well-being.

"If you really want to understand what creates conflict within the human being and, hence, within the world of human relationships, you will need to feel the urgency to create places where people come together to explore these issues, like this school. The Martial Arts have a unique and very important place in understanding conflict. As you well know, these Arts involve more than just physical self-defense skills. Even many 'experts'—people who glorify themselves as "Grand Masters"—actually create illusions and do not bring about understanding and intelligence.

"Young people, please listen to what we have to say. Question to find out if all this is true or not. Don't be fooled or mystified by the Martial Arts. We have used some unique ways to bring you face-to-face with yourself. But don't be fooled by the language. Look at the truth in the words to see if what they point to is real or false. In this way, you become you own 'master.' At the same time, understand that no one ever masters life! And, most of all, be humble and kind. It is so easy to think of oneself as someone important. Just remember—you are nothing! Oh, dear students, see the beauty of that!"

LOVE

Love is understanding that which prevent peace.

BELL RINGING IN THE EMPTY SKY
The Test of Love

The axe pierced the air, barely missing the student who had fallen backwards in defense of his life. The student swung the heavy sword up from the ground at the Ancient Warrior, meeting metal with metal as the two clashed in a violent struggle for dominance. On his feet again, the sword-wielding student lunged at the huge, armor-laden attacker, driving him up against the thick, stone wall. The student's arms were heavy with exhaustion, but there was not a second to rest; the Ancient Warrior fought on with animalistic ferocity.

Around these two combatants were hundreds of others, fighting to the death. Armed with every conceivable weapon and dressed in various military uniforms, the battlefield was teeming with war.

The student felt a sudden surge of energy and fought with renewed strength. The Ancient Warrior, in horned helmet and animal skins, fought back with equal power. But the battle was turning. The student slowly beat back the advances of the Ancient Warrior with continuous counter-attacks. Finally, the student swung his sword and hit the Ancient Warrior full in the chest. On impact, the Ancient Warrior vanished. Turning to face another oncoming foe, the student, gaining power with each moment, began to shift the tide of the war. Again and again, he defeated the Ancient Warrior in its many forms. Again and again, the Ancient Warrior charged at him with tremendous rage, but the student moved to meet each attack, vanquishing one after another with mighty blows of his gleaming, silver sword. Each contact with the enemy obliterated the Warrior, sending it back into the void from which it came, until there was only the student standing on a large expanse of battlefield, alone with the grass, trees, and sky.

He looked around for anyone, but all had disappeared. The day seemed peaceful and calm when, all at once, the earth cried out, trembled, and roared. The sky darkened; the momentary tranquillity vanished. The earth shook violently and cracked open in great fissures. About twenty yards from him, there appeared—out of the bowels of the earth—a gigantic demon dressed entirely in an Ancient Warrior's fighting gear. The demonic Warrior seemed one hundred feet high and looked down at the student with burning eye sockets. It was covered with thick, rusting chains. Bright red flames shot out of its mouth as it spoke:

"I have come to conquer you. You are my enemy and I must destroy you," it roared in a magnificent but evil voice.

The student raised his sword with outstretched arms and looked up at this towering demonic presence. He did not move, but rather, fastened his eyes on the eye sockets of the other. The beast was the great Ancient Warrior risen from the dead. Battle scarred from thousands of years of combat, the Ancient Warrior grew to immeasurable height, filling the sky, blocking the light. The darkness grew unbearable and the odor of fear was intense. Yet the student stood still with arms outstretched, grasping the bright, silver sword which pointed upwards at the underbelly of the tyrannical monstrosity above him. The great Ancient Warrior, bumping up against the sky, threw back its helmeted head and laughed, sending tremors through the earth.

"How can you defeat me?" it roared with a deafening bellow. "You puny little child! I am the God of War; I am Death and Destruction. I have leveled entire cities and brought nations to their knees. I have been worshipped by the high and mighty. There are great monuments to me. I am the Victor, the Terrorist, the Enemy, and Hero. I am all that which is violent, evil, warlike—and you dare to stand against me!"

The student did not waver but kept his sword true as the great Ancient Warrior looked down upon him with crazed black-holed eyes. Its body towered like a fantastic mountain range. The roar of cannons echoed through the valley as the Ancient Warrior raised its mighty axe overhead, chains rattling like thunder. The axe was bloodstained with millions of soulless, dead warriors. The axe reached its apex, and began its thunderous way down when the student—still focusing on his shimmering, silver sword—sent forth a tremendous burst of energy from its razor-sharp tip. Like a blinding bolt of lightening, the energy pierced the Ancient Warrior.

There followed a timeless moment where everything stood absolutely still—the student with arms outstretched, the towering Ancient Warrior with axe poised to strike its final blow. Then, slowly, from the deepest corners of eternity, there arose a scream like one never heard before, a scream so blood-curdling, so magnificently evil, that it enveloped the universe. Eyes, now blast-furnace red, burned through the empty black sockets of the beast. It roared its dying call and fell away, crumbling and spilling downward like a molten, volcanic eruption.

The student witnessed the titanic death as if it were the death of evil itself. Great bolts of lightning and claps of thunder broke the air as the chains encircling the Ancient Warrior began to break apart, rusted metal chunks spewing outward.

The sky filled with black smoke, tinged orange and red. Then, the sky opened and torrents of rain cascaded earthward, forming pools of water. The wind howled, bending trees to their breaking points. A sudden, gigantic blast of thunder set the student upright in his bed. Lightning flashed outside his rain-soaked windows. The fire in the small room had died out.

The student jumped up to peer out the window of his refuge from the storm raging outside. Pressing his face to the cold glass, he watched the sky as it lit up with nature's fireworks directly overhead.

✳✳✳

Today was the students' final day at the school; tomorrow they were all returning home to the far corners of the globe.

"Last night I dreamed of the Ancient Warrior," the student told his Teachers and fellow students after they had gathered in the old, wooden-floored hall that morning.

"And you slayed it," one Teacher commented.

"How did you know?" the student replied, surprised at the accuracy of her statement.

"Because either you give in to it or slay it. There is nothing in-between. I think we all have this dream eventually, perhaps in different ways, but of the same battle. The Ancient Warrior, as you have come to learn, is in you. You have inherited this violent legacy of war. And the only way to slay it is through love.

"Love is understanding how the Ancient Warrior was created and how it lives on in us, chaining our minds and hearts to past Warrior ways. This kind of love is not personal; it's not for another person. It arises in you when you least expect it. And, you can never expect it! It can only come when you have brought order to your lives, when you *live* the tests you have experienced here, when you are those qualities which make up an intelligent, kind, sensitive human being. Love is that quality which can shine even in a dark world, bring light to the shadow. Like the moon, this light does not discriminate, judge, or compare. It shines on everything equally.

"Your mind, through your dream, was allowing the shadow to surface into the light of awareness, of love. When you face the shadow in yourself without turning away, then there is the possibility the Ancient Warrior will be consumed in light, awareness, and love. In love, the enemy no longer exists. In love, the shadow becomes the light. In love, you wake up from the dream—*because it is only a dream!* The Ancient Warrior in you and in the world is a living nightmare. WAKE UP FROM THE DREAM! BREAK THE CHAINS!

"You must die to the known and the inherited warrior past. Do you know the word 'Karate' means 'empty self,' rendering oneself empty of all that which *prevents* peace, all that which blocks out the light of love? Please see this! This is real! We Teachers may express what we see in a way that is foreign to you, but the words we choose are accurate reflections of something that has not generally been inquired into before. Don't fall in love with words, because if you do, you will get lost in a never-ending maze of convoluted thinking and become vulnerable to Fire Dragons which will devour you. Stand in the Eye of the Hurricane and watch as the storm rages on just outside of your reach. In the still point of the eye is freedom. There, the chains do not exist. Be careful, for it's easy to fall asleep and get caught up in the storm again, in the wrath of the Ancient Warrior, to carry on the violent past in the present.

"Tomorrow, you will leave here to return home, bringing with you all you have come to understand. You are Martial Arts Peace Ambassadors whose challenge is to bring light to an ignorant and confused world. You have been trained properly, *both* physically *and* mentally. You know physical adeptness alone is not enough. You have passed the tests we set up for you here, but this is just the beginning. The real test starts when you leave and return to your lives at home.

"Just remember one thing—question! In questioning, you will become alert, intelligent, aware. Start with one unanswered question

149

and move from there.

"We wish you well, dear students. Perhaps you will come back again. We will be waiting for you, for you are our children, the young people of the earth."

The student sat in silence and listened. The storm had now passed and they all walked outside to greet the new day. The rain-soaked, green hills glistened and the air was fresh and clean. The brightness of the clear blue sky dazzled their senses. The odor of blooming flowers filled their heads with a delicate perfume. Overhead, a hawk circled, calling out its primal cry, "Enter here, enter here!" In that, there was nothing and everything.

The chains of the Ancient Warrior were broken by the flame of attention, by facing the warriors within themselves. That night they all slept well. The dream was over. Life was beginning.

To the Young Reader—

You have finished the tests in this book. Now the *real* test begins! What will you do now that you've understood the Ancient Warrior? How will this affect your life and the lives of others around you? Or are these "tests" just interesting stories to be enjoyed but not lived?

You are the creators of tomorrow's world—and tomorrow is soon to come. Either you will carry on as the generations before you have, or you will—because you've understood something of great importance in these "tests"—bring about a new society, a new and truly peaceful way of relating to others.

Do you have the strength of character?

Is your spirit brave?

Do you have the wisdom to understand the importance of all of this?

It is up to you.

In the cherry blossom's shade

complete strangers

do not exist

—*Issa*

Developing Character Through the Martial Arts

Martial Arts can be a unique, educational, and fun way to develop character (or "spirit") in young people. Learning patience from developing physical and mental skills is *one* of the values Martial Arts teaches. But there are many more.

It seems young people don't have much opportunity to develop character-building values so necessary to help them live in today's challenging world. As parents and teachers, we must give our children skills to survive and flourish. We have given so much of our time and financial resources to developing intellectual skills—the "3 Rs"—that we've neglected giving our children the greatest gift of all—the "4th R": relationship-building skill.

As I was growing up, relationship-building skill, or character development, was taught as an integral part of my overall education. Values such as respect, courtesy, and kindness were a part of my everyday life, as were studying and taking care of my health.

It seems that teaching young people values—character development or relationship skill—has become a thing of the past for the most part. It is not that we don't want to teach them; rather, we don't seem to have the time as we are so busy preparing young people academically. We have gotten caught up in the notion that academics or knowledge will solve all our problems. And there is also the matter of competition, that our children need more and more knowledge, and need to be more and more aggressive in getting and using that knowledge.

There is one other issue which, I think, has contributed to the decline in teaching values to our children. This is *how* we teach them. The "how" is, to a great extent, a process of punishment and reward, which translates into pain and pleasure. In our well-intentioned but misguided attempt at teaching children values, we create people to whom morals, ethics, or manners have a painful, underlying negative feeling. In the process of trying to bring about goodness, we judge behavior in favor of the ideal of "right" and "good" behavior. We create conflict within ourselves and our children by the very means which were to bring about freedom from conflict. Goodness is held up as an ideal, something that we *should be*. What we are, our *actual* behavior (such as anger, greed, lust, and so on) is judged as something we *should not be*.

Simply said, we create unethical behavior by the very process that we are using to bring about ethical behavior! To be good means judging our "negative" qualities as "bad," while conforming to a standard or ideal of goodness. To be good feels good, rewarding. But, to be "good" also feels bad, and therefore painful, because the process of becoming good means that one judges oneself as bad in light of the ideal of goodness.

This all may sound complicated or merely one of those strange paradoxes of life. But, in fact, it is neither. It is just an inappropriate notion of *how* to bring about moral behavior and develop character. So, if the approach of judgment and conforming to ideals creates conflict , then what does work? How do we create ethical behavior? How do we teach values and build character without the pain and fear of punishment or the pleasure of rewards?

In my view, the seemingly contradictory practice of the Martial Arts might hold the key to answering these questions—*if* taught intelligently. By looking at the popular Martial Arts films, magazines, video games, and many schools of Martial Arts, one might wonder why anyone in his or her right mind would suggest such a thing.

In order to demonstrate the possibility that the Martial Arts might have the capacity to teach young people the "right" character-building values—ethical behavior—we will need to put aside for the moment our preconceived notions, our prejudices about the Martial Arts, and look at the Martial Arts anew. This is exactly what I am trying to do in all my books, because I see the potential within these Arts not only to build character and teach values, but also to help people understand and resolve conflict—individually and globally. This may sound grandiose, but it is a statement based on decades of inquiring into this premise.

It would take quite a few pages to demonstrate how this can come about. I have done so in all my books. Or without further reading, you can begin to examine for yourself whether the Martial Arts can be a means to help explore the "Martial" within us, to begin to discover how we create conflict in relationships, by *preventing* ethical or peaceful behavior.

I have attempted to create a context within which young people could come to understand themselves. The "tests" are mirrors for behavior, *without passing judgment!* Seeing what actually is, our actual behavior without judgment, without needing to conform to some ideal, creates the ability to understand that behavior. It is this understanding, this intelligent observation, which frees one from a behavior. There is no need to live according to any conditioned dictates of how one shall or shall not act. By bringing awareness to one's behavior, one's life, one is awakening intelligence. Intelligence is alive and active. It brings about understanding and, therefore, the value of goodness without trying to *be* good.

A unique way to bring about values without the reward/punishment method of "normal education" is through "tests" designed to take young people through character-building situations. The word "education" comes from the Latin word *educare* meaning to "lead" or "draw out." The tests in this book, and real-life situation roleplaying, "draw out" the strength of character from those who participate. A young person becomes self-disciplined through the events or circumstances that prove his qualities. In this way healthy, humane values are drawn out of a young person's intrinsic nature.

But there is a deeper "value" that is called for in this book, as well as in life. It is understanding our inherited militaristic predisposition to war, respecting the "Ancient Warrior" within that has and continues to cause tremendous conflict and suffering in our lives. Teaching young people merely to be polite and well-mannered isn't the answer in creating "right" and "good" relationships. Many polite and well-mannered people still create conflict even though, on the surface, they seem to be respectful. Respect goes much deeper than social skill.

Developing strength of character, more importantly, involves understanding the roots of disorder and fear in living. And it is fear which creates personal and social disorder, keeping the Ancient Warrior alive and continuing to perpetuate warlike attitudes of mind which have been passed on generation after generation for thousands of years.

The essence of Martial Arts practice is to develop an understanding and resolution of human conflict—individually and socially. With all the violent Martial Arts images in the media, one would naturally be skeptical of such an intent.

Putting aside the false view of Martial Arts, one can recognize their underlying theme. One first sees that teaching Martial Arts involves teaching Martial Arts "ethics"—a code of conduct. For without this code of conduct, teaching people lethal self-defense skills is dangerous, to say the least. But on deeper inspection, one begins to uncover the fundamental intent of the Martial Arts—that of discovering the roots of conflict within us. It is this fundamental intent that has been ignored or generally misunderstood.

If one is to study the Martial Arts seriously, as they were meant to be studied, one has to take into account not only the ethics of Martial Arts, the "code of conduct," but more importantly, this fundamental intent of understanding and resolving conflict, conflict that in the extreme leads to war. For conflict is conflict whether within a person, or between groups people; the basic structure is essentially the same in all its aspects.

The Western world is beginning to recognize the Asian Martial Arts as much more than merely techniques for self-defense or competitive sports. As the challenges of life increase, we adults look for ways our children can learn to cope with them successfully. The Martial Arts, *if* taught properly, can be a means of character development and conflict resolution. When this is recognized and practiced, then these Arts will demonstrate to society what their full potential can be, and will be placed in a respected position in the education of children worldwide.

Note for Adults Working with Young People—

The questions presented here will help you to stimulate young people's thinking about what these "tests" have to offer—in understanding destructive conflict, both individually and socially. Reading the stories together with young people and then using these questions can assist you in creating the right image and intent of the Martial Arts. There are no right or wrong answers. The most important thing is to open students' minds to a new way of looking and understanding. Generally, questioning is only intellectual—wanting an answer from a body of knowledge already memorized. These questions ask the reader to *observe* what the question is pointing to. Therefore, this type of learning through questioning is not mere memorization of information, but more importantly, it is learning which is immediate, bringing clarity of mind and action into the moment. It is this "in the moment" learning which is needed to understand and end the inherited, conditioned, war-like attitudes which have been passed on from generation to generation, creating tremendous suffering and sorrow.

Please note: students need to read the stories themselves before considering these questions. It will be helpful if each student has his or her own copy of the book to refer to when asked these discussion questions.

Breaking the Chains: *The Test of Respect*

1. What creates the Shadow?

2. What can we do to stop being influenced by the Shadow?

3. What does it mean to say "we all leave footprints in time?"

4. What keeps us chained to the Ancient Waririor?

5. What is the most important intent of the martial arts?

Hall of Battle: *The Test of Bravery*

1. Why is it important to be "disturbed," to "wake up"?

2. What does the statement, "Most people are asleep," mean?

3. How does "fear take charge of your life"?

4. What was "bravery" in the past? What does it mean in this test?

5. What is intelligence? How will it help you understand and be free of the chains of the Ancient Warriors?

6. Why is the "first step the last step"?

7. Who was the unknown person "by their sides"?

8. What was that cleanliness which "pervaded their whole being"?

9. Why did the voice call out, "Don't look back!"?

10. Can you see anything in this test that can help you better understand your life?

Way of the Golden Dragon: *The Test of Selflessness*

1. How can the "Way of the Dragon" take a lifetime to learn, yet take no time at all?

2. What does "expect the unexpected" mean?

3. What is "Mental Freestyle"? Why is it important to the Martial Arts? To life?

4. Why is the "Art of Listening" so important in the Martial Arts and in life?

5. Again, the teacher commands, "Don't look back!" Why is this so

important?

6. Before the students entered the woods, they sat quietly in Nature and their fears left them. Why did that happen?

7. How did the students see without seeing, hear without hearing, feel without feeling, know without knowing, in that pitch-black night?

8. What does "emptiness cannot be trapped; nothingness cannot be captured" mean? How is this important in the Martial Arts? In everyday living?

9. What does it mean when "the brain has come to a still point"?

10. What does "time had ceased and there was nothing, and everything" mean?

Curse of the Ancient Warrior: *The Test of Honor*

1. Why can't you get away from the "Ancient Warrior within you"?

2. What is the lesson of the "Chinese Puzzle"?

3. How can you free yourself of the Ancient Warrior? Through effort (to *try* to get away) or through understanding?

4. How does condemning or judging the Ancient Warrior within you just make it worse?

5. What does it mean to "honor" the Ancient Warrior within us?

6. Why did the Assistant Instructor fight so hard with the younger student? What was the Assistant trying to accomplish? Why?

7. Whom did the younger student see in the mirror? Where did that

image come from?

8. What did the younger student do when he saw that reflection? Why was what he did *not* do so important?

9. What does respect have to do with understanding what happened to the younger student when he saw his reflection in the mirror?

10. How can this test help you in your everyday life? As a young person? As an adult?

Mind Like Moon: *The Test of Unity*

1. What was the lesson of the cat and mouse? Why is it important in understanding the practice of the Martial Arts? In understanding your life each day?

2. Why are there "no answers" to this test? Why is there "nothing to say"?

3. What was the "division between them"? How did it fall away?

4. Why was there no "remembrance of what had gone before, no hoping for what was to come"?

5. Why is this test so important in understanding the Martial Arts' real meaning?

Gordian Knot: *The Test of Spirit*

1. What meaning did cutting three bundles of hay have?

2. What is "Spirit" and how is it important to Martial Arts training? To daily life?

3. How do you just let the board break?

4. Why is the movement to break a board not of will-power? What "power" breaks it? Why is this important to understand?

5. What does sword cutting and board breaking represent?

6. Why is it important to understand thinking?

7. How can you be free of confused thinking?

8. What kind of learning can help you be free of the mind tied up in knots?

9. What does, "Should you meet the Ancient Warrior on the road, 'slay it'" mean?

10. How can you end confusion or danger at the root?

Games Martial Arts Masters Play: *The Test of Trust*

1. What feelings did the students have when they were in the Ceremonial Hall? What caused these feelings? Are these feelings dangerous? If so, why?

2. What was the white-robed man at the alter doing to make the students feel that way?

3. What did the white-robed man ask the students to obey? How should they obey? Is this intelligent?

4. Why did the Teachers trick the students?

5. Why are the students "so susceptible to what we adults tell you"?

6. Why would adults take advantage of young people?

7. Why was the experience in the hall "pleasurable"?

8. Are there necessary rituals in the Martial Arts? In life? Are there unnecessary and even dangerous rituals in the Martial Arts? In life? What are they? Why are some necessary and beneficial and others unnecessary and destructive?

9. What is trust? How can it be abused by another?

10. What is an authority? Are some authorities necessary? Who? Are some authorities unnecessary? Who? Is it important to question authority? If yes, why?

Gift of the Moon: *The Test of Charity*

1. Why did Teshu give the thief his clothes?

2. How did this affect the thief?

3. What was the gift of the beautiful moon?

4. Why did Teshu want to give it to the thief?

5. What meaning does this test have for Martial Artists?

Attacking Nothingness: *The Test of Compassion*

1. How did the Teacher respond to the drunken man? Did her response help the situation? How? What is the lesson in this for the Martial Artist?

2. Why was the drunken man so angry?

3. Did knowing this reason help the Teacher act calmly towards him? Why?

4. Why didn't the Teacher use her Martial Arts physical self-defense techniques against the drunken man? What kind of Martial Arts skills was she using?

5. How did the Teacher help the man? What does this have to do with the Martial Arts?

Defeating the Enemy Without Fighting: *The Test of Understanding*

1. What does the saying mean? Why is it important to understand this? Why is this a part of the Martial Arts?

2. What is your greatest "weapon"? Why it is the greatest?

3. What does "conditioned" or "brainwashed" mean? Does "conditioning" create conflict? How?

4. In this test, how are violence and war created?

5. What is "the greatest challenge for the Martial Artist"?

6. How is the "enemy" created? How do we protect ourselves from the "enemy"? Where does the need to protect ourselves come from?

7. What does "we are the world, and the world is us," mean?

8. How does "destructive thinking" get carried over from the past? How does this past destructive thinking affect the present? The future?

9. What is "our challenge"? Why is it important?

10. Can understanding how thought works, how we create the enemy, affect global peace? How?

Unbroken Flame of Attention: *The Test of Harmony*

1. How did the Teacher hit a target without seeing it?

2. Why were the targets placed just a few feet away from the students?

3. Why did the Teachers ask the students to shoot their arrows at sewing needles? What was the point of this lesson?

4. Why was it so important to try very hard to hit the eye of a sewing needle when it was virtually impossible?

5. Why were the students' dreams important? How did the dreams help them?

6. How did shooting arrows while blindfolded help them?

7. What does it mean, when shooting arrows, to "just let it fall—like ripe fruit from a tree"?

8. What did the Teacher mean when he said, "*You* get in your way"?

9. What does "'It' shoots! 'It' hits!" mean?

10. Can one try to bring about harmony? What is the flame of attention? Does this "make way" for harmony?

War of the Rose: *The Test of Strength*

1. What did it mean when the Teacher told the students, "You are defeating yourself"?

2. What was *not* ordinary about the old man?

3. How did one old man defeat younger thugs?

4. Why did the older man ignore Carlos' plea to be his student?

5. Why did the old man ask Carlos to attack him?

6. How did Carlos lose before he started?

7. How was the rose a way to power?

8. Why did sitting and watching a rose create "a battle of wills" for Carlos?

9. What was Carlos' state of mind at dawn? How was it different than the day before? What does this have to do with the Martial Arts? With everyday life?

10. What does comparing yourself with another do? Can this "defeat" you? How?

Quest for Peace: *The Test of Order*

1. Why was cleaning the school an honor?

2. Why weren't the explanations of order correct?

3. What is the difference between an explanation and an example (of order)? An experience of order?

4. Can order come about by an explanation, an answer? If not, why?

5. After the students learned order was in the doing of it, how come they couldn't line up in an orderly manner?

6. Why was there the most commotion at the head of the line?

7. Why is order important? In the Martial Arts? In life?

8. How does only knowing an explanation of order prevent order?

9. What is "insight"? How is it different from knowledge?

10. What does the Teacher mean when saying, "Understanding that which prevents order brings about order"?

Fighting the Paper Tiger: *The Test of Focus*

1. What is the lesson of the woodpecker? How is it important to Martial Arts Training?

2. Is breaking boards similar to punching at a flame? What different skill do you need to put out a flame than to break a board?

3. What is the lesson of the wet towel?

4. What kind of power is needed to strike at hanging paper?

5. What are the qualities necessary to defeat the Ancient Warrior? How are they important in the Martial Arts? In everyday living?

Way of the Sword: *The Test of Excellence*

1. Why was the young man assigned by the Sword Master to learn the Art of the Tea Ceremony instead of learning Swordsmanship?

2. Why did the young man's Teacher tell him to approach the outraged Master Swordsman as if he were serving him tea?

3. What helped the young man remain calm in the face of his opponent?

4. Why did the Master Swordsman become confused and begin to waver?

5. What did the young man master? Why is this important?

Beginner's Mind: *The Test of Wisdom*

1. What were the three students doing sitting on the hillside? What were they trying to attain? Could they attain what they wanted by sitting like this?

2. What lesson did the Teacher show the students by rubbing two rocks together?

3. Were the students being greedy? How? Why?

4. What made the students think they were correct in this type of sitting practice?

5. Did the students question authority or accept it? Which is more intelligent? Why?

6. What does respect mean in this test?

7. What did the Teacher ask the students to do besides questioning?

8. Was the Teacher their authority? Why not?

9. What does repetition of slogans do to the brain? Why?

10. What is a "Beginner's Mind"? Why is it important to understand? What does it have to do with the Martial Arts? With life?

Faceless Face: *The Test of Purity*

1. What death did the students face?

2. What "killed" them?

3. What is "dying to the known" mean? What is the known? What is the unknown (death)? Can you capture the unknown?

4. When "you" die, what also dies? How? Why is this important?

5. In the realization of the tremendous mystery of life, what happens to "me"?

6. Who am "I"? What makes up "me"? What are "the chains of the past"? How can we be free of them?

7. What prevents you from "entering the unknown"?

8. What is your "faceless face"?

9. What is purity?

10. What it "the ending of time"?

Face of the Enemy: *The Test of Humility*

1. Is the Ancient Warrior only an image? Can the image hurt you?

2. What is the popularized image of a Martial Artist? Is this the correct representation?

3. Physical self-defense helps you to do what? What other skills will you need to stop a conflict *before* it becomes one?

4. What does practicing the Martial Arts do for you? Why is this important?

5. What are "Martial Arts Peace Ambassadors" and why are they important?

6. Are the Martial Arts an "eye for an eye," "might is right" way to resolve conflict? If not, what is the intelligent way for Martial Artists to resolve conflict?

7. Are the Martial Arts merely a set of gymnastic skills? What is

their other side? Why is it valuable to study "the other side"?

8. What is the basic intent of the Martial Arts?

9. What do we sometimes get fooled by? Why is it important not to be fooled?

10. What does the Teacher mean when saying to the students, "You are nothing"? How is this important in bringing about an end to conflict, individually and globally?

Bell Ringing in the Empty Sky: *The Test of Love*

1. How did the boy defeat the Ancient Warrior?

2. What is the only way to slay the Ancient Warrior?

3. What can happen when you bring order to your life?

4. What does it mean to say, "Wake up from the dream!"?

5. What does the Teacher warn the students about? Why is it important?

6. How will you get caught up in "a never-ending maze of convoluted thinking"?

7. What is the one thing to remember? That which will begin to break the chains of the past, of the Ancient Warrior?

8. What will happen if you "fall asleep"?

9. What do all these tests have to do with the Martial Arts? With life?

10. Where will you go from here? Have you really learned something or did you just memorize what has been said to get all the "correct answers"? Who will tell you?

BOOKS BY DR. TERRENCE WEBSTER-DOYLE

For young people:

Breaking the Chains of the Ancient Warrior: *Tests of Wisdom for Young Martial Artists*

Operation Warhawks: *How Young People Become Warriors*

Tug of War: *Peace Through Understanding Conflict*

Fighting the Invisible Enemy: *Understanding the Effects of Conditioning*

Facing the Double-Edged Sword: *The Art of Karate for Young People*

Why Is Everybody Picking on Me: *A Guide to Handling Bullies*

Eye of the Hurricane: *Tales of the Empty-Handed Masters*

Maze of the Fire Dragon: *Tales of the Empty-Handed Masters*

Flight of the Golden Eagle: *Tales of the Empty-Handed Masters*

For adults:

Karate: *The Art of Empty Self*

One Encounter, One Chance: *The Essence of the Art of Karate*

Growing up Sane: *Understanding the Conditioned Mind*

Brave New Child: *Education for the 21st Century*

The Religious Impulse: *A Quest for Innocence*

Peace—The Enemy of Freedom: *The Myth of Nonviolence*

ABOUT THE AUTHOR

Dr. Terrence Webster-Doyle is the Founder and Chief Instructor of Take Nami Do Karate and the Director of the Shuhari Institute, a center for the study of the Martial Arts. He has studied and taught Karate for over 30 years, has a doctorate degree in psychology, and is a credentialed secondary and community college instructor. He earned his Black Belt in the Japanese style of Gensei Ryu Karate from Sensei Numano in 1967. He has worked in juvenile delinquency prevention, taught at the university level, and developed counseling programs for young people. He and his wife Jean are co-parenting five daughters.

ABOUT THE ARTIST

Rod Cameron was born in 1948 in Chicago, Illinois, but has lived in southern California most of his life. He studied painting with the renowned illustrator, Keith Ward, and at the Otis/Parsons School of Design in Los Angeles, California.

Mr. Cameron has been designing and illustrating for over twenty years; his work has been shown on major network television and has received seventeen awards for illustrative excellence.

ABOUT THE PUBLISHER

Atrium Society concerns itself with fundamental issues which prevent understanding and cooperation in human affairs. Starting with the fact that we are conditioned by our origin of birth, our education and our experiences, the intent of the Atrium Society is to bring this issue of conditioning into the forefront of our awareness. Seeing who we actually are, not merely what we think we are, reveals the potential for a transformation of our ways of being and relating.

If you would like more information, please write or call us. We enjoy hearing from people who read our books, and we appreciate your comments.

Atrium Society
P.O. Box 816
Middlebury, Vermont 05753
Tel: (802) 388-0922
Fax: (802) 388-1027
For book order information:
(800) 848-6021

SPECIAL BOOK DISCOUNTS

Atrium extends special low prices to public and independent schools, libraries, youth centers, and other educational customers who buy our peace education books in bulk quantities. Discounts apply to the "Education for Peace" books for young people, and to adult titles suitable for teacher training, parenting, and adult education.

HOW TO USE THESE BOOKS

Many caring and motivated Instructors have made a real difference in the lives of children by incorporating "Martial Arts for Peace" books into their classes. Try reading and discussing a story with young students at the start or close of class. Have students perform the role-playing situations described to defuse bullying situations nonviolently or better understand the nature of the Martial Arts. Use with Atrium's Martial Arts school curricula, which are full of games, activities, and discussion questions. Present a book to new students along with their uniform when they join your school—or award books to your students for rank advancement or improvement.

MARTIAL ARTS FOR PEACE

The Atrium Society operates the Shuhari Institute—a center for the study of the Martial Arts, dedicated to promoting the Martial Arts as a means for self-understanding and of confident, nonviolent avoidance of physical conflict. Seemingly contradictory to the aims of peaceful conflict resolution, a martial art—if properly taught—reveals itself as a safe, fun, healthy and direct way for young people to see conflict within themselves, gain self-esteem, and use their new insights and confidence to *avoid fighting*.

Atrium Society works to bring together people who, and resources that, give an intelligent perspective to the Martial Arts as a tool for the understanding of conflict. Its comprehensive "Martial Arts for Peace" program helps create an understanding of the martial arts as a way to peace, assisting young students in their education about relationship—what it means to live with dignity, caring and beauty in their daily lives.

Classes for young people, teens and adults are offered in Vermont and in northern California. The "Martial Arts for Peace" project also encourages martial arts schools, youth centers, and schools nationwide to host Dr. Webster-Doyle's workshops for young people. For information on these activities, or for special instructor-training programs, please contact:

Atrium Society/"Martial Arts for Peace"
PO Box 816
Middlebury VT 05753 USA
Tel: (802) 388-0922   Fax (802) 388-1027

174

International Praise for Dr. Terrence Webster-Doyle's Previous Books

The award-winning "Education for Peace" and
"Martial Arts for Peace" books have earned
widespread acclaim as resources for the understanding
and nonviolent resolution of conflict.

- "It would be wonderful if children all over the U.S. would read *Facing the Double-Edged Sword.* Adults too."
  —George Leonard, Contributing Editor, *Esquire*

- "These books are an asset to Martial Arts instructors, students and parents of all styles, ages and rank levels. Don't just place them on your shelf! Read them again and again!"
  —Marilyn Fierro, Owner and Chief Instructor
  Smithtown Karate Academy, Smithtown, New York

- Dr. Webster-Doyle has been awarded the Robert Burns Medal for Literature by Austria's Albert Schweitzer Society, for "outstanding merits in the field of peace-promotion."

- "Thank you for *Eye of the Hurricane.* We are unaware of any other resources which address the concept of using the Martial Arts for peaceful purposes. At last someone has presented a healthier view of karate for children, and for their concerned parents."
  —Hampton Educational Center
  Grand Rapids, Minnesota

- Winner of Benjamin Franklin Awards for Excellence in Independent Publishing

- "Every publication from the pen of this author should make significant contribution to peace within and without. Highly recommended!"
  —*New Age Publishers and Retailers Alliance Trade Journal*

TALES OF THE EMPTY-HANDED MASTERS

Can You Discover the Secret of the Empty-Handed Masters?

The "Martial Arts for Peace" books offer young people a view of the Martial Arts as they should be seen: as healthy and humane activity that can help them live with sensitivity and intelligence in their daily lives.

EYE OF THE HURRICANE embarks on the journey into the heart of "Empty Self," the path of self confidence and nonviolent inner power, by recognizing the root of human conflict with a fresh or "beginner's" mind. $14.95 (paperback) $17.95 (hardcover)

MAZE OF THE FIRE DRAGON travels further with symbolic challenges that lead the reader to understand his or her real strengths, guiding the individual toward insights for personal wisdom and peaceful social skills. $14.95 (paperback) $17.95 (hardcover)

FLIGHT OF THE GOLDEN EAGLE depicts the profound mental and physical training of martial arts students and presents powerful and sensitive classic tales to guide the martial artist to live with awareness and intelligence. $14.95 (paperback) $17.95 (hardcover)

© 2009 The Little Bookroom
First published 2009 by Alastair Sawday Publishing Co. Ltd

Copyright © 2009 Alastair Sawday Publishing Co. Ltd
Photos ©

Mark Bolton
La Traversina Agriturismo
Agriturismo Cascina Folletto
B&B Valferrara
La Piana dei Castagni Agriturismo
Antica Casa 'Le Rondini'
Tenuta di Pieve a Celle
Fattoria Barbialla Nuova
Sovigliano
Locanda Casanuova
Azienda Agricola Le Tore
Lama di Luna - Biomasseria
Masseria Serra dell'Isola
Masseria Il Frantoio
Masseria Impisi
San Teodoro Nuovo Agriturismo
Hotel Villa Schuler
Hotel Signum

Lucy Pope
Agriturismo Cervano B&B
Ca' del Rocolo
Agriturismo La Faula
Casa del Grivò
La Sosta di Ottone III
Agriturismo Rendola Riding
Relais San Pietro in Polvano
La Locanda
Frances' Lodge
Podere Salicotto
Il Rigo
Podere Le Mezzelune
Pieve di Caminino
Locanda della Valle Nuova
Locanda del Gallo
Casa San Gabriel
Villa Aureli
La Palazzetta del Vescovo
I Mandorli Agriturismo
La Torretta

Helena Smith
Villa Michaela
Le Due Volpi
Villa Campestri
Casa Palmira
Azienda Agricola Il Borghetto
Fattoria Viticcio Agriturismo

Odina Agriturismo
Fattoria Tregole

Ross James
Il Pardini's Hermitage

Series editor: Alastair Sawday
Editorial Director: Annie Shillito
Editor: Jackie King
Editorial Assistance: Florence Oldfield
Writing: Alastair Sawday, Jackie King
Production (UK): Julia Richardson, Rachel Coe,
                Tom Germain, Anny Mortada
Production (US): Adam Hess
Maps: Maidenhead Cartographic Services
Cover design (US): Louise Fili Ltd

Sawday, Alastair.
Go slow Italy : special local places to eat, stay and savor /
by Alastair Sawday ; with Jackie King ; foreword by Giorgio
Locatelli ; photographs by Lucy Pope, Mark Bolton, and
Helena Smith.
    p. cm.
Includes index.
ISBN 978-1-892145-81-9 (alk. paper)
1. Italy—Description and travel—Guidebooks.
2. Ecotourism—Italy—Guidebooks. 3. Slow food movement—
Italy—Guidebooks. 4. Restaurants—Italy—Guidebooks.
5. Sustainable living—Italy—Guidebooks. 6. Ecology—Italy.
I. King, Jackie. II. Title.
DG430.2.S227 2009
914.506'193—dc22
                                    2009011571

Published by The Little Bookroom
435 Hudson Street, 3rd Floor
New York, NY 10014
www.littlebookroom.com
(212) 293-1643 Fax (212) 333-5374

Printed on 10% PCW recycled paper with soy-based inks.

0 9 8 7 6 5 4 3 2 1

Go Slow Italy

Alastair Sawday
with Jackie King

Foreword
by Giorgio Locatelli

Special places to stay

Contents

7   Foreword by Giorgio Locatelli
9   Introduction by Alastair Sawday

The North
22   Maps and regional information

26   La Traversina Agriturismo, Piedmont
30   Agriturismo Cascina Folletto, Piedmont
34   Agriturismo Cervano B&B, Lombardy
38   Ca' del Rocolo, Veneto
42   Agriturismo La Faula, Friuli-Venezia-Giulia
46   Casa del Grivò, Friuli-Venezia-Giulia
50   B&B Valferrara, Emilia-Romagna
54   La Piana dei Castagni Agriturismo, Emilia-Romagna
58   La Sosta di Ottone III, Liguria

Tuscany
64   Maps and regional information

68   Villa Michaela, Tuscany
72   Antica Casa 'Le Rondini', Tuscany
76   Tenuta di Pieve a Celle, Tuscany
80   Le Due Volpi, Tuscany
84   Villa Campestri, Tuscany
88   Casa Palmira, Tuscany
92   Fattoria Barbialla Nuova, Tuscany
96   Sovigliano, Tuscany
100   Azienda Agricola Il Borghetto, Tuscany
104   Fattoria Viticcio Agriturismo, Tuscany
108   Locanda Casanuova, Tuscany
112   Odina Agriturismo, Tuscany
116   Agriturismo Rendola Riding, Tuscany
120   Relais San Pietro in Polvano, Tuscany
124   La Locanda, Tuscany
128   Fattoria Tregole, Tuscany

132   Frances' Lodge, Tuscany
136   Podere Salicotto, Tuscany
140   Il Rigo, Tuscany
144   Podere le Mezzelune, Tuscany
148   Pieve di Caminino, Tuscany
152   Il Pardini's Hermitage, Tuscany

Central
158   Maps and regional information

162   Locanda della Valle Nuova, Le Marche
166   Locanda del Gallo, Umbria
170   Casa San Gabriel, Umbria
174   Villa Aureli, Umbria
178   La Palazzetta del Vescovo, Umbria
182   I Mandorli Agriturismo, Umbria
186   La Torretta, Lazio

The South
192   Maps and regional information

196   Azienda Agricola Le Tore, Campania
200   Lama di Luna – Biomasseria, Puglia
204   Masseria Serra dell'Isola, Puglia
208   Masseria Il Frantoio, Puglia
212   Masseria Impisi, Puglia
216   San Teodoro Nuovo Agriturismo, Basilicata
220   Hotel Villa Schuler, Sicily
224   Hotel Signum, Salina, Aeolian Islands

228   Italy by train
230   Italy on a bike
233   Index

Foreword by Giorgio Locatelli

Food inspires conviviality and it is central to all that is Slow. I remember the lovely atmosphere at mealtimes at home in Italy when I was little—the sense that everyone had come together to join in with the preparation of a meal. My grandmother would be stirring something, my mother chopping, my grandfather grating the parmesan and I would lay the table. Everyone played a role. I learnt about cooking, too, especially their respect for good ingredients, and I absorbed a lot of knowledge.

I always ask my children to help at home because I want them, too, to have that sense of creating something together. Mealtimes are important for families.

Sometimes when friends invite me for supper, I can see that they are really stressed —there is smoke coming out of the kitchen and their hair is on end. I hate to see that. I would rather that they just put out a nice piece of cheese, some bread and some wine, then we could all relax. Spending time with people is the important thing, not what you eat.

Lots of people have this idea that food is a problem and they sigh when they wonder what to cook for supper. You don't find that in Italy. Nobody minds the little bit of work because they love the end result, the bit where they stop and sit down together. Food seems to bring more happiness in Italy than anywhere else.

The Slow Movement is reconnecting people with their regional culture—I am totally in tune with it and so are the people in this book. They can work a special magic for you.

Giorgio Locatelli
Chef proprietor of Locanda Locatelli

Introduction by Alastair Sawday

Its time has come. "Slow" is upon us and it is the least controversial "new" idea I have ever embraced. Who can argue against it, especially if lying in a hammock after a good lunch with friends in Italy? As the heat settles like a blanket over the soft browns of the landscape, you haven't the heart to give yourself a hard time.

That is one view of Slow: harmless idleness, eating and drinking good and honestly produced food and wine, enjoying good conversation and convivial company. But, of course, below the placid surface of that picture swirl the turbulent currents of food politics, competing production systems, attitudes to progress, global struggles for trade dominance, land ownership and more. Slow is a political movement; it is in deadly earnest, a powerful idea with the capacity for changing the way we think and act. Peaceful and non-confrontational, but reaching deep into our lives, it has some of the underlying power of Ghandi's revolutionary pacifism. But before we take ourselves too seriously let us go back to the foundations of it all.

Carlo Petrini, an Italian food journalist, was so saddened to see that a McDonald's had opened near the Spanish Steps in Rome, one of Europe's most iconic and beautiful cities, that he resolved to battle the growth of fast food with its logical alternative—Slow Food. He had seen how fast food had threatened to undermine much of Italy's traditional food production, had driven young people into the arms of an alien and damaging culture, fattened them and filled them with junk. Much that he loved about his country was under threat from this invasion of shallow, industrial food marketing. He saw it as the thin end of a long and dangerous wedge.

Luckily he had hit upon an idea with its own momentum and commercial potential.

Back in Bra, a small town not far from Turin in northern Italy, Carlo Petrini created the Slow Food movement and launched a series of devastating attacks on the way that his country, with others, had allowed itself to be duped into accepting fast food. Far more powerfully, he encouraged people to think of Slow Food as a creative and wholly enjoyable phenomenon. This part wasn't difficult. Suddenly, those who had always been happy to pay a bit more for food grown well, by local people, were made to feel part of something bigger and more significant. Pig farmers who rejected factory farming, raised their pigs in the forest, fattened them on acorns and apples and refused to feed

them unnecessarily on hormones and antibiotics—they were now serious players in a movement that celebrated them. They were never going to

get rich, but not all of us want to. For people who like doing things their own way, the Slow movement has been a tonic.

The Slow movement can give us meaning, a conceptual framework into which we can fit ideas that range more widely. In Italy there began the CittaSlow—Slow City—movement in response to the modern obsession with speed. Some of those languidly lovely Tuscan hilltop towns, such as Greve in Chianti, began to bed Slow ideas into town planning and governance. Why not encourage Slow production methods by giving priority to artisans? Why pollute the sky with street lighting when it could be directed downwards? Why not give people priority over cars, allow public transport to serve the public? In many towns the local Slow Food chapters have seen off bad planning applications.

Cynics might suggest that the Slow movement is bound to thrive in Italy, of all places, because everything moves at a crawl there anyway. Try getting the bureaucracy to shift, a phone installed or planning permission granted. Is Slow merely making a virtue out of the inevitable? However, another view is that Italians can get things done at high speed when they need to, often just ignoring the system that lies in the way. Perhaps Slow thrives there because Italians are so happy to ignore the rules; the UK Health and Safety regulations are, of course, anti-Slow because they insist on new and complex ways of doing old, well-tried, things.

The reach of Slow ideas is enormous—into energy, food security, the way old people are treated and children taught, waste is handled and houses built. Slow cities are booming in Italy, though they are usually "towns." In the UK we have a few too—Ludlow, Dereham, Aylsham, Diss, Mold, Berwick, Cockermouth, Perth and Linlithgow—and they are thriving. It appears that people want to live in them. It is obvious, isn't it?

It is indeed obvious, but not so obvious that we all get the message. I went to a play in Bristol last year in which the frantic madness of our obsession with movement, change and speed

was played out on stage. Young executives, plugged into their mobiles and laptops, walked on conveyor belts, rolled around at speed on their executive chairs, were gaily caught up in a clashing kaleidoscope of technology and optimism. They were going nowhere, but were exhilarated by the journey. Standing back and taking a look was not an option.

This introduction is perhaps not a place to be too serious, but I can't pass by without saying

why, beyond all other reasons, I am keen to promote Slow ideas. It is because they go far, far deeper than it might seem. They embrace the vastness of the ecological crisis that is threatening us all. While we are taking fossil fuels from the ground and recklessly burning them at irretrievable cost to the planet, those who adopt a Slow approach are burning less. While globalization creates inconceivable wealth for a few and impoverishes many, a Slow economy acknowledges the need for local solutions and restraint. I won't press on with this argument here, but I did want to touch on it.

Slow is serious too. And it is sophisticated, as the recent international banking crisis might suggest.

So, perhaps one can describe Slow as a bridge from panic to pleasure. Out of distressing awareness Slow brings hope. Others may be hell-bent on destroying the planet but if we eat that locally-reared pig, drink organic wine from the region, buy our bread from the baker, then we are acting, and perhaps being, positive. If we want to think of it that way, we are even being radical.

I have just mentioned organics, which brings me to another reason for embracing Slow. At work celebrations we try to eat only organic food; no other form of quality control really works at such a demanding level. Organic agriculture provides an impressive package of benefits: lower pollution rates, increased habitat for wildlife, higher employment levels, lower fossil-fuel use, community stability—and so on. A partnership between the organic and Slow movements was inevitable. The former works at creating the highest standards and ensuring that they are maintained; the latter is less demanding, wider-ranging and gets closer to people's hearts. There is no such thing as a Slow grower, just a grower who likes Slow ideas. Nobody polices his performance, but that is why the movement has grown so dramatically. It is an Idea—a sophisticated justification for continuing to do things the old way, or a platform for serious thinking. It is—and this is very appealing to Italians—an honor system.

Now I come to Italy. When we published *Go Slow England*, our best-selling book in 2008, we knew that the fun would continue when we took on Italy for our next project. *Go Slow Italy* has been a book-in-waiting. Here the Slow Food movement began, here the loss of traditional ways of growing food, eating and drinking, living in communities has been slower than elsewhere in western Europe. That is why we go there in such numbers, year after year, decade after decade. Italy remains lovably resistant to the clarion calls of "progress." They do progress well when they want to, but there beats in the heart of every Italian a preference for human beings over systems and over commerce and speed. Yes, they are keen on "*la bella figura*," not a very Slow notion, but it is fairly harmless and undermines any obsession with ideas that have more complex expression, and unintended consequences—like efficiency and success.

Searching among our Special Places to Stay in Italy for the ones that are genuinely Slow was a delightful task. Choosing those to include here was difficult. Growing their own food? Taking it easy after rejecting hectic lives? Spending half the day preparing great food and the other half eating it? This is what lucky Italians do. They always have. It is hard to go to any corner of Italy without encountering the ancient Romans,

epicures and lovers of the Good Life when they weren't battling barbarians. I love, beyond almost anywhere, the Italian lakes. Around Lake Como are the remains of some gorgeous villas to which rich Romans would retire to write their memoirs or enjoy lives of ease and good food. They rarely retired abroad, knowing that Italy was where life could be well lived.

Italians still stay largely in Italy. They take their holidays there, they retire there. Why do the English retire and holiday abroad in huge numbers? It can't just be the weather. Maybe it is also because they are, often unconsciously, seeking a Slow life. They like people talking to them in the street, even if they resent it at home. They love taking their time over meals and eating with others, even if they rarely do at home. They admire the way Italians have kept their small shops, though they flock to Tesco like lemmings at home.

Have we, in England and elsewhere, lost so

much that what we have lost is seen as nostalgia rather than as part of our reality? Have we destroyed so many town centers that we can no longer imagine a beautiful one as part of our lives? We have erected so many brutally ugly buildings that we now see them as inevitable, perhaps. Italy has retained so much that is beautiful that they see beauty, I believe, as their birthright. Slow has its roots in a love of beauty. It is fundamentally an aesthetic movement. It cannot thrive where ugliness rules.

This book is titled *Go Slow Italy* because it is about far more than Slow Food. It invites you to get there slowly, stay awhile, to float serenely through the days—conversing, enjoying every experience rather than longing for

whatever might be over the next hill. It invites intimacy, simplicity.

You will discover some lovely people in this book, people who have made the sort of life-changing decisions that we only dream about. If you have dreamed of abandoning the rat-race, you will enjoy meeting those who have done it. Rather than embracing conventional "progress,"

then inevitable frustration with bureaucratic inertia, they have adopted Slow as a life-enhancing form of progress.

Slow Travel is part of the new Slow Movement, as are slow sex, slow business, slow everything. And how we need it! We have an inalienable right to travel—which nowadays means fast travel—under the UN Declaration of Human Rights. The UN in 2001 even declared that "obstacles should not be placed in the way of... participation in international tourism." So it is hardly surprising, if you add the seductivity of the budget airlines, that we gad about all over the world as if there were no consequences. Well, the consequences are vast and are coming home to roost. I won't go into total "eco" mode, for you are here now to enjoy the best of Italian Slow, but do remember that by adopting Slow ideas you are playing out a new and positive role. You are, even, part of a subtle but powerful revolution. If it keeps McDonald's at bay, it will have achieved something.

If this book tempts you out of your armchair, look up these special places on our website (www.sawdays.co.uk) to find lots more useful information. And, when you travel to Italy, don't forget to travel slowly—by train. We've given the nearest train station for each place and, at the back of the book, there are features on getting about by train and bike.

Piedmont   Lombardy   Veneto

Friuli-Venezia-Giulia   Emilia-Romagna   Liguria

[THE NORTH]

THE NORTH

The rich and powerful north is closer to the rest of Europe in many ways and, with France, Switzerland, Austria and Slovenia at its borders, it has a multi-cultural feel. It is a huge Alpine area stretching from the Golfo di Genova in the west to the Golfo di Venezia in the east. To the south, the Po River winds its way through the vast and fertile Lombardy Plain, emptying into the Adriatic; the southern border of Emilia-Romagna reaches across the northern range of the Apennines before descending to the flatlands. The cities of the north have drawn people in droves from the historically poor south in search of jobs.

Piedmont is a border region with its sights turned firmly to Europe, ever receptive to progress, yet with more small farms and tiny villages than most regions. It has spawned huge industries such as Fiat and Olivetti and yet is still deeply rooted in tradition and has a strong sense of place.

The Royal House of Savoy made Turin its capital in 1563, triggering a grand period of baroque construction. It is a handsome, elegant and stylish capital city, more French than Italian, with wide streets and a geometric street plan. It regained its crown as a capital when the Kingdom of Italy was united. Turin is well worth a visit during the colder months when the city lives its understated fashionable life. At weekends the locals take off to the mountains—only an hour or so away by train.

Don't miss the fine museums, such as Il Museo Egizo, or a hot chocolate and some freshly-baked *pasticceria* in one of the beautiful porticoed piazzas. Turin also hosts the bi-annual Salone de Gusto, the internationally-acclaimed Slow Food fair.

In the Piedmont valleys you will find dishes unique to each—each, for example, has its own twist on the *bagna càuda*, a fondue made with

"rich and powerful, the north has a multi-cultural feel"

garlic, anchovies and walnut oil served with seasonal vegetables.

Chiavenna, a medieval village to the north of Como in **Lombardy**, has bubbling mountain waters coursing through its center and surrounding nature parks draw bird-watchers. The towns of Bergamo and Brescia have the most famous piano festival in the world, the Festival Michelangeli.

Venice! No adjective is worthy of her, "a maiden city bright and free." Today, tragically, the jewel in **Veneto**'s—the world's?—crown is slowly but inevitably sinking into the sea but her beauty survives: in squares, quiet backwaters and residential *calli* (lanes) where real people live and work just a short hop from heaving Piazza San Marco and the Rialto. An early-morning walk is a good way to get a feel for it all; for real serenity share a silent Basilica di San Marco with those at prayer. Modern art enthusiasts should time their visit to catch Venice's Biennale art show.

Don't overlook Treviso, Padova or Mantova (the latter is just in Lombardy), each as charming as Verona, nor the Veneto countryside, rich in elegant Palladian villas.

The Alpine region of **Friuli-Venezia-Giulia** is a name little known outside Italy. The Friuli part of the name originates from Forum Iuli, named after Julius Caesar, now known at the city of Cividale. Italian, the Friulian language, Slovenian and some German are spoken here.

The clear mountain air, crystal clear waters and sheltered river valleys produce outstanding wines and food: renowned grappa, good meat and trout, San Daniele ham, salamis made from goose and a huge variety of unusual cheeses.

The July Folkfest, held every year, spans 30 towns here and in neighboring Veneto.

Bologna—"*la rossa, la dotta e la grassa:*" "red" for its politics and its stone, "learned" because of its academics, "fat" thanks to its reputation for gastronomy—has the oldest university in Europe and is a handsome, rewarding city. The duomo and its towers are all built of local pink stone and glow red as the light fades and the cobalt sky starts to fill with stars.

There are many fine towns in **Emilia-Romagna** connected by a rail system that runs the width of the region from Piacenza in the west to Ravenna on the Adriatic coast. Ferrara, Modena and Ravenna are all World Heritage sites and many small towns have achieved CittaSlow status.

Much of the region's produce is world-famous —Prosciutto di Parma, Parmigiano Reggiano, *aceto balsamico*—but there is much more to discover including outstanding wines such as Lambrusco Grasparossa di Castelvetro, L'Albana di Romagna DOCG, Sangiovese and Trebbiano.

Liguria is a rainbow-shaped land running around the Gulf of Genoa with a narrow coastal plain dotted with sparkling bays; the land behind rises sharply into towering mountain terrain. Its mild climate earned it a reputation as Europe's flower garden; every bit of contoured fertile land is ringed and stepped with greenhouses, vineyards or olive trees. The food is richly interesting: *La torta pasqualina* is filled with rice, vegetables and seasonal wild herbs and *pansooti*, big ravioli, are filled with *preboggion,* a delicate mix of wild herbs. Taggiasca olives make the sweetest oil.

The road that links France with Italy disappears deep into long mountain tunnels only to appear again on lofty viaducts high above the sea. Magnificent.

Lindy Wildsmith

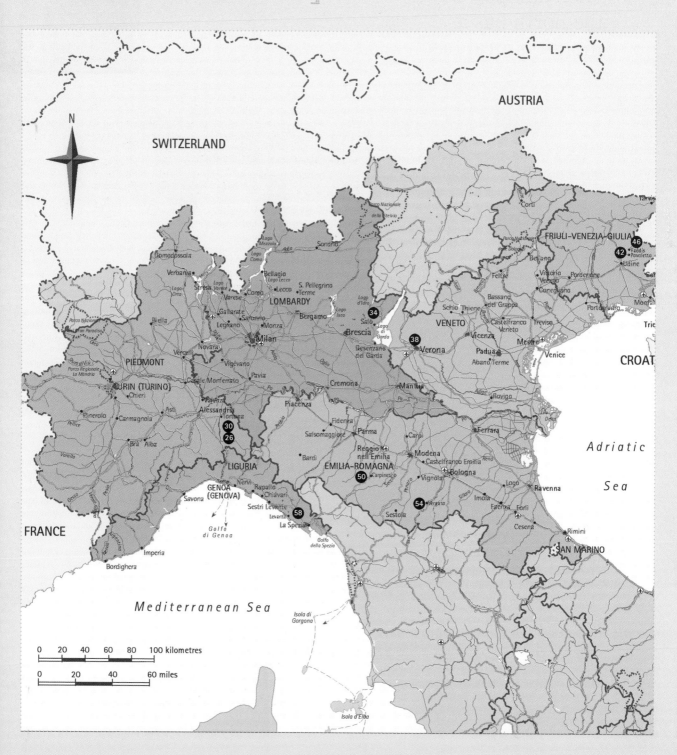

AUSTRIA

SWITZERLAND

FRIULI–VENEZIA–GIULIA

LOMBARDY

VENETO

CROAT

PIEDMONT

Milan

Brescia

Verona

Padua

Venice

TURIN (TURINO)

Cremona

Mantua

Alessandria

Piacenza

Parma

Ferrara

Adriatic

LIGURIA

EMILIA–ROMAGNA

Bologna

Ravenna

Sea

GENOA
(GENOVA)

La Spezia

Rimini

FRANCE

SAN MARINO

Mediterranean Sea

N

0 20 40 60 80 100 kilometres

0 20 40 60 miles

Special places to stay

Piedmont

26 La Traversina Agriturismo

30 Agriturismo Cascina Folletto

Lombardy

34 Agriturismo Cervano B&B

Veneto

38 Ca' del Rocolo

Friuli-Venezia-Giulia

42 Agriturismo La Faula

46 Casa del Grivò

Emilia-Romagna

50 B&B Valferrara

54 La Piana dei Castagni Agriturismo

Liguria

58 La Sosta di Ottone III

La Traversina Agriturismo

PIEDMONT

"I tried being an architect but my heart was too tied to the countryside, to the perfumes of the grasses and the lush woodland, to the fireflies which during the summer nights transform the little valley into an amphitheater, to the birds and their song. My life here is pure poetry, the poetry of the joy of small but important things. That is why we decided to open our house, to share the joy."

Thus writes Rosanna when asked to describe her journey to this place. She is one of life's "radiators," radiating joy and life-force in everything she does. She and Domenico really do consider their guests as friends; their attitude to hospitality is shaped by their humanity. There is no talk of "we and our guests;" it is "we." The experience of dining together at their big table is pure "Slow"—convivial, light-hearted, happy, open-minded. "I adore my work. The rhythm of our life and that of our guests is the rhythm of the forest and its animals. This is not pure fancy; I love getting to know new people and sharing with them my passions for flowers, good food, art. After a hard day's work I give thanks that destiny has enabled me to realize my dreams."

For 300 years this house and farm, high on a wooded hillside, have been in Rosanna's family. Was it ever so beautiful and full of life? She gave up a career in architecture to create her version of paradise only 40 minutes from Genoa. If you came for the roses alone you would be happy. One, an attention-seeking star, has climbed all over the front of the house; the air is fragrant with lavender, oregano and roses. But the irises, the hostas, the 230 varieties of plants—they are a magnificent chorus in colorful support. Rosanna has achieved here a level of happiness that is contagious. Her exuberance is manifest in the garden, where plants run riot and the feel is, surprisingly, of an English country cottage garden.

The arrival at La Traversina is memorable: Ollie the dog, accompanied by the five cats, may well be the first welcome. You know instantly that you have arrived somewhere special. People love the homey, imaginatively decorated bedrooms with handsome furniture, books and pictures. One visitor wrote of excellent dinners served at a long communal table with friends, guests and family joining in, happily chatting, and enjoying the local produce. She writes: "I was invited to sit at the kitchen table and chat with them while they got dinner under way. Domenico is the perfect foil for spirited Rosanna, who is so organized and efficient that in half an hour she had made a sauce for the pasta, two enormous savory tarts and two lemon pies, all the while chatting gaily with me."

Vijaya is the young Nepalese Sherpa who is now very much part of the family. He trained as a yoga teacher and they hope soon to create a space in the garden where he will be able to give classes.

Domenico is upholding the desire of Slow Foodies everywhere to protect rare and unusual species of plants. He nurtures a strain of tomatoes that can grow—each one—to an enormous one kilogram! Straw has to be laid beneath each plant to nurture the huge fruit until he decrees it is ready to be harvested—and it is soon on its way to Rosanna's kitchen to be transformed into a delicious dish. All this is part of La Traversina's charm—Rosanna and Domenico have worked a special magic of their own and swept others up into it.

Rosanna & Domenico Varese Puppo

La Traversina Agriturismo,
Cascina La Traversina 109, 15060 Stazzano

* 1 double, 1 family room, €90–€110.
  Half-board €70–€80 p.p. 4 apartments, €115–€135.
* Dinner €25–€32, by arrangement. Wine €7.
* +39 0143 61377
* www.latraversina.com
* Train station: Arquata Scrivia

Agriturismo Cascina Folletto

PIEDMONT

"If it's not in season, it's not on the menu." This simple statement from Andreina sums up her approach to food.

"All the food we cultivate here is organic, and GM-free, naturally, and almost all from old varieties that are protected by the Slow Food Presidium. Around 80% of what we serve is organic and is our own produce; what we can't supply ourselves we buy locally from other farmers and producers who are Slow Food members."

At Cascina Folletto's little restaurant—one that is open to the public—it is a privilege to have Andreina and her mother MariaRosa cooking for you. MariaRosa was born in this 18th-century Tortonese farmhouse.

"I help the guests choose their meal and I explain the ingredients; Mamma does most of the cooking," explains Andreina. "Many of our dishes have a local, historical significance. We have done a lot of research to rediscover forgotten foods and recipes."

The family effort extends to Andrea, Andreina's husband, too. He is a wine specialist and genuinely enjoys telling guests about the local grapes, wines and grappas. He can organize courses, too, for guests who want a deeper understanding of how wines are produced and the flavors achieved.

For him wine is far more than a drink. "Educating people about the wine they have chosen gives them a richer eating experience, a more complete evening. We can introduce them to the *vigneron*—the wine maker—too. I enjoy teaching cookery and particularly like teaching couples. Sometimes we get one partner to prepare the first course and the other to create the second course. Afterwards they will enjoy the meal together on the terrace.

It's a romantic experience for them and they can take the recipes home."

Two crops grown here are of local importance: the wonderful "Scented Strawberries of Tortona"— a Presidia Slow Food—and the *Ceci di Merella* (chickpeas certified as a Traditional Product of Piedmont). An ancient strain of saffron from the Middle Ages, Scrivia River Valley saffron, is also

> "Many of our dishes have a local, historical significance. We have done a lot of research to rediscover forgotten foods and recipes"

grown. The chickpeas are bottled and preserved to last the whole year. Andreina makes wonderful chickpea foccacia and risottos, too.

There are few producers of the famed Tortona perfumed strawberry—they can be difficult to cultivate and many of the farmers that grew them have retired or died. They are similar to a blackberry, are large, sweet, and unusually scented. They are harvested in one ten-day period each year—usually the second half of June.

A whimsical elf sitting on top of a strawberry is an apt house emblem for Cascina Folletto: once you have tried the *fragola profumata* you are hooked. No other strawberry will ever satisfy you.

You are encouraged to explore the landscape that gives up all this produce; bikes can be borrowed and trails are discussed. Much of the landscape is surprisingly flat, cultivated agricultural land (a lot of rice is grown in the flatlands of northern Italy).

The nature park at Torrente Scrivia and the Roman city of Libarna are nearby and it's a shortish hop to the coast. They know all the local festivals, events and concerts and take pleasure in

constructing an enticing itinerary for their friends and guests whatever the time of year.

Folletto is a simple farmstead deeply respectful of its place in its community, of its history and traditions. Don't expect luxury laid on specially for you. This is an authentic house with engaging owners, the sort of place that makes you feel you have really gotten under the skin of Italy—an experience rarely available in hotels.

The farmhouse is, in turns, cheerful and somber: there is a bright front parlor for tea or coffee, a dining room hung with plates and an upstairs sitting room with balcony views of the fields. A mellow brick archway frames the stone staircase to bedrooms that hold well-polished family furniture, iron-and-walnut beds, brocade spreads, a rocking cot. ("Folletto" has elf-green in its tartan curtains and cushions and is a large suite.)

Tortona is a very ancient town, once an important military station for the Romans. Flattened, stone by stone, by Frederick Barbarossa in 1155, it was then virtually flattened a few more times before finding some sort of peace under the House of Milan and finally of Savoy. Like a dazed boxer, it has survived pummelling from all sides— like so many Italian towns. There are a fine cathedral, a ruined castle and a Roman museum. This is the Italian hinterland—fascinating and rich in its own way, and free from the worst of modern tourism. It is, simply, very "real."

Agriturismo Cascina Folletto

strada Veneziana 9/1, fraz. Bettole,
15057 Tortona
- 2 doubles, €80–€100. 1 single, €50.
  1 triple, €110–€120.
- Dinner with wine, €25.
- +39 0143 417224/ +39 339 6749917 (mobile)
- www.cascinafolletto.com
- Train station: Tortona – Novi Ligure

Agriturismo Cervano B&B

LOMBARDY

The Apennines, 150km away, can be seen on a clear day. Does that say something about the air quality? Snow-topped mountains, the deep-blue, glassy Lake Garda and an enormous sky—they are an uplifting spectacle.

Gino and Anna have impeccable eco-credentials and run Cervano with the tiniest impact on their stunning surroundings. Remarkably, too, they have held onto a joie de vivre that is often lost in the quest to live cleanly. "We do all we can to minimize our energy use and as most of our guests are not very green we pass on our tricks to them, too!" says Gino. "I hope they don't think we are being stingy, but we simply don't want to waste the earth's resources. We try to live an ecologically responsible life without driving ourselves, and others, mad!"

Gino's words will resonate with those who take the environment seriously. One of the hotel owners from our *Go Slow England* book wrote: "It is not until you set off down the eco road that you realize what a very long road it is."

There are daily dilemmas: which is the most responsible food to buy; balancing your carbon footprint with the need

to run your life efficiently; weighing up one method of heating over another... the list goes on.

The Massaranis have used the most effective insulation, installed 32 square meters of solar panels that supply half the power for the house, use wood from their land to fuel boiler and fires, have a ground-source heat pump and a condensing heating system. Their lighting is light- and movement-sensitive and there are double-glazed windows to keep the heat in. They have won, quite properly, recognition and green certification from ISNART, Italian tourism's Chamber of Commerce.

Avoiding light pollution is an important aspect of the CittaSlow philosophy, and important for wildlife here, too: "Wildlife thrives when we don't flood the land with light—we are surrounded by pheasants, deer, and hare and we want to preserve their natural habitat."

Cervano remains a comfortable villa, an artful restoration of a once-crumbling family home. Built in the 1800s, it is a fine example of Lombard "fort" design: horses would pull carts laden with hay into the central, narrow, cobblestoned courtyard. Four families once

lived here and many features from the 1800s remain unchanged, such as the lanes and paths to the house and the flow of the mountain spring that irrigates crops of figs, persimmon, apricots, apples, almonds, grapes, nuts, medlars, hazlenuts and tomatoes. Gino and Anna now have two-tenths of the original land—the rest has been divided among other family members. "We have the comfort of knowing that the land remains pure. For 100 years it has been cared for organically and we produce the best oil on the Lake—anything from 200-1,000 liters per year."

In 1877 the owners, the Fiorini brothers, channeled the natural springs into two underground pipes, one going to a fountain where barrels from the cellar were washed and another to a marble fountain for washing clothes. They are still there and you'll sometimes spot crayfish that have been carried down from the brook water.

Much, however, has changed inside the house with the arrival of the B&B rooms and self-catering apartments. The bathrooms and kitchens have yielded to modern ideas; everything else has been left much as it was at the time of construction. There are slick bathrooms, a marble breakfast bar in a luminous kitchen and decorative floors in a rare, speckled, marble from Verona. Bedrooms are simply and traditionally furnished (one, "Monte," is suitable for wheelchair users). One guest wrote "Every morning Gino and Anna would deliver fresh bread and croissants with such a kind touch. They can't do enough for you and, what is more, are immensely knowledgeable about Italian art."

Children are wholeheartedly welcomed; Gino and Anna have even created a hideaway for them in the garden, the "Roccolo," a blue Smurf house that was once a small hunting cottage. "It has two rooms and is for children only, away from the grown-ups," says Gino. He has even crafted pop-guns from elder tree branches that use berries from the laurel as pellets. "We show them how to make the berries bang and smoke." He makes bubble wands from bamboo

canes, too. Paths through the woods are ideal for spotting wildlife: roebucks come to drink in the brook at the back of the villa and fireflies add a sparkle to the garden's night.

"We have created a meditation spot on our small 'mountain' behind the house. The 'Dos' is a little structure flanked with oaks and cypresses and with a terrace onto a spectacular view of the lake."

Mountains and lake are majestic, and the weather is kind; the vast lake creates a micro-climate that helps keep the temperature up, even this far north, and enables farmers to produce the finest olive oils, wines and fruits. The cross-lake ferries are a fun and efficient way of exploring the lake's shores. The endlessly kind Gino and Anna may even take you to local markets and introduce you to their favorite restaurants. You could not be in safer hands or with nicer people. And in the lakes one rediscovers the meaning of beauty.

Gino & Anna Massarini

Agriturismo Cervano B&B,
via Cervano 14, 25088 Toscolano Maderno
- 3 B&B suites, €110-€150;
  4 apartments, from €100 per night.
- Restaurant 1km.
- +39 0365 548398
- www.cervano.com
- Train station: Brescia

Ca' del Rocolo

VENETO

It seems impossibly dreamy, too good to be true. Once upon a time there was a beautiful farm up in the hills above Verona with something to catch the eye at every turn: wooden horses on the terrace, carvings on the walls, flowers on the roof. Children set off to see their friends on horseback, Dad created beautiful objects in his workshop, Mum climbed the hill to collect honey for breakfast. Yet it is all very real, and there is a real streak of steeliness, too, running through Ilaria and Maurizio. This is evident in their determination to be forces for environmental good; their commitment to living responsibly means that while you are with them you'll feel far from the excesses of consumer culture.

"Every day we have to make choices that affect us, our guests and the land," says Ilaria. "We spend a lot of time thinking about the right choices. Our electricity comes from a green provider that puts profits into research on renewable energy; we heat the water with solar panels; we reduce our waste, save water and travel only little and responsibly. But we are involved in tourism—albeit in a small way—and that has a huge impact on the environment. Most of our foreign guests arrive by plane and then hire a car—they need one in these hills—and that has a negative impact that cancels out some of our work. But these conflicts are a common part of being aware; if we opted for a career in conservation in a far-off place, we would fly back and forth. We try to do our best and hope to show guests that it's possible to make a difference."

So you will be encouraged to explore the hives, the eight organic hectares and the woodwork studio. The extension—the *sala desgustazione*, the tasting room—is made from wood and hemp and has a "living" roof planted with bright flowers; the turf on the roof insulates the room. These living roofs are still pioneering experiments but will one day be

common as we struggle to find more intelligent ways of saving energy and growing food.

The Corazzas are keen supporters of local agriculture. "Our farm is organic and we use as much organic produce as possible but we often choose to buy local—food we trust but which hasn't got an official organic label. The goats cheese from the neighboring farm, for instance, has to be a better choice than an organic cheese made elsewhere, packaged and sent here. I find the organic craze a little hard to understand—has it become a status thing?"

(Note from Alastair: it is harder to understand in Italy than elsewhere, for Italy has such a long tradition of small producers known and trusted by their community. Organic is, indeed, often the choice of city dwellers, removed as they are from food producers. Certainly it is rare to find such a passion for organic food among country dwellers who are confident in the integrity and competence of their neighboring farmers. I, though, am nevertheless a stalwart defender of the organic system, knowing something of the grim industry that is most food production.)

Ilaria and Maurizio organize tasting sessions of local produce and of their own honeys, oils and jams. You can buy all these, plus hand-crafted presents and other local produce in the tasting room. The wood from the land around Rocolo, used to fuel their house, is also made into furniture by Maurizio; he makes toys, picture frames and walking sticks, too.

There are animals everywhere. "They are part of the equilibrium of our lives. We all respect them and the children know how to look after them. Our guests can even bring their own animals. We like cooking vegetarian food, even if we do occasionally eat meat." Maurizio ran a restaurant in Verona, and Ilaria has written three cookbooks; so you know the food will be exceptional.

Maurizio bravely restored part of the structure—which dates from 1800—himself, and the result looks authentic and attractive: big and airy rooms

have simple cotton rugs over stripped bedroom floors, rough and whitewashed plastered walls, solid country furniture and excellent beds and bathrooms. There's also, usefully, a shared kitchen. Breakfast is delicious, with seasonal cakes and home-grown fruits. Conversation usually bubbles.

Plans were underway to install a salt-water pool but were blocked; they had wanted to heat it entirely by solar panels but the number needed were not authorized. "Aesthetics still rule in much of Italy's planning strategy so we can't always make the choices we would like. But we are optimistic that we will realize our plan," says Ilaria.

There is, nearby, a WWF-managed forest and there are nature trails galore on the farm and beyond. It's an easy place to be, even though there is a keen sense of purpose. Join in with it all or simply settle into the quiet that is everywhere.

Ilaria & Maurizio Corazza

Ca' del Rocolo, via Gaspari 3, loc. Quinto, 37142 Verona
- 2 doubles, 1 family room, €60–€75 (€410–€450 per week).
- Snacks available on request, €15.
- +39 045 8700879
- www.cadelrocolo.com
- Train station: Verona Porta Nuova, 12km; Verona Porta Vescovo, 8km.

Agriturismo La Faula

FRIULI-VENEZIA-GIULIA

The story of Luca and Paul's journey at La Faula is worthy of one of the ubiquitous-but-amusing documentaries that appear to be on every television channel. Two successful businessmen are living and working in London and enjoying the metropolitan life. Neither wants a country life but when the call goes up to lend a hand on a farm, the daring duo dash off as full of good intentions as they are devoid of appropriate skills.

Idanna and Franco, Luca's parents, needed to step back from the hard physical work of running a large farm on a hilly site but didn't want to retire completely. The obvious solution was to see if their urbanized son wanted to take over the reins. As soon as the seed of the idea was planted, it blossomed into a reality for Luca and partner Paul. One day they were on the London Underground, commuting to their jobs in law and marketing, and the next they were working on the land learning quite how little they knew about agriculture. "A huge wave broke over us as soon as we arrived. We needed to learn about forestry, viticulture, viniculture, animal husbandry," says Paul. "Suddenly our days were full of tractor-driving, wood-cutting, vine-pruning, delivering calves, digging drains, making wine. At times it was a daunting struggle."

Their tenacity paid dividends, and they have created a modern working farm where rural laissez-faire and the commerce of a serious winemaker happily mingle. As often happens when someone makes a "discovery" about a corner of the world they barely knew, there is an urge to share the secret. So Paul, now an eloquent evangelist for the area, had the brave idea of opening the house for bed and breakfast. "We realized that our joy could be shared and that there could be a powerful synergy between

the farm and its work and the house guests. Luca's mother Idanna still helps us with rooms and guests and she and his father are very much a part of La Faula."

An exuberant miscellany of dogs, donkeys, guests, friends and family co-exists happily, all apparently aware of boundaries but providing the sort of mixture that most people enjoy. Bedrooms are simple, with good antique furniture, a rustic feel and modern bathrooms. There is a bistro-style

"An exuberant miscellany of dogs, donkeys, guests, friends and family co-exists happily"

restaurant where wonderful home-reared produce is served (free-range veal, beef, chicken, lamb, just-picked vegetables and fruits); on summer nights there may be a barbecue. People do, indeed, love walking around the vineyards and the farmland and learning about food and the farm's considerable wine production. That's what agritourism is all about, of course.

Luca and Paul have become wine experts and have brought the winery on since they took over in 1995 with slightly dated machinery. Their grapes are organic and they make their wines with as little mechanical intervention as possible. Luca, who made wines here with his father in the 70s, consulted wine expert Emilio Del Medico and now they plan to reduce the number of vines and concentrate on producing smaller amounts of very high quality wines.

Luca explains the history of their hamlet, just outside the village of Ravosa: "'Faula' was the name given by the old Friulani to the beech tree grove at the bottom of the first hill that rises up from the Friuli plane. The Lombards gave it the name 'Gion' and it was considered a place difficult to reach, surrounded by marshland and

a river that was prone to flooding. Before the Lombards were here, the Romans built a quarry at the base of the same hill where they excavated fine clay, formed it into bricks and then fired it right there in a kiln to build the city of Aquileia."

Founded in 181BC, Aquileia was significant during the last days of the Roman Empire and was one of the first places in Italy to accept Christianity. Its basilica, begun in 313, is awesome, and there is a Paleo-Christian Museum. Just outside the city walls there is a small cemetery with votive altars—"an extraordinary place," says Luca. La Faula is just below the site of the Roman kiln.

This is an especially peaceful patch of Italy, close to Slovenia and mountainous, historic, rustic. An alpine charm washes over the small villages that soar above sea level. "I have found a life that suits me. I am now slower to respond to stress and strain," Paul says. "Sometimes I don't bother responding at all! I enjoy the seasons and love being outside: the smoky, pastel landscapes of winter, the brilliant blues, yellows and greens of summer, the promise of spring and the satisfaction and closure of autumn. And especially lovely is being embraced by the community. I'm a New Zealander but now I am considered 'one of them'. I am woven into the fabric of Italian-Friulano-Ravosa society and it doesn't get any better than that."

Paul Mackay & Luca Colautti

Agriturismo La Faula,
via Faula 5, Ravosa di Povoletto, 33040 Udine
- 9 twins/doubles, €40-€45. Half-board €56-€66 p.p.
  4 apartments for 2-4, from €65.
- Lunch or dinner €18. Wine €9.
- +39 334 399 6734 (mobile)
- www.faula.com
- Train station: Udine

Casa del Grivò

FRIULI-VENEZIA-GIULIA

The smallholding is in a hamlet on the edge of a plain; behind, densely wooded hills extend to the Slovenian border, sometimes crossed just for the gathering of wild berries. From the bedroom balconies there are wonderful views over the treetops; in autumn, the smell of wood-smoke wafts around the chalet, and, with the low sun's long shadows, creates a wonderful, almost alpine, atmosphere.

The task of relaxing here is made easier by the family's palpable happiness. Guests have spoken of the artistic atmosphere and of Toni and Paola's absolute commitment to doing the right thing environmentally, socially and communally.

"The reconstruction has been done largely by ecological methods," says Toni. "We used all the original building materials that we could find around the property, all that had been discarded because they had fallen out of place or were too damaged. We repaired hand-made roof tiles, chestnut beams, floor tiles and hand-carved flagstones. These materials happen to be worth a fortune now but we used them to save them from waste and because they bring with them

a sense of their past life here. They add extra pleasure to the building."

Simplicity, rusticity and a "green" approach are the keynotes here; so you'll sleep on traditional, and immensely comfortable, wool and vegetable fiber-filled mattresses, some with blankets and some with handsome quilts. Children will adore the open spaces, the ready-made playmates, the animals and the little pool that's been created by diverting a stream. It is a convivial space, shared easily by the family.

Everywhere there are little displays of old tools, antique jugs, pretty plates. "Our guests say that it feels like stepping into a fairytale. There are many old objects, too, as in a museum, but this is a living house, our home, so it is not static and silent."

Toni celebrates traditional farming—growing for yourself and for your community—for the self-sufficiency it gifted. "There was no middle-man and a farmer had independence. Farming then stood for everything that totalitarianism does not."

They delight in each season and the fruits that

CASA DEL GRIVÒ

each gives them. Each crop sets off a spell of conviviality as friends, neighbors and family gather to help harvest and preserve the organic fruits and vegetables. The main crop is grapes and 2009 marks the Costalungas' 20th year of organic farming. Wine from this region is considered by many to be the finest of all Italian wines and Toni and Paola make three.

"Our Tocai Friuban is a dry white, good with prosciutto, the Refosco dal Peduncolo Rosso is a ruby red dry solid wine for meats and intense flavors and Verduzzo, a tasty straw yellow wine, excellent with risotto or strong cheeses," says Toni. There's a touching story behind the labels, which are exquisite, and Toni will tell you if you ask.

> "Days draw gently to a close at Casa del Grivò: fires are lit, tables laid, glasses polished and fine dinners are cooked by Paola"

They point to the Slow philosophy of wine production: an elderly gent holds a rake and with it he is drawing the lines for a musical score. "Producing our wine is like working on a melody," says Toni.

Maps are laid out at breakfast, and there are heaps of books on the region; the walking is wonderful, there are a castle to visit and a river to picnic by. It is an area as rich in art, architecture, monuments and history as any in Italy. To ignore the Friuli would be a great shame, so do add it to the list! It is steeped in fascinating history yet is small enough to be navigated easily by bus, train or bike. A visit to Cividale del Friuli will plunge you into the history of Julius Caesar's arrival in 50BC. It was called Forum Iuli in honor of the Emperor and from those origins came the word Friuli. Market day is lively and you will see influences in the food from Yugoslavia, Slovenia and Austria.

The art collections of Udine are well known, and the whole area has more than a flavor of Venice. Aquileia has important early Christian history and the basilica shields extensive remains of a Roman port. From its mosaic floor, depicting ocean scenes, soar mighty Corinthian columns. Friulanos are proud of their history and the language of Friuli is enjoying a renaissance: you may even see road signs in Friulano. The Società Filogica Friulana in Udine houses studies on the fraught history of Italy's much-invaded north-eastern corner and has cataloged important developments in the dialect.

Days draw gently to a close at Casa del Grivò: fires are lit, tables laid, glasses polished and fine dinners are cooked by Paola using old recipes and their own and local produce. There is candlelight and wine, too, and maybe even music and singing.

Toni & Paola Costalunga

Casa del Grivò,
Borgo Canal del Ferro 19, 33040 Faédis
- 1 double, 4 family rooms, €60. Half-board €50 p.p.
- Dinner with wine, from €25. Lunch in summer only.
- +39 0432 728638
- www.casadelgrivo.com
- Train station: Udine

B&B Valferrara

EMILIA-ROMAGNA

There is an endearing simplicity in the bones of this Emilia-Romagna tower house, for its personality has been nurtured by Cosetta and Giuliano. They arrived at the 17th-century sandstone Casa a Scale—"tiered house"—in 1994 and wanted to do nothing more than allow the old ruins to breathe again and reveal their natural beauty.

Nothing has been overdone; all is understated, and fittingly so, in this silent hamlet on the ancient road that once linked Canossa with Carpineti. When it was a travelers' lodge, weary merchants would stop here, absorbing the protective calm of the surrounding forested hills before resuming their journeys to market. There were less benign travelers, too—the *briganti*, or bandits; but it's unlikely that a well-defended *fortezza* such as this would have come under attack. The house survived all sorts of turmoils and sits securely in the Tuscan-Emilian National Park.

Here you can slough off the self-absorption and frenzy of the modern world. There are three bedrooms for guests and an unusual amount of space to inhabit: a red-sofa'd living room and a large log-fired dining area that opens onto the garden. The feeling is of staying as friends, and the gentle hospitality of Cosetta and Giuliano has been praised by many a happy guest.

Cosetta's passion is furniture restoration. The house is full of antiques, gleaming wood, and even a parquet floor made from reclaimed roof timbers. "I always try to work faithfully. I want to be sure, even, that every key and lock is the right one for the age of the house. My greatest pleasure is when guests appreciate it all," she says.

Cosetta's story embraces Slow cooking, as it does so often in Italy. She creates jams that most of us would never think of, such as rosemary and fig and experimental berry mixes. She bottles

them, not always to sell but often to give to guests—a typically generous gesture. Her shelves sag under the weight of cookbooks ancient and modern and, thus equipped, she is able to produce wonderful local dishes such as spinach and ricotta wrap with locally ground wheat. "We love inspiring our guests with our recipes and helping them discover the farms that sell produce. In Latteria there is a famous place to buy parmesan and there are many traditional restaurants in the area."

Local produce includes honey and home-grown vegetables from the *orto*. Her own garden is grassed but it is seemingly without boundaries and tumbles into a prettier, wilder, landscape.

You can see the delicate tower of the Carpineti castle from the house. Nearby Canossa is rich in architectural and historical interest and its own castle, in a strategic position above the Secchia and Enza valleys, is where Emperor Henry IV was made to stand outside in the snow for three days as penance for his interference in the ecclesiastical appointments proposed by Pope Gregory VII.

Cosetta's ambition is to open three little apartments in the grounds so that guests will stay for a week or two and properly explore the area. "We have Slow Food festivals and can organize walking tours. I plan to hold music events in our own garden, too." She is a gentle helmswoman and imbues the whole place with a sense of family and home that is appreciated by all.

Cosetta Mordacci & Giuliano Beghi

B&B Valferrara,
via Valferrara 14, Pantano, 42033 Carpineti
- 3 doubles, €76–€90.
- Restaurants 1–4km.
- +39 340 1561417
- www.bb-valferrara.it
- Train station: Reggio Emilia

La Piana dei Castagni Agriturismo

EMILIA-ROMAGNA

Roughly etched into a piece of wood leaning against a wall by Piana dei Castagni's front door are these words: "I awake with the scent of the forests wafting in through the open window; I look out and watch the hawks soaring effortlessly through the sky. The smell of freshly baked biscuits floats up the stairs to where I am standing." Valeria's words are simple, home truths. "I'm no poet!" she laughs. "They just come from the heart. Mornings here really are like that!"

And life here couldn't be simpler or more genuine. You won't trip up over any ostentatious gestures; quite the opposite. The tempo is slow, to the point of being almost at a standstill, the mood relaxed. "We want guests to feel that all this is theirs; only then will they really, truly relax."

Valeria's father restored the simple farmhouse nearly 20 years ago. Now she and her husband and young son live a little way away down a tree-lined track which only boosts your sense of blissful, restorative isolation.

Baskets overflowing with geraniums dangle beneath brown-shuttered windows. A pale yellow rose clambers boldly over a window arch, pinning itself to the weathered bricks as it goes. The lovely lawns aren't manicured and are dotted with fallen leaves and shady trees; the garden's boundaries and wild borders beyond are blurred. In fact it's hard to tell where Valeria's land stops and the rest of the valley begins as the uneven, grassy slopes tumble down to the valley below. The whole place seems to thrive on its isolation.

Although historically an *agriturismo*, Piana dei Castagni doesn't produce its own oil or press its own grapes. Their sense of what is Slow is more subtle, though no less tangible. "It's not the activities that we do which are Slow, it's the way that we live," explains Valerie. "And that has drawn many types of

guests—particularly artists who are drawn to the peace and seclusion and, of course, to the landscape.

"Guests turn up, a pile of books tucked under one arm, and maybe an easel and set of paints under the other, and they're content. They don't need anything else. I'm just happy that I have the space for them so that they can enjoy doing the things they love in such peace."

La Piana is productive in another way. There is something, hidden in the surrounding greenery, that they produce in abundance. "This is the land of the chestnut tree (*castagno*)!" Valeria claims, proudly. The chestnut trees have been here since medieval times and are as poignant a feature of the landscape of Emilia-Romagna as rows of cypress trees are to her western neighbor, Tuscany. Surrounding the farmhouse is acre upon acre of this ancient woodland. Guests can follow the paths which wriggle their way through the trees, skirting around huge trunks, some of them over 300 years old. "*Il pane dei poveri* (the bread of the poor)

"When the time's right, in the autumn, we collect the chestnuts then dry them in the kiln"

played an intrinsic nutritional role during the Second World War. At that time everything was made from chestnut flour and polenta; that's all anybody ate!" says Valeria.

The significance of the chestnut tree appears to be as important in local life today as it was then. "When the time's right, in the autumn, we collect the chestnuts then dry them in the kiln. Just before Christmas, we make chestnut flour." The water-mill next to the farmhouse still churns away, grinding up the chestnuts, just as it has been doing for hundreds of years. "These ancient woodlands are so rich in history and tradition. And that's why we protect the *castagni*, because they have been such an integral part of our livelihood for generations."

Piana dei Castagni's menu has come a long way since the 1940s and Valeria is a wonderful cook. Nowadays you're more likely to come across regional dishes, with the occasional unusual one thrown in, such as Valeria's *tortelloni alle ortiche* (tortelloni in a nettle sauce). They're all accompanied by vegetables plucked straight from the well-tended garden. "Sometimes we'll all muck in together in the kitchen, my husband, father and son. It's a team effort!"

Plaques on the doors of the simple, snug bedrooms depict fruits of neighboring forests, with one exception, of course; "Chestnut" is brighter and more spacious, with wooden floors topped with colorful rugs.

"It's strange to think of us as part of a movement, a Slow movement," Valeria says. "This is just the way we are. But it is rewarding that people appreciate what we do here."

Signora Valeria Vitali

La Piana dei Castagni Agriturismo,
via Lusignano 11, 40040 Rocca di Roffeno
• 2 doubles, €60–€90. 2 triples, €80–€100.1 single, €40.
• Dinner €17. Wine €8–€15. Restaurant 3km.
• +39 0519 12985
• www.pianadeicastagni.it
• Train station: Vergato

La Sosta di Ottone III

LIGURIA

At La Sosta, 200 meters above sea level and on a large ridge, the views up and down—and all around—are riveting. Angela and Fabio thoroughly appreciate that they owe much to their local Slow chapter for, as well as communicating the Slow Food philosophy to the broader community, it is a vigilant guardian of the landscape, the culture and even the mood of the town.

"The fact that Levanto is a Slow city, and that we are on the edge of the Cinque Terre National Park, does give a sense of security; it is unlikely that much of what we love about living here will change," says Angela. "We exist in a democracy yet there is a moral onus on those applying for planning permission to respect our environment and to bring something of quality to the area. A five-year planning program means that all interested parties have a chance to vet proposals and give their opinions."

Fabio, Angela and her mother, Jo, are devoted members of the Slow Food movement. They attend chapter meetings and have twice heard Carlo Petrini, an inspiring speaker and the movement's founder, talk in Levanto. Naturally, they source the best local food to serve in their own restaurant, but such dedication requires careful planning. "We ask guests to pre-book dinners because we buy what we need for that day. We don't have frozen or pre-made foods and can't suddenly conjure up extra meals for late guests."

Fabio cooks with the help of Fulvia; she is the pastry and puddings expert and he the sommelier. The wine list includes carefully selected Ligurian wines and some regional varieties that are not well known outside Italy. The restaurant is in the converted cellar and its terrace opens onto a long-reaching view of Chiesanuova, Levanto and the Mediterranean.

The steep hills that tumble down to the jumble of multi-colored houses on the famous Ligurian Cinque Terre coastline are dotted with neat allotments, pretty gardens and lines of billowing washing. There is one narrow road through Chiesanuova but cars are not allowed; so enjoy the peace and be prepared to carry your luggage down a footpath to the house.

La Sosta di Ottone ("*sosta*" means stopover) is named thus for it is said that Otto III stayed here on his way to his coronation in Rome in 996. The listed 16th-century house has been restored with the required reverence, using Ligurian stone and local marble. Bedrooms and bathrooms are exceptionally comfortable and large.

There is great comfort at La Sosta but this is not a hotel. There are spaces to sit and read yet you will not find staff dashing about to cater to your every whim. Sybarites may lament that the

> "My favorite path is the 8B. It overlooks one Cinque Terre town after another with the sea laid out beneath. It is breathtaking."

nearest bar is a 15-minute walk. The comfort of the rooms and the high quality of breakfast and dinner are evidence, though, that behind the scenes wheels are turned energetically on your behalf.

"Guests looking for great walking will be delighted," says Angela. "Several footpaths, some of which lead to the National Park and others to villages in the Levanto valley, cross Chiesanuova. It is 35 minutes to the Levanto beach and 45 on the way back up. One three-hour trail, with only one 15-minute stretch on a road, delivers you to one of the most spectacular parts of the national park. There are many choices of paths, high and low. My favorite path is the 8B. It overlooks one Cinque Terre town after another with the sea laid out beneath. It is breathtaking."

The faint-hearted or less mobile can get around the area with remarkable ease too. Any combination of boat/train/bus can be arranged to get you to and from the five marine hamlets of Monterosso, Vernazza, Corniglia, Manarola and Riomaggiore. Angela, Fabio and daughter Constanza have posted details of lots of walks on their website. They have done them all and have uploaded stacks of photos to inspire you to pack your boots.

Happy are they who have found their corner of paradise before their time is up. To have your corner of paradise within a stone's throw of Levanto, one of Italy's Slow cities, is enough to fill your cup to overflowing. The best part of belonging to a community that is dedicated to all things Slow is that much of what you love will remain unchanged.

Fabio & Angela Graziani

La Sosta di Ottone III,
loc. Chiesanuova 39, 19015 Levanto
- 1 double, 2 family rooms for 2–4, 1 suite for 4, from €180.
- Breakfast €10. Dinner €35. Restaurant 5km.
- +39 0187 814502
- www.lasosta.com
- Train station: Monterosso

[TUSCANY]

TUSCANY

Tuscany, the cradle of the Renaissance, and Florence its capital, are a treasure trove of architectural, painted, and sculpted gems, each one seeming to outshine the next. Its towns—such as Lucca, Pisa, Siena, San Gimignano—are as familiar to us as the names of its sons Michelangelo, Leonardo, Botticelli, Galileo and Dante. So too are the names of the galleries: Uffizi, Accademia, and Bargello. The landscape of undulating hills clad in disciplined rows of vines, blue mountains, cypress trees and medieval hilltop towns peeping through morning mists has been so celebrated by Renaissance masters, Oscar-scooping directors and advertising agencies that it is in danger of becoming clichéd. Yet we never tire of Tuscany.

Venus, the mythical goddess of beauty, broke her necklace and its seven pearls dropped into the sea. As they touched the water they turned into a string of islands—the Tuscan archipelago. The largest is the island of Elba, best-known as Napoleon's place of exile. The second is the tiny Isola di Giglio, a short trip by ferry from Porto Santo Stefano. As the boat approaches the simple little houses that cluster around the port one sees that Il Porto is in fact an animated little town with diminutive sandy beaches. A steep, winding bus journey takes you to the cool and peace of Il Castello, the walled town at the top of the island.

Before the arrival of the Etruscans, Tuscany was inhabited by Apennine peoples. Over the centuries, city states grew and prospered and, by the time the Romans came in the first century, the Etruscans had ceded all power. Lucca, Pisa, Siena and Florence were established; roads, aqueducts, sewers, domestic and public buildings were built.

"blue mountains and hilltop towns peeping through morning mists"

After the fall of Rome, Goths and Longobardi picked up the mantle and there was more building—Vicenza, for example. During the medieval period, pilgrims travelling across the region on their way from France to Rome brought huge wealth to the area and new communities grew up around churches and inns.

The conflict between Guelphs and Ghibellines split the Tuscan people but increased the wealth of communes such as Arezzo, Florence, Lucca, Pisa and Siena. Florence became the Renaissance capital, Pisa its port (it was once on the sea), Siena and Lucca centers of finance.

The Medici family ruled Florence in the 15th century and annexed the surrounding lands to create modern-day Tuscany. In the 18th century the Duke of Lorraine took over from the Medicis and Florence became part of the Holy Roman Empire. This was later dissolved by Napoleon and became part of the Austrian Empire until it was transferred to the newly unified nation of Italy. (Austrian troops had even occupied Venice, much to the disgust of the proud Venetians.)

Tuscany has vast swathes of lush forest and woodland of beech, chestnut and oak. From September to January you can join the Tuscans in their passion for hunting and foraging. In season you may find mushrooms, truffles, chestnuts and berries, or just walk and savor the sounds, scents and beauty.

In the gentle hills of Val d'Arbia there is a network of 67 tracks for walking, biking and riding; take the medieval pilgrim's way along the Via Francigena; follow a route connecting historic fortifications or discover Etruscan ruins and tombs along the Valle dell'Ombrone.

Many Tuscan villages are famous for their crafts: Scarperia is the town of knives and its charter for apprentices and master craftsmen was drawn up in the 16th century. You can watch a horn-handled knife being fashioned in one of the little knife shops. Other villages produce goods crafted from leather, wood or alabaster. Impruneta is well known for its clay quarries and terracotta furnaces, some of which date back to the 16th century and are still used to fire fine terracotta pots.

Massa Marittima is a fascinating hill town with distant views to the sea at Follonica; a puzzle of tiny streets and staunch *palazzi*. The colorful Torneo della Balestra (crossbow) is enacted in costume. In the evening young lovers, silver-haired gents, mothers and small sons dance together to the booming sounds of the town's brass band.

The fashionable coastal towns of Punta Ala and Castiglione della Pescaia are choc-a-block in August. Further north is Viareggio—home to the most flamboyant of all Italian carnivals.

Arezzo hosts a summer Polifonica music festival and Cortona the Tuscan Sun Festival of classical music, Renaissance art, food, literature.

Each Italian region has its own dialect but the 12th-century literary language of Florence and of its sons Dante, Petrarch and Boccaccio, was the basis of the Italian language and Florentines maintain they speak the purest, most sophisticated Italian.

Lindy Wildsmith

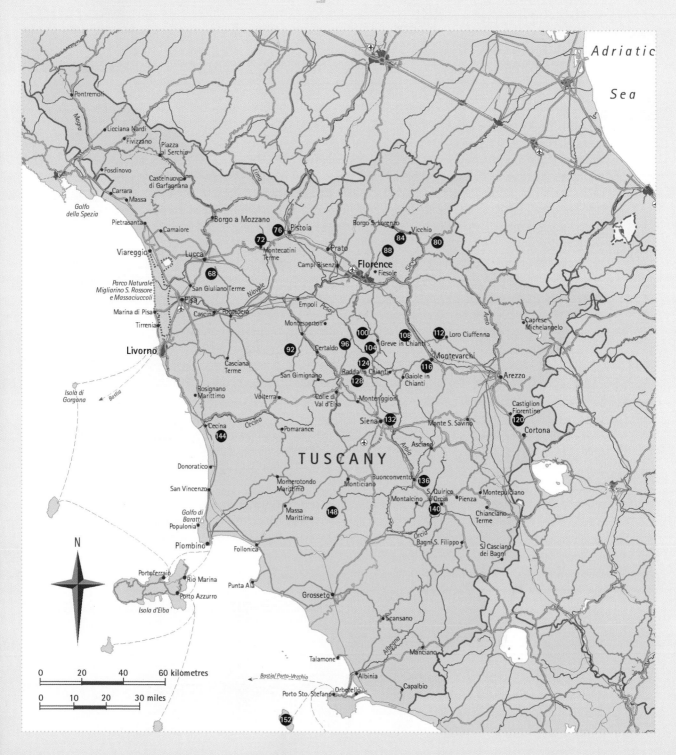

TUSCANY

Adriatic

Sea

Pontremoli

Licciana Nardi
Fivizzano
Piazza
al Serchio

Fosdinovo
Carrara
Massa
Castelnuovo
di Garfagnana

*Golfo
della Spezia*

Pietrasanta
Camaiore
Borgo a Mozzano
Borgo S. Lorenzo
76
Pistoia
Vicchio
84

Viareggio
72
Montecatini
Terme
88
Prato
80

68
Lucca
Campi Bisenzi
Florence
Fiesole

San Giuliano Terme
Pisa
Cascina
Pontedera
Empoli

Marina di Pisa
Tirrenia

Livorno
Montespertoli
100
108
112 Loro Ciuffenna
Caprese
Michelangelo

*Parco Naturale
Migliarino S. Rossore
e Massaciuccoli*

92
Certaldo
96
104
Greve in Chianti
Montevarchi

Casciana
Terme
San Gimignano
124
Radda in Chianti
116
Gaiole in
Chianti
Arezzo

*Isola di
Gorgona*
Rosignano
Marittimo
Volterra
128
Colle di
Val d'Elsa
Monteriggioni

Cecina
Siena **132**
Monte S. Savino
Castiglion
Fiorentino
120
Cortona

Cecina
Pomarance
144

Donoratico
TUSCANY
Asciano

San Vincenzo
Monterotondo
Marittimo
Monticiano
Buonconvento
136
S. Quirico
d'Orcia
Montepulciano

*Golfo di
Baratti*
Populonia
Massa
Marittima
148
Montalcino
Pienza
Chianciano
Terme

140
S. Casciano
dei Bagni

Piombino
Follonica
Bagni S. Filippo

Portoferraio
Rio Marina
Punta Ala
Grosseto

Porto Azzurro
Isola d'Elba

N

Scansano

Manciano
Talamone
Albinia
Capalbio

Bastia/Porto-Vecchio
Porto Sto. Stefano
Orbetello

| 0 | 20 | 40 | 60 kilometres |

| 0 | 10 | 20 | 30 miles |

152

Special places to stay

Tuscany

68 Villa Michaela

72 Antica Casa 'Le Rondini'

76 Tenuta di Pieve a Celle

80 Le Due Volpi

84 Villa Campestri

88 Casa Palmira

92 Fattoria Barbialla Nuova

96 Sovigliano

100 Azienda Agricola Il Borghetto

104 Fattoria Viticcio Agriturismo

108 Locanda Casanuova

112 Odina Agriturismo

116 Agriturismo Rendola Riding

120 Relais San Pietro in Polvano

124 La Locanda

128 Fattoria Tregole

132 Frances' Lodge

136 Podere Salicotto

140 Il Rigo

144 Podere Le Mezzelune

148 Pieve di Caminino

152 Il Pardini's Hermitage

Villa Michaela

TUSCANY

Just ten minutes from the beautiful city of Lucca. To get here you follow a tiny road called Via di Valle which takes you past the Vorno church and winds up the hill, through olive groves and onto the mountain where it becomes a track and finally peters out. There is little traffic and all you hear is the whisper of the breeze and the occasional chiming of the church bells.

Tuscany does it again—another eye-popping house looking over a vast range of hills and forests, in this case 50 acres of pine with the olive groves beyond. Here you also have a fine garden, heady with gardenias, plus a tennis court and a pool. There is more than a touch of opulence too, something often found with foreign owners driven by the magic of Tuscany. The grander bedrooms have frescoed ceilings, lavish fabrics, huge beds and double sinks. "Puccini," "Verdi" and "Dante" are the names of those rooms, and you may well find yourselves listening to opera music while you float around in a haze of admiration.

Vanessa bought the villa in 1984 when it was a com-paratively simple structure.

"It was a bit like a grand country barn and, like many of the houses up here, it was the second home of a Lucchese family. These old villas were traditionally used for little more than six to eight weeks in summer when their owners would flee the heat of the city and take off to the hills in their horse and carriage."

The renovation was a project on a grand scale—taking it on today would be even more challenging.

"Commendably the Italian government has put in place stringent regulations to ensure buildings are energy efficient," says Vanessa. "We have converted an outbuilding and we must install solar panels and rainwater reservoirs. We embrace the measures.

"We have a heat-exchange system for the pool and the air-conditioning and use long-life bulbs everywhere. We ask guests to be mindful of water usage. The English take it well but some others have an 'I have paid and I will indulge myself' attitude. They think we are simply trying to save money so I need to present a more scientific argument to persuade all to join in happily!

"Recycling collections are

efficient and regular. We aim to constantly reduce our waste; we buy fresh stuff at markets and buy in bulk. In England I can't believe the waste created by supermarket packaging.

"We are enthusiastic supporters of Vorno's wonderful village store run by Alba; she sells fresh produce that she buys from local people and is something of an institution locally. We buy our breakfast croissants there."

Scallop Risotto
Serves 6

1 kg (2 lb) scallops, shelled and cleaned
125 g (4 oz) butter
4 tablespoons brandy
sea salt and freshly ground pepper
3 shallots, finely chopped
500 g (1 lb) Carnaroli rice
1.5 liters (3 pints) hot fish stock
2 tablespoons flat leaf parsley, finely chopped
3 tablespoons double cream

• Separate corals from scallops.
• Heat half the butter and sauté the scallops for 2-3 minutes, turning once.
• Pour on brandy and ignite it. Season when flames die down, and put to one side.
• Sauté shallots in remaining butter until soft.
• Add rice and mix. Heat until the rice is crackling hot and shiny.
• Pour in a ladleful of hot stock. Stir and let the grains absorb the liquid. Repeat until the rice is almost cooked.
• Add the scallops, corals, juices and parsley. Stir and resume the cooking process as before.
• Take off heat when rice is creamy and velvety but has a slight bite. Stir in the cream and cover.
• Leave to rest for 2 minutes. Spoon onto a warmed platter. Serve at once with chilled white wine and arugula salad.

Vanessa has organized Slow Food house-parties by liaising with the Slow Food movement's Presidia in Tuscany. For instance, for one event they gathered together little-known cheeses for tastings from one of Tuscany's forgotten areas—the north-western corner within which lies the alpine-like Garfagnana National Park.

Vanessa is at the villa for six months of the year. In her absence Robert and Massimo take care of guests. Massimo is an architect and art historian and has stacks of knowledge that he is happy to share so you are in intelligent hands.

Vorno is famous for its spring—people arrive with empty bottles to fill up and take home. It is collected each day for the villa's guests, too.

You can get here easily: train to Lucca, hourly bus to Vorno and then five minutes of walking to the house. To get your fix of medieval Tuscany you need only drop down into Lucca. There you can cycle around the entirely intact city walls and take in a concert; this is Puccini's birthplace and the city is alive with music.

If you are assailed by delusions of grandeur during your stay at Villa Michaela you can hire two sopranos and a tenor to sing to you in the garden. This is more of a palazzo than a villa, and the mountain belongs to it—as does the chapel, so you could even marry here.

Vanessa Swarbreck

Villa Michaela,
via di Valle 8, 55060 Vorno
- 10 doubles, €200–€300. Entire villa on request.
- Dinner with wine, €50.
- +44 (0)7768 645500
- www.villamichaela.com
- Train station: Lucca

Antica Casa 'Le Rondini'

TUSCANY

Expectations soar on the approach to Antica Casa. The village of Colle di Buggiano is resolutely medieval: narrow cobbled streets, towering church towers, a tiny village square where elderly ladies sit in the shade playing cards for money, dogs lie in the sun and the church clock solemnly declares the time. The scene is so exquisitely set for something magnificent that you might wonder if your chosen place to stay could possibly measure up and keep the fairy tale alive.

Antica Casa exceeds expectations. Imagine a room above an archway within the castle walls of this ancient hilltop village, a room with 200-year-old frescoes depicting swallows swooping and diving and where, when you lean out from the window, you realize it is all for real as the swallows (*rondini*) flit in and out of nests in the archway.

Embracing Slow can mean many things; here

it is celebrated in Carlo's determination to restore and renovate the shell of the 500-year-old house that he found nine years ago. As an architect he had the credentials to do the job creatively and knowledgeably; he is Vice President of Bio-Architecture at Pistoia University. "We travelled widely," says Fulvia, "and when we first returned to Italy I taught P.E. and martial arts at a school in Venice. When we adopted a six-year-old boy from Russia, Federico, we decided upon the move to Tuscany. It was so important to us to find something special. We found this house, which has foundations dating from 900, in a state of abandonment. It was far too big, but we fell in love with it and refused to be deterred!"

It is impossible to resist. The combined charms of the house, the garden, the owners, the nearby hilltop restaurant with memorable views—they vanquish you. "One lady was in tears when she told

me that we had the house that she had dreamed of. I do feel proud and lucky," says Fulvia.

An archway off the Via del Vento ("where the wind blows") leads to the house. You step into a lovely room, a study in white—fresh lilies and snowy walls and sofas—dotted with family antiques and paintings; everywhere there is elegance. Delightfully different bedrooms have wrought-iron bedframes, big mirrors, thick padded eiderdowns, daybeds, pretty headboards; the suite is especially attractive.

The garden, opposite, was nurtured as gently as the house and was created from the plot of an ancient derelict property. It is now alive with lemon trees, flowers and scented herbs, a sensuous place to which Fulvia takes breakfast for guests. It is an oasis in the middle of the village. The hillsides beneath scramble down to the Montecatini Terme plains and are tinged with the silver of olive trees. Such is the architectural significance of this village and many of its buildings that Carlo has been unable to introduce many of the ecological innovations used in his professional projects. "There are many rules and regulations that apply because of the age of the house. We can't have solar panels, for example. We are making small changes where we can, though, and have managed to harvest rainwater from the roofs into an ancient central cistern."

Their restoration has been a nine-year journey— "a demanding one," says Fulvia, "but one that has brought us happiness and great satisfaction."

Fulvia Musso

Antica Casa 'Le Rondini',
via M Pierucci 21, 51011 Colle di Buggiano
- 5 doubles, €75–€115. Apartment for 2-4, €65 for 2.
- Restaurant 200m.
- +39 0572 33313
- www.anticacasa.it
- Train station: Montecatini Terme

Tenuta di Pieve a Celle

TUSCANY

Unity is a leitmotif running through Pieve a Celle, something that Fiorenza Saccenti values above most things: the unity of guests and family, of conversation and conviviality, of their life and the life of the community.

The Saccentis—three generations of them—live at the ochre "*colonica*" at the end of the cypress tree-lined drive. For them Pieve a Celle is an island, a paradise—albeit a hardworking one. They run it in a delightful spirit of inclusivity, encouraging others to join in with the rhythms of their family life. "We have our own perfect ecosystem and are lucky enough to be able to produce our own organic olive oil, wine and vegetables. We appreciate, too, being in a part of the world where respect is given to tradition, to local food and to artisan producers."

Fiorenza does something that we can all do, wherever we live, and that is focus on the little things that make us happy. If we fall into the trap of seeing happiness as a big goal to achieve, we miss out on an easily-achievable sense of contentment.

"I have a deep love of small pleasures for they bring

me the greatest happiness. It is something sweet taken from the oven and filling the room with a beautiful smell, a good coffee poured for friends, flowers from the garden on the kitchen table, even the dog wagging its tail!" And these are the things that can bring happiness to us all, slow though we may often be to recognize it. We need, perhaps, to give ourselves enough time to celebrate our fortune.

"We have had many wonderful times with guests, sitting on the terrace under summer skies and stars, or around a fire in winter, sharing some good wine. These are the things that people appreciate and savor when they are on holiday with us."

Among the many fine things here—the beautiful fabrics designed by Cesare, the family antiques, the luxuries that give deep comfort to your stay such as lovely bathrooms and beds—the practical things that make the farm work are respected, almost revered. "The olive mill, for example, is very important. Every year for many years people have gathered around it, tended it, and appreciated the conviviality of working with it at harvest time."

The house reflects the warmth and elegance of its owners. There are cabinets with pretty china, hand-printed bedspreads and curtains, African art,

> "I have a deep love of small pleasures; these bring me the greatest happiness. It is something sweet taken from the oven and filling the room with a beautiful smell, a good coffee poured for friends, flowers from the garden"

antique rugs on terracotta floors. Bedrooms are pretty and undeniably Italian in style; one has its own private entrance from the patio.

Cesare and Fiorenza share a deep love of art and music. Cesare studied art and archaeology and has his own workshops in Prato producing fabric for clothing. Together they have chosen sculptures, pictures, and bronzes for the house and garden; the previous owner was a sculptor and his work is displayed in the grounds.

This patch of northern Tuscany has saved its charm from the ravages of modern times. There are beautiful, medieval working cities with markets and fine food shops. These tightly built communities were at the center of the Renaissance. Many throb with musical life and festivals. The vitality of Italian cities feels like something we should be attempting to reproduce all over the world.

The charms of Pieve a Celle are considerable. The pool—immaculate and with panoramic views from many meters above sea level—is delightful, and handsome with its decking. Lawns, hedges, olive groves and vineyards stretch out in all directions. "We find that people who appreciate our way of life are attracted to stay here," says

Fiorenza. "They, like us, enjoy the sense of being in a working community with people who have greater aspirations than simply earning money in the city. It's an organic way of life."

Fiorenza spends much of her time, happily so, in the family kitchen. She makes bread in a wood-fired oven, does imaginative things with vegetables from the kitchen garden, and with mushrooms foraged from their ten-acre woodland. She makes jams and fruit puddings when the 17 acres have been particularly productive. Dinners are important celebrations, all of them, and have a light-heartedness that is so Italian. They serve their own wine made from Sangiovese grapes. "We don't make lots of wine but enough to share with friends, family and guests. Our oil is sold to local restaurants.

"When we found this house we wanted to make a Slow life here and have embraced the whole philosophy of the movement." One happy guest wrote: "I have never experienced a property more beautiful, a family more genuinely friendly or food more beautifully prepared."

This is praise indeed—and it is richly deserved.

Cesare & Fiorenza Saccenti

Tenuta di Pieve a Celle,
via di Pieve a Celle 158, 51030 Pistoia
- 5 twins/doubles, €120–€140.
- Dinner €30, by arrangement. Wine €8.50–€10.
- +39 0573 913087
- www.tenutadipieveacelle.it
- Train station: Pistoia

Le Due Volpi

TUSCANY

From your eyrie in the Mugello, in this northern corner of Tuscany, it's a short tumble down the hills to the art-soaked cities of Florence, Siena and Arezzo. But once you are here your focus may shift; there is more to Tuscany than art.

"People retreat into the peace and the shade of our garden, away from the crowds," says Heidi Flores. "We are far from a main road and, most importantly, Lorenzo and I don't rush about or live by the clock. We work with ease and I am sure this sense of ease transfers itself to guests."

Instead of sightseeing you may want to walk in the hills, on routes marked out by the Italian Alpine Club, take a short trip to Lake Bilancino, do yoga or have a massage. There is a tangible sense of contentment and playfulness around Heidi and Lorenzo. In a rather typical Slow story they ditched demanding careers and city life for something more satisfying. "I became ill in 2005 and looked hard at my lifestyle," says Heidi. "I was an education administrator, at the beck and call of too many people. Friends pointed out that making a change might be a good idea and we landed here in 2006.

"I have never looked back. This house was a cure. I have become a different person!" Their enthusiasm for guests is very real and they are genuinely happy for you to linger all day. "There is space enough for everyone to be undisturbed. Time has less significance here," says Heidi, "and seeing guests unwind is rewarding for us."

Lorenzo owns a cantina in Fiesole in the hills above Florence, a shop where you can buy the wines and delicacies of Tuscany. He shares his knowledge with all those wanting to learn more about Italian wine and can arrange tastings, too. As a young man his passion was cycling; he was an all-Italy champion and his Lycra shirt is framed and

hung just near the breakfast room. His hobby is renovating antique radios and gramophones; from his little workshop in the garden may drift the sound of a Neapolitan folk song. The names given to the bedrooms are his favorite models of radios.

Heidi is a polyglot and true cosmopolitan with a particular passion for England. Her large kitchen has been built around a handsome four-oven Aga. It arrived from England in pieces and took the ever-patient Lorenzo two days to assemble.

The bedrooms are pretty, thanks to the English country-house feel. Windows give onto the oak and chestnut woods above and the valley below. Further seduction may come from a massage in a therapy space below the house with windows that give onto panoramic views. The sunny slopes are perfect for the solar panels installed as part of their growing campaign to become more eco-friendly.

Snowy, the Westie, and Heidi will take you to collect eggs from neighbor Silvano. He stores them in his cellar, richly filled with flagons of wine and legs of ham and salami.

Lorenzo will tell you tales of the *sagres* held in local fields. *Sagres* revolve around a seasonal product, maybe the new wine, the first chestnuts or truffles. The closest English equivalent to these Tuscan fairs is the village fête, though a *sagre* is far more rambunctious; eating, dancing, drinking and energetic partying are encouraged.

Come in early October and help Silvano during the *vendemmia* (grape harvest) or for Canta Maggio, when folk singers and musicians roam from village to village: they sing to the locals and the villagers offer cheese, salami and a glass of wine. Heidi and Lorenzo have asked them to make Le Due Volpi one of their stop-off points, so May is a good time to visit if you'd like to join in.

Twice a week Heidi and Lorenzo cook for

guests. At a communal table under the pergola you can try her *panzanella* and salads, Lorenzo's Florentine steaks and Silvano's wine—bottled by Lorenzo.

Lorenzo describes these evenings as "a night with the Etruscans"; he is keen to point out that modern Tuscans are upholding the party spirit of their famously feasting, drinking, Etruscan ancestors. Their jollity was celebrated by D.H. Lawrence in *Etruscan Places*—he derided the empire-building Romans, who "crushed the free soul in people after people".

Heidi runs cookery courses, too; she'll collect you from the train, take you to markets, share her recipes and then create a party atmosphere in which to celebrate the bounty of Tuscany. Is it possible to resist?

Heidi Flores & Lorenzo Balloni

Le Due Volpi,
via di Molezzano 88, 50039 Vicchio del Mugello
- 3 doubles (one with kitchenette), €75–€95.
  Extra bed €20–€30. Half-board option.
- Dinner €25, with local wine. Picnic, with wine, €15.
- +39 055 840 7874
- www.leduevolpi.it
- Train station: Vicchio

Villa Campestri

TUSCANY

Once upon a time in Tuscany, olive oil was worth more by weight than the choicest cuts of beef or veal. Then, virtually all oil was of the finest quality. Now that it is a staple foodstuff, prices have tumbled, but so has quality.

At Villa Campestri the olive is revered, even by Italian standards. There is an "Oleoteca" in the old cellars, cooled by spring water, where you can attend a course on all aspects of the oil: historical, cultural, scientific and gastronomic. Inaugurated in 2002, it was Italy's first to be devoted to olive oil in such a wide-ranging way.

The Pasqualis—father Paolo and daughters Viola and Gemma—run the estate together. Paolo takes charge of the tastings.

"An important part of our oil tasting is to educate people about the right methods of production," says Gemma. "Olives must be crushed within 24 hours of harvest to ensure they are not oxidized. If oxygen enters during the processing, the oil, when ingested, will produce free radicals in the body that result in tissue damage.

"It is frightening that a lot of oil sold in Italy is not even from Italy—olives are simply shipped here to be processed. Many of them are old and have been harvested carelessly."

Gemma can speak with authority: she studied agricultural engineering and gained a PhD in bio-technology at the University of Florence; molecular biology is her speciality. One part of her role at Campestri is to source the best type of trees for the micro-climate. "We are 450 meters above sea level and winters are slightly colder than most tree types like, so we choose carefully."

Their oil is widely used in their restaurant— there is even an "olive oil menu" that includes chocolate soufflé.

Although Campestri is large, with its 25 rooms, it succeeds in behaving like a private villa. There is little about it, in fact, that is like a hotel. It has a warm, homey mood, with charm and delightful staff to provide it.

Viola looks after guests. She is a genuinely nice woman, soft-spoken and very much there for you. The family bought the villa in 1989 and restored it using local architects and appropriate, original materials. It opened as a hotel in 1991.

Most rooms are in the villa itself, others are across the courtyard in the old farmhouse and dairy where they used to make cheese and butter.

The oldest part of the villa was built in the 13th century and was once the property of the Roti Michelozzi family, who lived there for 700 years. It is said that they commissioned one of Giotto's pupils, Lorenzo Bicci, to fresco the tabernacle at the entrance to the villa. At the same period a chapel was built, and is still consecrated. The frescoes from the 1600s are still there, discovered under the plaster and now revealed. They are superb, and only slightly faded in parts. Inside the house there is a well, too, still there after 600 years. It meant, of course, that the family never had to go outside the villa in the cold to get their water.

Although much has changed inside, there still remain wonderful wooden ceilings, terracotta floors, coats of arms, and some wonderful art-deco windowpanes created in the early 20th century by Galileo Chini. They are still much admired today.

The bedrooms, in Renaissance style, are wonderful—and ineffably comfortable. On each floor there is a big sitting room for your use, with antique furniture, rugs, old fireplaces and massive beams. Each one is charming and invites frequent use. Some of the higher rooms are vaulted with old red brick; bathrooms are beyond criticism.

Breakfast is served in a magnificent room with huge Murano glass chandeliers. You won't, now, be

surprised to be offered eggs and bacon with your homemade cakes, fruit and yogurt. The food is memorable, generous and superb value.

There are 140 hectares of land in which you can wander, land rich with fauna and flora, ancient olive trees, wild cherries and maples. The cypress-lined avenue and fine green lawns set the grand Tuscan tone, as does the big swimming pool with its views over the Mugello Valley and the Chianti Rufina hills.

Gemma is pleased she returned to the Villa with her own family. "In my twenties I wanted to discover the world. In my thirties I realized the best place is home. Here I can combine work with motherhood with ease. We each have our roles and responsibilities and work very well as a team."

Viola Pasquali

Villa Campestri,
via di Campestri 19/22, 50039 Vicchio di Mugello
- 10 doubles, 3 triples, 1 single, 2 suites, 5 junior suites, 4 apartments. €120–€310.
- Dinner €52.
- +39 0558 490107
- www.villacampestri.com
- Train station: Vicchio

Casa Palmira

TUSCANY

It is easy to think of Tuscany as a golden land where everything just appears on a plate: dreaming villas on hillsides washed by the sun, with hardly an effort in sight. *Under the Tuscan Sun*, the American tale of a rich woman settling into Tuscany with the help of an amusing gang of Polish builders, merely made us think that there are always others to do the work. Most of us don't think DIY when we think Fiesole. But Stefano and Assunta are a reminder that this is a land of grit and sweat too. They couldn't afford to hire help to restore the house, so they did it themselves—over ten years. Hence the passion in every brick, their obvious delight in showing it to visitors. They still do everything themselves. Stefano seems capable of making anything the house needs, and more. He uses local wood for furniture, and they have even made their own rugs. Ask—and he will show you how it was done. They grow their vegetables for meals, take guests for walks or bike rides, run cookery classes and churn out huge quantities of pasta and pizza with the help of their students and their wood-fired oven.

It is inevitable that a book on "Slow" will discuss local food production at length, but these folk are genuinely excited by the production virtues of their region. The cookery classes are offered once a week, so you can take something home with you. They are especially proud of the local flour, made in a mill that still uses the old millstone.

The farm is medieval, and beautiful. When the couple arrived in Tuscany in 1985 they met Signora Palmira, the farmer who had spent her life in this house. She led a tranquil and self-sufficient existence. Inspired by the serenity, Assunta and Stefano bought the farm's barn and began to renovate it. They lived next to Signora Palmira for

15 years until she died. Much has changed since then "but," says Assunta, "we hope that people feel her spirit is an enduring presence."

Fiesole is up on the hill above Florence; numerous celebrities and literary people have lived,

> "They do everything themselves. Stefano seems capable of making anything the house needs, and more"

and live, up here. It is only half an hour from Florence's bustle, with superb views on the drive up. Not to explore the countryside on a bike, or on foot, would be a shame. Stefano will ferry you about in his van, taking you to the start of your walk or ride, and Assunta will prepare a picnic basket for you. Irresistible, and in just one and a half hours you can be in Fiesole after walking through the woods. There is no need for a car here.

The rooms are charming: a log-fired sitting room setting the tone, and bedrooms opening off a landing with a brick-walled little garden in the center, created by Stefano. Two rooms have four-poster beds dressed in Florentine fabrics; all have polished wooden floors.

Casa Palmira is imbued with a sense of substantiality and sustainability. It comes from the considerable skill and love poured into it by its gifted and visionary guardians.

Assunta & Stefano Fiorini-Mattioli

Casa Palmira,
via Faentina 4/1,loc. Feriolo, Polcanto,
50030 Borgo San Lorenzo

- 7 rooms, €85–€110. Apartment for 3–4, €95–€120.
- Dinner with wine, €30. Restaurant 700m.
- +39 0558 409749
- www.casapalmira.it
- Train station: Caldine, 6km

Fattoria Barbialla Nuova

TUSCANY

If you spend your working life and your spare time in contact with nature you are almost bound to have a streak of authenticity running through all you do. There are many modern thinkers who believe that the answer to many of our greatest man-made problems is to reconnect with nature distinctly not man-made. Only thus will we relearn how to live, how to adopt healthy rhythms, how to coexist with the complex and interdependent world around us, how to see beauty.

*The poetry of earth is
never dead;
When all the birds are faint
with the hot sun,
And hide in cooling trees,
a voice will run
From hedge to hedge about
the new-mown mead.*

Keats

Guido Manfredi Rasponi, who manages the rugged 500-hectare organic Fattoria Barbialla Nuova with Gianluca, explains: "A Slow way of life can't be forced—if people are not utterly committed it shows. We are Slow through and through: we wait for just the right moment to collect

truffles, we raise our cattle in a leisurely way, giving them all the time they need to grow naturally. We run our *agriturismo* in a way that we feel helps our guests to leave behind the stresses of life in the modern rat race."

He speaks with burning passion and commitment and goes so far as to decry some of the hundreds of *agriturismi* that have sprung up all over Italy. "Many of these farms only have one small line of produce and concentrate almost entirely on accommodation. We have olive oil, grains, hay, honey, white truffles, chickens and cattle."

The farm, in a nature reserve, is carved out from a larger estate that was left to Guido; the land has been organic since the early 90s and is perfect for grazing their prized, almost biblical, white Chianina cattle. Raising this breed has been a labor of love for there is double certification involved—one for rare-breed status and another for organic.

They have a little shop on the estate, managed by Sabali, that sells the fruits of their labors—bottles of golden oils, precious preserved white truffles, beef—so that guests can take a flavor of the place home with them. Guido and Gianluca have worked hard to provide somewhere beautiful to stay, even if they themselves still have to keep working hard while you loaf about!

They didn't want to create an agricultural fantasy but wanted to keep their rooms genuinely rustic; they shunned anything showy or ostentatious. "English people particularly appreciate the simplicity of our rooms; they like the spaces and the colors and prefer that they are not out of keeping with the work of the farm or with nature," says Guido.

There are three self-catering farmhouses dotted around the estate, all with sweeping views, all on the top of a hill; "Le Trosce," with four fireplaces, has several levels but is all open-plan. The three "Doderi" apartments, embraced by an olive grove, are minimalist; Gianluca's joyous bedcovers and 60s-style furniture in Tuscan colors add style,

"A Slow way of life can't be forced—if people are not utterly committed it shows"

originality and color. The apartments in "Brentina," a *casa colonica* (traditional farmhouse), deeper in the woods, are a touch more primitive, though many will love the simplicity of the whitewashed walls and the handmade staircase; all have delightful bathrooms. Outside are pergolas, patios and pools, cheerful with deck chairs and decking; there are also orchard and hens.

It is a place for the independent, but the pair are always around to help if you need anything. There will be space soon for cooking courses but meanwhile you can invite the resident chef, Lucia, to your apartment for a personal lesson, or just sit back with an aperitif while he works his special magic with an abundance of local produce.

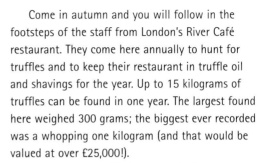

Come in autumn and you will follow in the footsteps of the staff from London's River Café restaurant. They come here annually to hunt for truffles and to keep their restaurant in truffle oil and shavings for the year. Up to 15 kilograms of truffles can be found in one year. The largest found here weighed 300 grams; the biggest ever recorded was a whopping one kilogram (and that would be valued at over £25,000!).

"Imperio is our truffle hunter and he has 40 years of experience," says Guido. "He manages the land year-round and controls the growth of the grey poplars which are rooted in volcanic tufa rock. These poplars are the only trees under which the truffles grow and Imperio knows the best spots to dig. His dog, Toby, seeks them out and many Italians now use dogs rather than the traditional pigs for they are trainable."

So a stay in October or November will bring you closer to the rhythms of nature in this part of Tuscany; the woods yield porcini mushrooms, too, and all around there are autumn berries. Stay in spring and you can join in wildlife walks or take off on your own with special route maps.

The Fattoria is a richly interesting place to stay, run with such verve by young owners who cleverly manage to maintain the best of traditional farming values while wholly embracing the most modern ideas about the future of agriculture. They do it all with panache.

Àrghilo Società Agricola

Fattoria Barbialla Nuova,
via Castastrada 49, 50050 Montaione
- 7 apartments: 2 for 2, 3 for 4, 2 for 6. €420–€1,320. Farmhouse for 8, €1,250–€2,000. Prices per week.
- Self-catering. Restaurant 3km.
- +39 0571 677004/0571 677259
- www.barbiallanuova.it
- Train station: Fucecchio S. Miniato

Sovigliano

TUSCANY

"Our daily life is serene, guided by the rhythms of nature, and not a single day is like another. Each is full of the symbolism of nature and its extraordinary richness, its colors and smells. We lead a life that weaves the past with the present, tradition with innovation." That is Signor Bicego speaking. How many of us wish we could say the same of our own lives?

The story of Sovigliano started 27 years ago when a young family from the Vento, Claudio, Patrizia and their three children, began the search for a different existence. The ancient farmhouse was alluring enough; the pure air, the hills, the views, the light finished the process of seduction. "We had moved from the city and of course we wondered if it would suit us. Now we believe that anybody who finds what we have here would give in to the charms of the countryside."

They came with a huge respect for the history and tradition of the place—its distinctiveness—but wanted, too, as any young family would, to create their own story. They have done so with respect for the architecture, the locals and the landscape.

Claudia, their daughter, has remained at Sovigliano to help her parents; her two brothers work in Paris and Florence. "She is the future of Sovigliano," says Claudio proudly.

It is a very special place, halfway between Florence and Siena: a pretty loggia opens onto distant views of San Gimignano, barbecues are held by candlelight, B&B and self-catering guests seem equally happy; the latter have a delightfully rustic kitchen to share. One guest wrote to tell us that they had gone to a "village night" in Tavarnelle, nearby—a convivial occasion where you gather with locals, choose

your own steak and wine from the village shop and watch while your meat is cooked on a communal fire.

Sovigliano is a productive estate. Correggiolo, Frantoio and Leccino are the olive species that the family have cultivated to produce their exceptionally good extra virgin oil. These trees thrive in exposed southern hill sites—the parts of the land here which straddle the Pesa and d'Elso valleys and where the soil is clay-based. They collect the olives by hand and use traditional pressing methods to extract the oil. When first bottled, the oil is a light, vibrant green and then it matures to a deep buttery yellow. It is fragrant and fruity and aficionados like to taste it as they would a wine—straight

> "We lead a life that weaves the past with the present, tradition with innovation"

from a little glass—or sometimes by dipping in a piece of bread.

They produce their own wine, too, and the Sangiovese red grape thrives on the soil. The harvest is done by hand, and the grape juice is transferred to steel vats before being poured into wooden oak barrels to mature. "We do a lot of it ourselves," says Claudio, "but for the bottling we call in a specialist. The conditions have to be perfect." The wine varies from ruby to crimson to garnet according to the climate and growing conditions. It's a robust companion for roast meat and game, cheese and grilled meat.

"We make grappa too, of course—what else do you expect from a family from the Veneto?" smiles Claudio. "It's made here from our grapes and we add walnuts—picked, according to tradition, on San Giovanni's day when they are still unripe—which are macerated in the grappa for a few months. It is

sweet and fragrant, delicate with a soft touch on the palate."

They work with what the land is happy to give them—sometimes a lot, sometimes less, but always quality is prized over quantity. Some of what they produce is sold here at the farm and guests are encouraged to learn about their family recipes and their Venetian and Tuscan cooking. They can then try their hand at bringing together a meal of entirely local produce in the wonderful large kitchen that is set aside for those who self-cater.

There is much to engage any traveller and Patrizia enthusiastically gathers information for guests on local music festivals and exhibitions.

"Next year will be the 20th anniversary of our belonging here and we hope to celebrate with as many guests as possible. We have grown older but our spirits remain young and our values and philosophy are unchanged."

Signora Patrizia Bicego

Sovigliano,
Strada Magliano 9, 50028 Tavarnelle Val di Pesa
- 2 doubles, 2 twins. €130–€160.
  4 apartments for 2–4, €150–€390.
- Dinner with wine, €35.
- +39 0558 076217
- www.sovigliano.com
- Train station: Florence

Azienda Agricola Il Borghetto

TUSCANY

Can the English make good wine? Well, the wine-
making here is in the hands of an Englishman, Tim
Manning—an idea which would have been
preposterous to Ilaria Cavallini's grandparents. But
Tim and Ilaria's brother, Antonio, are making a
huge success of it, concentrating on the finest
quality grapes from the small parcels of land, each
with a different soil type and different grape
varieties. "We practice small-batch fermentation
here," says Tim. "Because we grow different
varieties of grapes the harvest is a more long-
winded and relaxed affair than elsewhere."

Tim is very serious about the organic aspect of
their wine-making, and properly hostile to mono-
culture. He has the full support of the family, with
whom he works closely. The wine is Chianti
Classico and Merlot. "We aim for quality, not huge
quantities," says Ilaria.

Il Borghetto is almost hidden; you could drive
past and miss it, behind its tall hedges, private
gates and lofty cypress trees. Slip inside and you
feel you have stumbled upon a lost world. The
main building is 15th century with pantile roofs
sloping towards a central tower. The Cavallini
family rescued it, along with the vineyards and
olive groves, in 1982, with plans to live there and
keep heads above water with the help of rooms for
visitors. Much of the work, and most of the

decorative ideas, came from Rosi, Ilaria's mother.
Now, Ilaria and her husband Michele live on the
estate and have taken up the reins. Father,
Roberto, lives in Milan but comes back when he
can, to his own house in the grounds.

They hold cookery classes in the superbly
equipped modern kitchen, with its big mirrors for
demonstrations. It is a beautiful old room, however,
and still has a farmhouse feel to it: terracotta floors,
marble sinks, high ceilings. Wine tasting courses are
offered, too, and dinner, as you would expect, is a

treat that combines the best local foods and wines. Francesca Cianchi, the founding chef of New York's Mezzaluna restaurant, has held week-long courses here. Cookery lessons can be combined with art tours of Florence and Siena.

The whole place has been beautifully restored. The rooms have a timeless elegance, unshowy but rich and welcoming. The dining room opens airily onto a veranda, a fine place for breakfasts of brioche, local cheeses and homemade jams.

Bedrooms have tiled floors, stencil friezes, and beamed ceilings, and are understatedly luxurious with soft colors, antiques, fresh flowers and many individual touches—such as pretty wallpaper, or a

> "We practice small-batch fermentation and because we grow different varieties of grapes the harvest is a more relaxed affair than elsewhere"

sleigh bed, a writing desk or hand-painted wardrobe. They are all generous and comfortable, with good beds and their own bathrooms. There are French beds, antique family furniture, cotton fabrics in soft mellow colors. The top bedroom has magnificent views and there is a suite, too, with two bedrooms and two bathrooms; things have not been half-done. Bathrooms are simple, fresh and luxurious, with beams and uncluttered space.

There is a tidy garden with solar panels dotted about and little paths here and there. The kidney-shaped pool is hidden away. Beyond is a terraced water-garden and pond—and eye-stretching views. There is an herb garden, an orchard, and paths mown through the vineyards and olive groves.

Florence and Siena are close and staff will help you plan a trip, or borrow a bike and explore the surrounding countryside. But in the chapel of

the Villa Caserotta near Calcinaia is a stunning 16th-century fresco by Ghirlandaio: wonderful art without the crowds. There is another gem right here: a 12th-century BC Etruscan tomb in the garden. It is one of the most ancient monuments in the Etruscan region and is said to be the final resting place of a famed archer. To get a bird's-eye view of Chianti you can book a balloon trip in Tavarnelle.

Ilaria is very much in charge, and gets things done in spite of having two young daughters; Michele, her husband, is a guitarist and producer. They, along with Antonio and father Roberto, are a delightful family and their very typical Italian togetherness is a solid underpinning for their admirable Slow ambitions.

Antonio & Ilaria Cavallini

Azienda Agricola Il Borghetto,
via Collina 23, 50026 Montefiridolfi, San Casciano V.P
- 3 doubles, 5 suites. €130–€260.
- Dinner, 3 courses, €50. Wine €12–€80.
  Light lunch €15–€35.
- +39 0558 244442
- www.borghetto.org
- Train station: Florence

Fattoria Viticcio Agriturismo

TUSCANY

Nicoletta insisted on telling us the story behind the ubiquitous tiramisù dessert... it apparently has a noble history, having been created in Siena especially for Cosimo de Medici III at the end of the 17th century, to reflect all his qualities, such as "importance" and "strength!" It was christened the "*zuppa del Duca*" and travelled to Venice where it was rapturously received by the courtesans, who ascribed aphrodisiacal properties to the humble dish and insisted on consuming it before their amorous encounters. Thus it gradually became known as "*tiramisù*"... "pick me up."

As the name suggests, the Fattoria is a hard-working winery, not just a place dedicated to the gentle pampering of international guests. But that is why it is so rewarding to be there, for one feels part of the working throb of Tuscany rather than an uncomfortable interloper bent on idleness and introspection.

"He who is born under the vine has better luck than he who was born under the cabbage" goes the local saying. Put like that it is hard to disagree. Alessandro and Nicoletta do, genuinely, feel thrice blessed: by their vines, their countryside and their ability to welcome visitors. "Creating wines teaches you to be patient, to watch the wines mature in the barrels or bottles, to oversee every detail, to be aware of the effect they have on those who taste them." Visit the vaults and taste for yourselves. The wines have an international reputation—and deserve it. two hudred thousand bottles are produced annually.

The 35 hectares are planted with Sangiovese Grosso, Cabernet Sauvignon and Merlot grapes. There are more than 300 barrels of French and American white oak for the aging of their super-Tuscans: the Prunaio, from the Grosso vines and Monile from Cabernet Sauvignon and Merlot.

Their vin santo is classically light and sweet. But the winery is known best, of course, for its Chianti Classico.

Agritourism can, like so many other phenomena, be little more than a label cynically attached to receiving people in the countryside. For these two delightful people it is much more, a way of bringing the countryside and its work into harmony with the outside world, of showing what agriculture means. They are proud that their wines reach across the globe to distant places, where people can learn, through tasting, about the reality of the production in Tuscany. They are, indeed, romantic about their wine-growing. Nicoletta, by the way, is a sommelier—and the oldest daughter, Beatrice, worked on a wine estate near Bordeaux and is studying viticulture.

Tiramisù
Serves 6–8

4 shots espresso
one box Pavesini cookies
4 eggs
2 tablespoons sugar
500 g (1 lb) mascarpone
1 cup chocolate flakes
cocoa to dust

• Make the coffee and let it cool.
• Lay the cookies in a serving dish and pour over the coffee.
• Mix the egg yolks and sugar.
• Add in the mascarpone and then add in the beaten egg whites.
• Spread half the cream mixture over the cookies.
• Sprinkle dark chocolate flakes over the cream, then add the rest of the cream.
• Dust with cocoa powder.

Warning: This recipe contains raw eggs, the consumption of which the FDA warns poses a health risk.

Alessandro's father, Lucio, bought the farm in the 1960s, when others were leaving the land. The economy was in tatters, so it was a bold decision. The farm has prospered and the apartments are the icing on the cake. Delightful they are, too: plain walls, beams, terracotta floor tiles, brick arches and a mixture of family furniture or pieces they have collected on their travels. They are big, light and airy, with superb kitchens with all you could possibly need—plus a superb hand-painted barrel top mounted on the wall. The daughters who play such a big role in the farm have given their names to the apartments: Beatrice, Arianna and Camilla. The simplicity of the rooms is just right for this farm. Some of the walls have wine-themed frescoes painted by young artists who gave their work in exchange for lodging.

You can reach this estate in just an hour by bus from Florence, and it is within walking distance of Greve in Chianti—the home of the CittaSlow movement. Greve's piazza is a gem with a loggia all round the square filled with artisan shops. People are given priority over cars, lighting the pavements priority over illuminating the sky, and local producers have seen off the big boys.

It is fitting that the Fattoria is part of the Slow scene of Greve. "'*Viticcio*' means 'tendril' in English," they explain. "It is symbolic of our slow and steady growth. Like the tendril we are carefully reaching new heights."

Alessandro Landini & Nicoletta Florio Deleuze

Fattoria Viticcio Agriturismo,
via San Cresci 12/a, 50022 Greve in Chianti
- 2 doubles, 1 twin. €100.
  5 apartments: 3 for 2–4, 2 for 4–6. €683–€970.
- Breakfast €5. Restaurants 15-minute walk.
- +39 055 854210
- www.fattoriaviticcio.com
- Train station: Florence

Locanda Casanuova

TUSCANY

Tuscany has always had a way of inspiring dreams; the Locanda Casanuova is a dream-maker. It is a place of contemplation, too, and always has been, for it began life as a monastery. Casanuova's bedrooms are almost monastically simple, but have splashes of color and style to introduce a perfect measure of modernity. Another incarnation was as a farmhouse and the estate chapel is still there, for exhibitions and meditation.

The 23 hectares of vineyards and olives produce 7,000 liters of wine and a lot of olive oil; there is an organic vegetable garden too.

Holland and Germany come together in Ursula and Thierry, she behind the smooth efficiency of the place, and in the kitchen with four helpers, and he, tanned and easy-going, in his supervision of the estate and the wine-making. They are fine hosts, smiling, humorous and generous—easy with themselves and their guests. He was a P.E. teacher; Ursula worked as a social worker in a female prison but was brought up on a farm. "That the land should be run on organic principles was the most important thing for us," says Ursula, "and we were lucky that no chemicals had been used for a good number of years before we came. The land has now been managed organically for 50 years."

The atmosphere is wonderful for people who want to do their own thing unencumbered by hotel expectations. They are right to call it a "*locanda*" and not a hotel, for it has none of the mannerisms to be found in most hotels. It is an intensely personal place. It was 20 years ago that they came here and resolved to rescue it. They have done so much more: Ursula practices yoga in the early mornings—you are welcome to join her—and is a superb cook, the author of her own cookery book; meals are wonderfully convivial affairs in the refectory, off which is a library where you can pore over trekking maps at a big round table. Spontaneity is another feature; musicians, for example, might strike up at any moment on the terrace.

Ursula and Thierry rejoice in seeing their guests unfurl, the tension leaving them within days of arrival: "Those from towns and cities, particularly, arrive stressed. Often they will have planned an itinerary of sightseeing but relax into a different rhythm. In autumn, particularly, people love to get involved in the harvest. Spending time on the land and sharing a big spaghetti on the terrace at lunchtime can be really rewarding."

Just 500 yards from the house is a self-cleaning pond, set up as a swimming pool but rich in lily-pads and other vegetation. The light comes, dappled, through the branches of the lofty trees. The lovely garden has terraced steps, tables and delightful corners and nooks. Ursula is the goddess in the garden, as in the kitchen.

The area is densely forested with conifers; this eastern part of Tuscany is at a point where the cypress trees are giving way to another landscape. The views are far-reaching. You are close to Florence too, so you could, if you insist, burn yourselves up culturally with the greatest of ease.

There are two apartments, separate from the main house and down a bumpy track beside an ancient mulberry tree. They are rustically charming: attractive crocks, a collection of coffee pots and milk pans, candles and woodburner.

The mood of serene simplicity is at its most evident in the yoga room, a beautiful space with richly red silky curtains—a space that could lure even those most resistant to yoga.

The Casanuova is a natural candidate for Slow status, with its devotion to organics, its own vegetables, wine and olives, its lack of pretension and a commitment to doing things authentically. It also has that essential ingredient: great character.

Ursula & Thierry Besançon

Locanda Casanuova,
San Martino Altoreggi 52, 50063 Figline Valdarno
- 12 doubles, 2 suites, 4 singles. €90. Half-board €70 p.p.
  2 apartments, €75–€100.
- Dinner €25–€30. Wine €8–€35.
- +39 0559 500027
- www.casanuova.info
- Train station: Figline Valdarno

Odina Agriturismo

TUSCANY

You are 650 meters above sea level here and will feel on top of the world. The Arno Valley stretches away in the distance, as do the Chianti hills, and air is as pure as can be. The house is a solid, stylish, pale-blue-shuttered place, run by Gloria, who manages it all magnificently from her little office in the converted chapel.

If you arrive in a state of over-excitement, Valentina, the local herbalist who tends the magnificent herb garden, will perhaps recommend basil, which apparently helps with general restlessness—and sleeplessness, too. Having begun as a symbol of hatred in ancient Rome it became a symbol of love in Italy, with young maidens wearing a sprig in their hair to show that they were available for courtship.

Paolo, the proud owner, is a professional gardener and oversees the running of his herb farm "*con passione*." When he found Odina it was an abandoned medieval hamlet that he bought in its entirety. The self-catering apartments are all delightfully rustic and contemporary—the two styles cleverly combined. The overall effect is of softly muted colors, wood and sunlight. Each is different: some have kitchen surfaces of granite, others of local Pietra Serena. Bathroom walls are softly "ragged" in varying shades. Each apartment has French windows to a patio with wooden garden furniture. In the deconsecrated chapel there is an old bread-making chest and a little shop selling Odina olive oil, beans, lavender and honey.

At the heart of Odina lies the organic herb garden, entered at each end through two rose-covered arches. Labels tell you about the medicinal and culinary uses of each plant and every week Valentina, a biologist, guides guests through the

garden to explain it all. Afterwards everyone prepares lunch together with freshly picked herbs and vegetables.

A dish from their little cookery leaflet is pasta with sardines and wild fennel, that delicious bulb that acts as an aid to digestion and is a breath sweetener. It was in the root of a fennel that Prometheus hid the spark of fire he had stolen from Mt. Olympus. He was chained up for his crime and a vulture ate his liver. Those who know of the myth still consider it gauche to serve fennel with liver.

"Our British guests are intrigued by our herb garden," says Paolo. "Their interest is mostly in the

Spaghetti alla Crudaiola
Serves 1

5 cherry tomatoes
1 sprig each of fresh basil and parsley, chopped
1 teaspoon pine nuts, chopped roughly
1 tablespoon parmesan cheese
1 tablespoon extra virgin olive oil
half clove garlic, chopped
4–5 almonds, chopped
70 g (3 oz) spaghetti
chili and salt to taste

• Chop the tomatoes, add basil and parsley then the pine nuts, cheese, oil, garlic and almonds.
• Stir this mixture into just cooked spaghetti and stir.
• Add chili and salt to taste.

Parsley: rich in vitamin C, a tonic and a diuretic
Basil: a relaxant and sedative
Chili: a disinfectant, a digestive aid

culinary uses of the plants but the information that we lay out inspires them to consider their other uses, too."

Odina is one of those places which sap your will to move—there is so much to gaze upon, so much idling to be done. In the cool of the early morning you may want to walk out into the hills and the surrounding woods, where Paolo has laid out paths for walkers. There are also longer trails for the hearty, and then there is the local organic food market in Montevarchi on a Saturday. Massage and reflexology can be arranged.

Paolo, Gloria and Valentina are passionate about their wider environment and they are planning to install energy systems using biomass, the sun and the wind. Naturally, the apartments have been restored using natural materials. He has done a magnificent restoration job. Says Gloria: "Paolo was very careful to use only old materials and local stone and wood in the conversion—it is the ultimate recycling project!"

Signor Paolo Trenti

Odina Agriturismo,
loc. Odina, 52024 Loro Ciuffenna
• 4 apartments for 2–7, €550–€1,750.
  Farmhouse for 8–10, €2,050–€3,900. Prices per week.
• Restaurants 5km.
• +39 0559 69304
• www.odina.it
• Train station: Montevarchi

Agriturismo Rendola Riding

TUSCANY

Whether Jenny loves her horses, the Tuscan countryside or her guests most is hard to guess. She is a fascinating woman who embraced all things Italian when she moved here from England in the late 1960s. A dynamo, with a joie de vivre that seems to flourish in Italy, she sweeps everyone up into her enthusiasms.

Rendola is on the slopes of the Chianti hills, with 12 acres for 12 guests, 18 horses, paddocks and olive groves. Jenny pioneered equestrian tourism in Italy and thousands have come to ride with her—some having informal lessons in the ring surrounded by olive trees, some pottering gently along woodland tracks, some embarking on four- or five-day treks in the Chianti hills. For walkers there are many marked trails.

"People come back time and time again; we seem to have created something that appeals to a certain type of person. Rendola is not for those looking for elegance. Hens and ducks, never known for their respect for anyone's dignity, peck around the houses; our family dog lies on the doorstep and jackets hang on the backs of chairs. It is first and foremost a riding center and family home."

That is Jenny speaking—typically wanting to make sure that you understand the set-up and feel at ease. There is an absence of pomposity; you can just do your thing—whether in the garden, under a tree, or out on horseback.

"Guests quickly become friends," says Jenny, "and all who come—alone or with others—feel cherished. At meal times we sit together at a long table and there is plenty of merriment as well as good food." This is nourishing to hear—for Slow living needs a strong dose of conviviality. Imagine the scene at lunchtime: the outside world dozing in the sun, faint voices drifting up from the

vineyards, Tuscany working its magic upon another generation.

Jenny's team has been with her forever. There is Pietro—he with the red hat—who was a farmer between the 30s and 60s, before joining Jenny in 1970. He cooks simply, with home-reared turkeys and ducks and eggs, vegetables and oils and his son Sergio makes the puddings and can turn his hand to shoeing horses, building a wall, gardening and even installing a bathroom. Sergio's son, Marco, is a keen apprentice. Astonishing, in this age of fleeting phenomena, to have three generations working together.

"Pietro wrote his autobiography, *Pietro's Book*, which was published in English in 2003. It's his answer to *Under a Tuscan Sun*," says Jenny. The book reveals the hardships and the joys of working on the land; Pietro's local knowledge is unmatched and it is a fortunate guest who can

> "At the end of each full and purposeful day a cow bell is rung and guests, family and stable workers gather to dine together"

speak Italian and engage him in conversation. There is a ride that takes guests along a section of an old Roman road on the way to Mercatale. Pietro remembers when it was paved over; the paving was destroyed by the passage of the Allied tanks in 1944. After the war local farmers took the seemingly humdrum stones home to use, not realizing that among them were stones from the ancient Roman road.

The oak-beamed house is in the triangle formed by Florence, Arezzo and Siena, and is 1,000 feet above sea level. Jenny is keen, given how well-loved that area is already, to introduce people to "Toscana Minore"—the landscape, history and art of her immediate surroundings.

Places such as the rose garden of Gropina Cavriglia, the largest in Europe, and a Romanesque church with a 9th-century pulpit. "We like to take people to places which they would have difficulty in finding on their own, which do not attract hordes of people and which are all the more fascinating and enjoyable for that."

To complete the happy band is Nicholas, Jenny's son, who edits an ecology magazine, *Terra Nuova*. He helps Jenny with her computer and occasionally entertains guests with his piano playing in the evenings. His touch is as light as Jenny's and guests hugely enjoy his company.

At the end of each full and purposeful day a cow bell is rung and guests, family and stable workers gather to dine together. If they are lucky, Pietro will be in the mood to round off the evening with a tale or two.

Jenny Bawtree

Agriturismo Rendola Riding,
Rendola 66, Montevarchi, 52025 Arezzo
- 3 twins/doubles, 2 family rooms, €90. 1 single, €50. Half-board €65 p.p. Full-board €85 p.p.
- Lunch or dinner €15–€20, with wine.
- +39 055 9707045
- www.rendolariding.it
- Train station: Montevarchi

Relais San Pietro in Polvano

TUSCANY

Just a short hop from Florence, by train and then a quick taxi ride, here is a Tuscan paradise easily reached by the Slow traveller. Yet it is wonderfully secluded, high up and blessed with everything that makes rural Tuscany so idyllic. Its elegance is bathed in dreamy views and it is inspired by the immensely likeable Luigi Protti. He is a real gentleman, and takes enormous, and understandable, pride in his creation of somewhere that is so special.

Luigi had been in Milan for 50 years when he decided to seek a country life for his family. Ever since then, he and Antonetta have carefully whittled their home to its present perfect form. Bedrooms have gorgeous old rafters, generous wrought-iron beds, elegantly painted wardrobes, rugs on tiled floors, handsome shutters. For cool autumn nights there are cream sofas and a log fire. The pool—

although not the Slowest of accoutrements—is worth mentioning for it must have one of the best views in Tuscany: keep your head above water and you are rewarded with the blue-tinted panorama for which Tuscany is famous. In summer you dine at tables dressed in white on a terrace overlooking the gardens and views of the olive-grove'd valley beyond. There is a restaurant, too, serving local food and their own olive oil; bread comes fresh from the bread oven, as do *grissini* dotted with poppy seeds.

Behind the scenes the cogs turn on oiled wheels. "Even with helpful staff and the support of the family it is not easy to run a small hotel," says Luigi. "We always ask guests what they particularly enjoy about their stay and our greatest pleasure is to receive notes of thanks from them. Our intention has been to offer a place of stillness and silence. There are paths and lanes

for walking and cycling and we are surrounded by small historical towns and villages.

"The family character of San Pietro is especially appreciated, as is the cooking and the tranquility. My wife and I run our small hotel equally with our son Franco and daughter-in-law Franca and we are all in agreement that we should keep the scale of things small—then we can manage everything ourselves. The same applies to our land: we have 500 olive trees that produce enough olive oil for us, our friends and guests."

It is a tenet of Slow that small is beautiful. Ernst Friedrich Schumacher—the true godfather of Slow?—proselytized that businesses and communities keep things local and on a human scale. Operating on a large scale, things can become unwieldy and large mistakes can be made. So it is a wise decision of the Prottis, and of many Italians in this book, to keep things in the family.

Spaghetti with Wild Fennel Sauce

320 g (12.5 oz) spaghetti
150 g (6 oz) red onion, finely chopped
30 g (1 oz) fennel tops, chopped and blanched
30 g (1 oz) pine nuts
30 g (1 oz) raisins
chili flakes, to taste
4 anchovies, chopped
white wine
salt, pepper and olive oil to taste

• Gently fry the onion, then add the fennel and fry for a few more minutes until soft.
• Drown it all in the wine and add the pine nuts, raisins, chili and anchovies. Cook for 10 minutes, stirring, until the wine evaporates.
• Meanwhile boil the spaghetti and drain.
• Take the spaghetti to the sauce and stir. Do not add parmesan!

Tuscany is alive with festivals and *sagres*— there is almost one for every month, so productive are the land and the farmers. There are *sagres* for wild boar, mushrooms, polenta, chestnuts, even steak! Open-air concerts at Cortona, Piero della Francesca's art in Arezzo and San Sepolcro and the monthly antiques fair in Arezzo could threaten to overfill your itinerary.

Castiglion, sitting smugly between the treasures of Siena, Florence and Perugia, overlooks the Val di Chio and the beginnings of the Appenines. It is an archaeologically significant town: the remains of what is thought to be a 4th-century BC Etruscan city wall were discovered under the Piazzale del Cassero. Castiglion is known locally for its annual Palio dei Rioni, held in the main piazza on the third Sunday of June. Horses representing different areas of the city race around the main square, as in Siena, but this Palio is considered less treacherous.

"We feel lucky to have landed in Castiglion Fiorentino. It is a friendly place and we find the people to be spontaneous, polite and open."

And that is exactly as guests have described this family, too. Those attributes and their tangible contentment create a quietly winning combination.

Signor Luigi Protti

Relais San Pietro in Polvano
loc. Polvano 3, 52043 Castiglion Fiorentino
- 10: 4 doubles, €130–€200, 1 single, €100–€120, 5 suites €200–€300.
- Dinner €20–€35. Wine from €14.
- +39 0575 650100
- www.polvano.com
- Train station: Castiglion Fiorentino, 8km

La Locanda

TUSCANY

Most guests arrive in a state of shock, admit Guido and Martina. The postal address suggests the Tuscan tourist trail, but the reality is glorious isolation. The Bevilacquas' skills as hosts soothe the most ruffled feathers, and the astonishing panorama of Chianti and the medieval village of Volpaia does the rest.

"We give guests an 'unplugged' experience without letting them feel abandoned," says Martina. "We look after them, make them drinks, cook for them, help them make plans. We know when to leave people alone and when to join in. The joy is that everyone is different, so our experience is always different. We expect to adjust to their needs, not the other way around."

Guido is an ex-banker and Martina worked in the Stock Exchange. They found the old farm 12 years ago after it had been abandoned for 40 years. "It was a classic story: farmhouse left to rot, trees growing inside, land overgrown," says Martina. "The fortunes of Tuscany were at an all-time low after the Second World War. People were deterred from farming here because of all the ups and downs of the landscape and the stony soil. There wasn't the equipment to maintain the slopes, the Chianti grape had no status in the world wine market and people left the area in droves looking for work."

Eventually the European economies picked up, many properties were reorganized into bigger farms and modern machinery made farming a good prospect once again.

"Smart people in the 70s saw an opportunity to own a part of this amazing landscape and began buying property and land, agritourism started in the 80s, the area's reputation grew, and things turned around dramatically."

One would imagine, with the amalgamation of farmhouses into larger packages fit for selling,

that chaos would ensue over land ownership. But a Mediterranean generosity apparently reigns. Says Martina: "When you look at the hillsides you can see where one farmer's land ends and another's begins by looking at the way the crops are planted. But woods and forests are different. Here we are in the middle of a wood, there is no boundary but it really doesn't matter if it is my wood or my neighbor's. Our attitude is 'let's all enjoy it together!'"

There is a growing sense of responsibility towards the environment in Italy, some of it driven, of course, by economics. Many Italians, hit by expensive heating bills, are adjusting the

> "I prepare only one thing each night, just as you would at home. Sometimes we eat beautifully but simply, sometimes dinner is elaborate"

way they run their properties. "When we came here we were told that we couldn't install solar panels because they were ugly. Now we are encouraged by government grants to use them for pools and heating."

The couple are supporters of the Slow Food movement and revel in the respect given to food, particularly here in central Italy. Says Guido: "We are surrounded by 300 hectares of some of the best organic vineyards, olive groves and honey. We take a lot of care choosing our suppliers and, thank God, here it is still possible to find small artisan producers." A particular favorite of theirs is the protected Cinta Sinese breed of pig. "It is the ultimate Slow food: the pigs are expensive to feed and take longer to grow, so they are not an economic choice of breed for the farmer," says Martina, "but the result is spectacular."

They can look after as many as 14 guests and there are no rules and no budgets to follow. Martina, who does most of the cooking, prepares what is seasonal and good. "I don't watch my shopping bill. I prepare only one thing each night, just as you would at home. Sometimes we eat beautifully but simply, sometimes dinner is elaborate. I don't stress about making profit from my cooking. I imagined when we moved here that we would find a local lady from the village to cook for us. She never materialized and now I do it all and I love it. I like to stay in the kitchen and be the background girl. Guido, who is Neapolitan, with a beautiful southern warmth, is very good at front of house."

They are a dynamic pair, full of vigor and life and have created a memorable place to stay. The beautiful pool vies for attention with the heart-stopping view, there are a library/bar, fine antiques, lovely art, whitewashed rafters soaring over pretty beds and terraces upon which Guido alights with glasses of wine, maybe a grappa, or a restorative coffee.

They have discovered their own "*tempo giusto*"—the pace of life that suits them. They are vigilant guardians of the landscape and of local traditions. They richly deserve all the good company that is lured to La Locanda.

Guido & Martina Bevilacqua

La Locanda,
loc. Montanino di Volpaia, 53017 Radda in Chianti
- 3 doubles, 3 twins, 1 suite. €200–€300.
  Singles €180–€250.
- Dinner €35 (Mon, Wed & Fri only). Restaurants 4km.
- +39 0577 738832
- www.lalocanda.it
- Train station: Florence, 1hr

Fattoria Tregole

TUSCANY

What a spot! The mellow stone buildings are ringed by vines and woodland, with a high vantage point and long views over the Tuscan hills. Bolzano-born Edith and her architect husband Catello bought the rugged old farmhouse in the 1990s and transformed it into an idyllic place to stay.

As a professional art restorer, Edith had a keen interest in keeping the best of what is clearly a very ancient building. Its age was confirmed by the records of a local monastery, which showed that monks bought grain from Fattoria Tregole as long ago as 1003. The brick cellar, which now stores the Fattoria's precious stock of Chianti Classico, is 1,000 years old, as is a blunt tower now encased within newer parts of the house. The most unusual architectural feature is a 16th-century hexagonal chapel; ask Edith for the key as it's well worth having a look at the austere white-washed interior and the prettily peeling sky-blue paint of the dome. Throughout Fattoria Tregole though, sensitive use of stone, tile and wooden beams ensures that it's almost impossible to tell

the old parts of the building from the new extension.

Edith's approach within the building was admirably "slow," and the results are both harmonious and elegant. Using traditional powdered paint, she mixed the colors herself, with rich terracotta, pale peach, deep olive green and soft sage hues reflecting the colors of the Tuscan landscape. Overlaying these sweeps of color are stencilled oak leaves and trefoils, outlined with hand-painted swirls. And when you sink into a sofa you will be buoyed up by one of Edith's meticulously embroidered linen cushions, picked out in subtle, earthy tones.

Edith relishes her role as hostess and mixing her guests together, moves effortlessly between Italian, English and German. "I genuinely love people and I so enjoy having guests here, cooking and caring for them."

The main forum for conviviality at Fattoria Tregole is the twice-weekly dinner, eaten outside by candlelight on the terrace in summer. Edith says, "my guests come here to relax—and to eat! They can diet when they go home."

The long table groans with homemade food. You're likely

to be served a starter such as mushroom tart with crunchy *bruschetta*; a hearty pasta dish, perhaps Edith's classic pasta with zucchini and bright dashes of yellow zucchini flowers; a meat course which might be wild boar hunted in the nearby woods; and a fruit tart. All the food is, needless to say, local, seasonal and cooked with their own olive oil, and much of it comes from Edith's neat vegetable garden, which is edged around with bold, bright dahlias and climbing roses.

Food is a real feature of a visit here, and one of Edith's many passions. Join in with a cooking class that starts at 5pm and ends with the sharing of an evening meal. "Good food and wine bring people together," Edith says. Choosing wines to accompany the excellent food is Catello's considerable contribution to proceedings. His Chianti Classico made from Sangiovese grapes is

"Catello's Chianti Classico is reckoned to be one of the thirty best wines in Tuscany"

reckoned by the Camera di Commercio in Siena to be one of the 30 best wines in Tuscany. There's a lot of competition from excellent winemakers, so you can be sure this is the real deal. You might also want to sample their own vin santo and grappa.

Edith marks out the year with jam-making: marmalade is made in winter, next comes quince jam, and then strawberry, apricot and fig. All these await you on the breakfast table, as will homemade yogurt and a freshly baked cake.

You're in beautiful Chianti country and the hill towns and vineyards reward exploration; smart Castellina in Chianti is just 4km away and has substantial Etruscan ruins; tiny Radda in Chianti has an absorbing early medieval core.

The nearby village of Panzano looks out at the Golden Valley (Conca d'Oro) and has the fine Romanesque church of Pieve di San Leolino. Panzano has been called "*paese dei golosi*" (village of gourmands) and at its spiritual heart is the 250-year-old butchery, Antica Macelleria Cecchini. As you wait in line you can taste their specialities, maybe sip wine and listen to classical music. It's an institution and owner Dario a legend.

Siena, of course, holds some of the greatest works of the Renaissance: Martini's glittering *Maestà*; Ambrogio Lorenzetti's *Allegories of Good and Bad Government* which depict the 14th-century city; Pinturicchio's dramatic fresco in the Piccolomini Library in the duomo. Having explored the medieval masterpiece that is Siena, it is delightful to return to Fattoria Tregole. Thanks to the creative flair of Edith and Catello it is, in a quiet way, a work of art in itself.

Edith Kirchlechner

Fattoria Tregole,
loc. Tregole 86, 53011 Castellina in Chianti
- 4 doubles, €130. 1 suite for 2, €180.
  2 apartments: 1 for 4, 1 for 5. €200–€320.
- Dinner €35, by arrangement. Wine from €10.
- +39 0577 740991
- www.fattoria-tregole.com
- Train station: Siena

Frances' Lodge

TUSCANY

"No pictures can match the beauty," says Frances Mugnai about her home. The sheer loveliness of their farm, the space, the colors, the cool breezes, make being here something special. It is a wonder that it is so peaceful yet so close to Siena; apparently, when the Palio is about to start you can hear the mounting excitement of the crowd that is packed into the medieval walled city just across the way.

It is a ten-minute bus ride to Siena and its *campo*, the main tower of which, the Torre del Mangia, stands proud of the city's roofscape. The hill-top lemon-colored house and farmhouse, which belonged to the nearby 18th-century manor, was converted by Frances' family as a summer retreat. The lofty, light-filled *limonaia* (lemon house) is filled with beautiful things: vibrant art, deep sofas, and oriental touches.

It is a place of enormous beauty yet has its feet firmly planted in the traditions of Tuscany. Indeed, Franco is from a long line of Tuscans. In its eight acres of land—eight acres so close to Siena!—there are olive, lemon and quince groves and numerous fruit trees. From the fruits, Frances makes jams of every flavor. As for so many Italian cooks, recreating peasant dishes is a matter of pride for her—*pappa al pomodoro* for instance. "Even the poorest families had their own tomatoes, olive oil and leftover bread. It is a labor of love, it needs attention, but how beautiful it is."

Frances' new passion is saffron. There is one harvest in October each year and, when the crocus bulbs are ready, friends, family and the community roll up their sleeves to help. "We don't produce enough to employ a team but, because we need to work quickly, even with a smallish harvest we need help." Each bulb produces three flowers, with three strands of saffron to each

flower. During the ten-day blossoming the flowers have to be picked early each morning. A swift harvest is essential.

"We rise early and race the birds to the flowers," says Frances. "They are taken in a basket to the kitchen and we remove the saffron stems straight away. Then we dry them, near the fire in the winter and in a very low oven in the summer." Frances began her experiment with saffron in 2004 and last year she had a whopping crop of 200g. By 2008 she was the chosen supplier to the best restaurant in Siena.

Risotto alla Milanese is Frances' favorite dish for the prized ingredient—"saffron is the protaganist, the main flavor of the dish." She infuses the saffron in boiled water for 20 minutes to release the flavor, removes the stems (keeping

"Their own olive oil is decanted into little bottles for guests to take home"

them for decoration) and then cooks her rice in the flavored water. Guests, in raptures—we are told— over the flavors, go home with little packets of the flower to which Frances has pinned the recipe.

Their own olive oil is decanted into little bottles for guests to take home, too—as is her potent limoncello made with her own organic lemons. Some of her lemon trees are 150 years old and planted in handmade terracotta pots. They are used decoratively, in the 16th-century tradition of Italian garden design.

Three lemon harvests a year and a late-October ripening of olives provoke another flurry of activity as the groves come alive with friends coming and going. Everyone gathers for lunch and dinner on the terraces for restorative plates of pasta. It's a sociable and productive time of year; the guests have gone and the crops dictate the rhythms of life.

Frances dug a well to help irrigate the land— "I don't like to use water from the tap for the gardens." Solar panels heat water for big chunks of the year and she has "forever" had low-energy lighting, timer switches and sensors to cut down on her use of power.

The pool reflects the views of the city skyline; the loggia opens onto fields of wheat and the smell of rose, wisteria and lemon blossom drift around your breakfast table. The garden designer A. Fantastici introduced a touch of fantasy with the elegant birdcage temple in the early 19th century.

Franco, like every self-respecting Sienese, is a fanatical supporter of the Palio where *contradas* (districts) battle for supremacy in the twice-yearly horse race around the Piazza del Campo; people take up their positions days before the 73-second race. "His *contrada* is the 'Torre' and its flags hang in the house. The other *contradas* have historically fought about boundaries," explains Frances, "but the Torre's interests are not in this; its biggest adversary is 'Oca' and they battle for prestige."

The winning *contrada* pays dearly for the victory as it has to pay its jockey, handsomely, and pay bribes to other riders for their "help." If you can't win, you then hope that your biggest enemy doesn't win.

Or, hope the enemy will come in second—to come second in the Palio, many say, is to come last.

Franca Mugnai

Frances' Lodge, strada di Valdipugna 2, 53100 Siena
- 3 doubles, €180–€220.
  2 suites (1 for 2, 1 for 4), €240.
  Min. stay 2 nights; 3 nights during the Palio.
- Restaurants 1km–2km.
- +39 0577 281061
- www.franceslodge.it
- Train station: Siena

Podere Salicotto

TUSCANY

Relaxation requires effort and even in the bucolic setting of Salicotto, it isn't always easily attained.

"Guests arrive after hectic journeys and discover how different our rhythms are. The first thing that strikes them is the silence. It can be overwhelming for some and we understand that it takes time to adjust."

Silvia and Paolo moved here from Milan in 2004—they had demanding careers, busy social lives, and threw in, for good measure, the odd challenging cross-Atlantic sailing trip on their Hallberg Rassy boat. A three-year search for a new home in the country ended with a drive up to this 1820 farmhouse in Le Crete Senesi. It is 3km from Buonconvento, a thriving little town, but set apart from—well, everything.

"The most surprising thing to us was the all-enveloping silence. But I have learned to love the peace and now I crave it; silence makes space for new thoughts and that is a gift."

They began the hard work of renovating the two dwellings using local labor and materials and created six bedrooms and one apartment for guests. The beamed and

terracotta-tiled bedrooms are airy and pleasing, full of soft, Tuscan colors and furnished with simplicity: antiques, monogrammed sheets, great showers. Wherever you turn, the Tuscan landscape is laid out for you to admire for there are 360-degree views on top of the hill here.

From the poolside you can see Montalcino to the south and Siena to the north; there are plenty of garden seats all around for you to sit and absorb the colors, the smells and the wildlife. Emerging from the wood you may see a deer with her fawns; in the early morning watch the mists lifting as the temperature rises; in the evening the moonrise—Paolo says it is magical.

The organic farmland is spread over 46 acres and they produce organic grass for animal feed, walnuts, maple trees and, elsewhere, they grow olives and vines, too. There is a modern cellar that looks more like a smart shop where bottled oils and wines are kept. Everything feels polished and well-run yet Silvia and Paolo's feet are firmly rooted in the traditions of their community.

They join in with the local festivals—in Buonconvento

there is an annual food festival to which cooks from every neighborhood bring their local dishes for all to share; in September there is the Festival of Val d'Arbia and in June the Prima Luna d'Estate where villagers share a meal served at a long table in the street. The Classical Music Festival organized by the Academia delle Crete Senesi is at the end of July. Local buses deftly navigate the hills and villages delivering you from one extravaganza to the next. You can borrow Salicotto's maps and bikes, too.

Brunch—that most civilized meal—is a speciality at Salicotto and is a colorful jumble of Prosciutto Toscano, Pecorino di Pienza, melon, little cakes, fresh juices. "It can take two hours to

> "I have learned to love the peace and now I crave it; silence makes space for new thoughts and that is a gift"

prepare and we serve it on our terrace," says Silvia. It is a generous spread and thoughtfully sourced. "We invest a lot in it and we never compromise on quality. We have opted for local produce rather than prized produce that has to travel a long way and we think we have struck the right balance.

"We love to share our terrace in our own part of the house at mealtimes, and we do this happily because many of our guests are foreign—they have an ingrained respect for privacy. I would hesitate to do the same with Italian guests," she laughs. "I am Italian but I come from an international family and I do know that the Italian way is very different and they would maybe dominate our space!"

Perhaps surprisingly, Silvia thinks that most of her guests are more fervent than Italians in their search for Slow when they are on holiday. "The Italian sense of contentment is often fuelled by five-star service; our guests appreciate natural

beauty and the fact that they are in our home. They know how to move and how to be and that makes it a harmonious experience for us, too. We do not think in terms of us and them. When we say that we welcome them as family they are not empty words."

There is a kitchen for you to use if you don't want to order a dinner, so you can return from the villages below with your haul of fresh produce and create your own meal. "We point people to small local producers that make shopping a truly friendly Italian experience. And we do wine tastings here; Paolo is becoming quite an expert. Cooking your own evening meal would be anathema to Italians, too—they want to eat out all the time in the best restaurants!"

It seems that Paolo and Silvia find almost as much satisfaction from their guests as guests do from holidaying with them. To Silvia the greatest gift is to see people relax properly.

"If you live in a city—as we used to and many of our guests do—you are used to making every moment count. Life can be ridiculously busy. Here, there is a huge sense of space and time takes on a different meaning. These things help people to stop and breathe more deeply and that is rewarding to witness."

Silvia Forni

Podere Salicotto,
Podere Salicotto 73, 53022 Buonconvento
- 6 doubles, €150. €980 per week.
  Studio for 2–4, €1,330 per week. Sailing trips available.
- Breakfast €15. Dinner €30, sometimes available.
- +39 0577 809087
- www.poderesalicotto.com
- Train station: Buonconvento, 2.5km

Il Rigo

TUSCANY

The best cooks have the most fun with food. Not for them precision measuring and anxious minutes looking through the glass door of the oven. They understand what works with what, how things react and work or don't work; they experiment and go on building their skills.

Lorenza, one senses, has always been this way with food. She runs a cookery school in San Quirico d'Orcia, has taught in the States and is master of the menus at Il Rigo. "I love playing with pasta," she says. "I can change the proportions, the colors, the stuffings and the flour, and create hundreds of different flavors. I like making puddings, too, and cakes, so flour is my number one ingredient."

Lorenza celebrates amateurism in the kitchen; she would hate to think of everyone being trained.

"Over-education is the enemy of tradition," she says and the seasons are her guide to ingredients. "I would never use pecorino at the end of the summer, for instance. It's not fresh enough and the milk has a different flavor from the milk of spring, during the lambing season. It is rewarding to find the perfect seasonal partner for food. Nature dishes up perfect combinations, like an early crop of figs to go so perfectly with that pecorino. I am careful to get regionality right, too. Although I am Ligurian and love pesto I would hesitate to serve basil pesto because it is not a Tuscan dish and my guests from Liguria would notice!"

In spring Lorenza takes her cookery students to see that pecorino being made in nearby Pienza; in October they visit saffron farms together. Wild boar and venison appear on the menu in winter. Year round their farm supplies them with vegetables—greens, zucchini, peppers, lettuces and tomatoes.

The Orcia valley is a Unesco World Heritage site. The hills are of soft clay, the cornfields a

swaying sea of golden ochre; the landscape displays the full palate of Tuscan colors. There are two farmhouses on the hill: Casabianca,

Cantucci with Almonds

600 g (1 lb 5 oz) plain flour
pinch salt
8 g (1 teaspoon) baking powder
500 g (1 lb 1 oz) sugar
3 whole eggs
2 egg yolks
little glass vin santo
lemon or orange zest
300 g (11 oz) almonds in skin, lightly toasted
1 egg yolk to brush over biscotti

• Mix flour, salt, baking powder and sugar.
• Using only the tip of your finger, mix in eggs and yolks and vin santo.
• Add zest and almonds – you may need a bit of flour on your hands.
• Make snakes about 4 cm wide, 2 cm high.
• Place on buttered and floured baking tray and brush surface with yolk.
• Cook for 30 minutes at 180°C (350°F/Gas 4), cut into pieces, then cook for further 10 minutes. These keep well in an airtight tin. Good with coffee or vin santo.

dating from 1572, with nine rooms, and Poggio Bacoca, with six rooms. Each is rustic, woody, simple but with enough stylish touches to enchant us all. There are embroidered sheets, flowered bedspreads, gleaming white bathrooms. Everyone eats at Casabianca or drops by the cantina for wine tasting and exquisite seasonal snacks. There is a wood-fired oven in the courtyard.

Breakfast *ciambellone* (cakes) are home-made, as is the pasta. There are *bruschetta* and cold meats and cheeses for lunch, *cantucci* to go with a

glass of vin santo. You will eat like a king, led astray, not least, by the 60 wines in their cellar.

The couple were married 20 years ago—the cypress trees that line the drive were a wedding present—and their contentment is palpable. Their

> "Nature dishes up perfect combinations, like an early crop of figs to go so perfectly with fresh pecorino"

delight at being guardians of Vittorio's old family home transfers itself to guests. "Life is busy but when I am in my car on my way to town to shop or to the cookery school, I look every day at the landscape as a newcomer. When the light is beautiful I am happy for my guests—happy that they can share the beauty."

Guests staying at Poggio Bacoca farmhouse walk up to Casabianca to use the pool, or to eat. Lorenza asked a friend who works with wood to carve a sign to entertain them on the way. By the side of the track you come across an extract of a passage from Dante's *Divine Comedy*: "What negligence, what standing still is this? Run to the mountain to strip off the slough that lets not God be manifest to you."

Signor Vittorio Cipolla & Lorenza Santo

Il Rigo,
Podere Casabianca, 53027 San Quirico d'Orcia
- 15 doubles, €100–€110.
  Half-board €144–€156 p.p.
- Lunch or dinner €22–€25, by arrangement.
- +39 0577 897291
- www.agriturismoilrigo.com
- Train station: Buonconvento, 15km

Podere le Mezzelune

TUSCANY

Just where the hills rise from the plains above the ports of Livorno and Piombino, you will find Podere le Mezzelune. This is the region of Maremma, and from here views reach as far as the islands of Elba, Gorgona and even Corsica.

The Maremma is fascinating, and curiously ignored by the many travellers who pass by on their way to the more celebrated parts of Tuscany. All Italians think regionally rather than nationally and are fiercely protective of their birthplace, but here in Tuscany, those that live in the Maremma feel that their tiny corner of western Tuscany is its own universe. Italy is a nation of mini-universes.

Over 2,000 olive trees and 15 hectares of land surround le Mezzelune, and add to the magical seclusion of the place, gazing from the hills down to the coast. Luisa arrived in 1985 and has pulled off a triumphant restoration. She is a gifted designer—fabrics are her thing—and a calm emanates from the *podere's* interior: white muslin billows in the breeze, a delicate light filters into the bedrooms and well-chosen furniture decorates, rather than overpowers, the spaces. Upstairs are four bedrooms, two looking out to sea, private and secluded with their own fine views from their terraces. They have linen curtains, wooden floors, furniture made to Luisa's design, good fabrics, candles, fresh fruit and, maybe, vintage wooden pegs hung with an antique shawl. Colors are calming neutrals—a gentle mix of beige, taupe, cream. Bathrooms, too, are perfect. For longer stays there are two little private cottages in the garden with all the gadgets and equipment you could possibly need along with open fires, beams, sofas piled with cushions and lovely beds. Luisa created it all with her late husband Sergio. When he died Luisa decided to share the running of it with her friend, Renata.

An important part of their plan is for their farmland to be granted official organic status. Says Renata: "We produce our own IGP-labelled olive oil but for our farm to achieve organic status we have to convince our neighbors to become organic, too. We have received recognition from the Slow Food movement, which makes us very proud for they set the standard for all to follow. We use traditional methods of crushing the olives between large stones. The result," says Luisa, "is a sweet oil with a light bitter aftertaste. The oils are shiny with golden yellow colors and green reflective lights." The bottles are artfully displayed in the *bottega*, alongside bottles of preserved eggplant, zucchini and tomatoes from the kitchen garden.

The orchard produces lemons, peaches, cherries and strawberries—all to be found on the breakfast table, with charcuterie, cheeses and homemade cakes. Napkins are tied with twine and a sprig of lavender; this attention to detail is delightful.

The house has been heated, thus far, by a boiler fed with the estate's coppiced wood. "One of our ambitions is to protect our natural environment," says Renata. "A respect for nature should be at the core of all we do. It is worrying to see rapidly developing countries without a respect for the foundation of its culture. Europe is so green and beautiful; it could be regarded as the garden of the world. We have been blessed with this landscape and now we know how best to protect it. We all have a duty to be part of that preservation."

Luisa Chiesa Alfieri

Podere le Mezzelune,
via Mezzelune 126, 57020 Bibbona
- 4 twins/doubles, €166–€176.
  2 cottages for 2, €166–€176.
- Restaurants 3km.
- +39 0586 670266
- www.lemezzelune.it
- Train station: Cecina

Pieve di Caminino

TUSCANY

As pilgrims found shelter and warmth here 1,000 years ago, so will you. Pieve di Caminino is a former Romanesque church, its existence first recorded in the 11th century. It is built on Paleo-Christian ruins and it is said that three saints lived here: Feriolo; Egenziano, who met his end in Africa; and Luca, who turned the abandoned monastery into an agnostic hermitage. At the site of Feriolo's death, it was said, a spring sprung forth and from then on, even more pilgrims would come to stay at this "miraculous" hamlet.

The estate has been in Piero's family since 1872 and from that time the land, buildings and community have been thoroughly restored. Antonio Giuseppe Marrucchi created a hamlet in which farm workers would work and live and, following in the footsteps of the monks who produced oil here, he planted new olive trees, some of which are still here. By the 1960s Caminino was almost deserted again as workers left for the cities—a theme common in this book. The farm limped on until the Marrucchi Locatelli arm of the family took over in 1983.

The setting is dramatic—the landscape forms a natural amphitheater that on one side slopes down to the west coast of Italy; the Castiglione della Pescaia beach is a beautiful surprise for visitors, as are the sea views from here on a clear day. There are 500 hectares of farmland with olive groves, vineyards and a cork tree forest.

You drive through the big rusty gates and down the tree-lined drive to be greeted by Emiliano in what must be the most beautiful "reception" in the book, in the family's private quarters, lined with paintings by famous Locatelli artists. Among soaring columns, stone arches and vaulted ceilings you may well be invited to taste the estate's extra virgin olive oil. They have been

pressing their oil since 1872 and they serve it with toasted bread touched by garlic and salt. With a glass of red wine in hand, you can wander, feeling a touch diminished by the lofty surroundings.

Piero and son Emiliano are both heritage architects, working in Florence and at studios here. The Pieve has been the subject of dissertations by seven PhD students and the son and father have personally assisted each in their studies.

"I love our farmland but I regard it as a frame for the house. I know every inch of this place. Historical societies have used it as an archaeological, not an architectural, study. I have measured and know every stone and every tile."

As much thought has gone into the preservation of the ecosystem as of the Pieve and the apartments. Deer, wild boar, the many birds,

"Pieve is not a business,
it is part of our family.
I want to look after it myself"

butterflies, snakes and lizards are evidence of sympathetic land management, and Emiliano has created hides in the woods where you can observe the wildlife for yourself. Wildlife aside, the Maremma, in Tuscany's southwestern corner, is a fascinating region. It is 70% forest and has the lowest population density of all Tuscan areas. "There has been virtually no bad land usage," says Emiliano, "no big roads were built here and no airports. There aren't even any traffic lights!" Indeed, it is hard not to conclude that the motor car has led the historical assault on Slow.

"It is Slow—too Slow for some. It can take weeks to find a plumber or a workman. I explain to my guests that Slow Food restaurants can be slow through and through so that they go prepared for a wait and they are accepting! When my father came here in the 70s to hunt he would have to leave his car a good way away and ride a horse the last bit

of the journey. There was no electricity until the 80s and if he wanted to watch a soccer match he had to connect the television to the car battery.

"Thanks to technology I can live and work here. Very few houses come up for sale in the Maremma —those who live here realize how lucky they are. The clean air alone is a good enough reason to choose the area; the space, the peace and the coast make it exceptional.

"There are no televisions and no internet connection in the apartments," says Emiliano, "we want to encourage people to 'staccare la spina'— relax their spine—and spend their time quietly. To continue the Slow theme, we only suggest visits to outposts that are little-known, places where guests can get to know genuinely local restaurants that are family-run and where there may be only one dish on offer, cooked for you by the owners."

Emiliano's connection with the area is strong; his wife, Chiara, is the daughter of the famous Moris winemaking family and he has always hunted with her father. Now their daughter, Benedetta, will see her parents care for Pieve just as Emiliano watched Piero and Daniela.

"Pieve is not a business, it is part of our family. I want to look after it myself, which is why I am here 99% of the time to greet guests personally," says Emiliano. "I have had the loveliest people working with me but it is best when I do it. I light fires in the apartments, I lay out chocolates, I work hard to make sure that everyone is happy."

Famiglia Marrucchi Locatelli

Pieve di Caminino,
Strada Provinciale 89, Peruzzo, 58036 Roccatederighi
- 5 suites for 2–3, €120–€160. 2 apartments for 4.
- Breakfast €10. Restaurant 6km.
- +39 0564 569736
- www.caminino.com
- Train station: Grosseto

Il Pardini's Hermitage

TUSCANY

If you are alone, the family invites you to eat with them. When you relax in the garden, Federigo may appear, unprompted, with a glass of chilled wine. When you arrive, music is chosen for you and when you leave the family comes to the boat to wave you off.

Il Pardini's Hermitage is an institution, a heart-winner, an exceptional place in so many ways. The spirit of inclusion, openness and gentleness is second to none and the seclusion and necessary self-sufficiency create a thriving community. Deftly, guests are helped to feel part of it all.

This is much more than a place to stay. You can learn to paint, throw pots, practice yoga or take cookery courses, play music, meditate, or just find your own quiet space to read and enjoy the garden. The occasional yoga chant may catch the breeze and drift your way, further adding to the meditative atmosphere.

Tantalizingly close to the Tuscan coastline, Isola del Giglio is a 60-minute boat ride from the mainland but a world away. Once you arrive, a small boat then picks you up from Giglio Porto for the 20-minute journey round to the rocky outcrop beneath Pardini. If the weather isn't good, the brochure says, "the hotel can be reached on foot via a one-and-a-half-hour walk on uneasy paths." Now you get a sense of the seclusion; a journey here could feel like a pilgrimage, and many before you have done it on a donkey.

Barbara's great-grandfather came from Giglio and her family talked wistfully of their blissful life there. Federigo, whose father started Pardini, met Barbara when she was working in a bank in Geneva. His tales of island life mirrored the fond memories she had gleaned from her grandfather and it took little persuasion to get her out to the island to see the house where Federigo's father

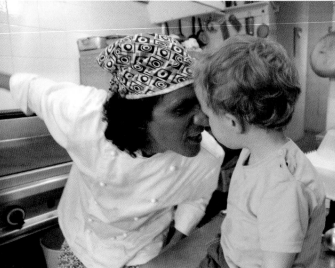

PARDINI,S
HERMITAGE

built a little house for family holidays. That was in 1962 and by 1966 the couple had moved to Giglio to help welcome guests in the, by then, much-extended Hermitage. It is not a house of cossetting luxury or many-starred facilities—there is a satisfying and very human assortment of family furniture, simple bedrooms, cool tiled floors—but you sense how it has grown organically and how much it is loved by the family.

"Every summer our daughter Veronica stays for three months with her young son Orlando; her cousin Antonio helps me to cook; Rosy, our friend, works in the office and helps us create a special atmosphere for the guests," says Barbara. "We respect that all our guests are different and need different things—we try to recognize what would

> "We respect that all our guests are different and need different things – we try to recognize what would make them more happy"

make them more happy. Giglio is more relaxed than the rest of Italy and we enjoy the fact that we have contact with guests. In big hotels sometimes nobody talks with each other."

Federigo's joie de vivre is evident at all times—especially when showing guests his garden that tumbles down the rock face towards the sea. He has terraces and vines, tomato plants and salad crops. Barbara copes with gluts of vegetables with aplomb: boxes of eggplants are sliced, baked and layered with cheese, tomatoes and zucchini for *melanzana parmigiana*; plentiful salads are a welcome light lunch for guests who gather on the terrace that seems to jut out over the sea. The small kitchen produces some spectacular meals, mostly made with home produce. "We have no menus but guests choose from a spread laid out in the dining room. We have lots of seafood and our own meats, too."

Federigo and Barbara together look after 11 donkeys, 35 goats and 20 pigs. They are all treated as pets although their presence comes from a practical need and desire for self-sufficiency. The Amiata donkeys are used when boats can't reach this side of the island, goat's milk is used by the cooks, and the pigs—an ancient Cinta Sinese breed—are slaughtered for prosciutto and *finnocchiona*, a special type of Tuscan salami made with home-grown fennel.

Drinks are taken together before dinner, with friends, family and guests gathering after the activities of their day. After dinner you can gather for a limoncello or port and, often, an impromptu music recital. Veronica says "The rhythm here is '*lento*'. We encourage guests to stay for a week. It takes time to get into it, but once they do, guests come back time and time again."

Federigo & Barbara Pardini

Il Pardini's Hermitage,
loc. Cala degli Alberi, 58013 Isola del Giglio
- 10 doubles, 2 singles, 1 suite.
  Half-board €95–€155 p.p. Full-board €130–€180 p.p.
- Wine from €15.
- +39 0564 809034
- www.hermit.it
- Train station: Orbetello

Le Marche   Lazio
Umbria

[CENTRAL]

CENTRAL

Arcing across the Italian peninsula, this band of regions has the majestic Apennine Mountains at its core. Le Marche borders the Adriatic and stretches across a long narrow coastal plain with rolling countryside that is cut off by wild and inaccessible peaks. Lazio has a rich historic and architectural heritage and a long coastline of dunes, salt marshes and pine forests facing the Tyrrhenian Sea. Evergreen, landlocked, Umbria nestles between.

The lusty, mysterious Etruscans ruled central Italy before the rise of Rome but they ventured no further east than Umbria. The Romans then built roads across the Apennines to establish colonies in Le Marche. After the fall of Rome, Goths and Byzantines struggled for supremacy. The Longobardi followed, then the Papacy ruled, apart from a brief period when the French took over before Italy became a unified kingdom in 1860. Lazio was finally annexed in 1871.

Le Marche's Adriatic coast is known for its regimented sandy beaches. However, Monte Conero is edged by small bays and coves, backed by steep white tree-covered cliffs. Mezzavalle is only accessible on foot and Le Due Sorelle by boat. Portonovo has a busy but pretty beach and a landing place for fishing boats making it the perfect place to try the local *brodetto* (fish soup), mussels and other seafood dishes. After lunch, visit the 11th-century Romanesque church that sits peacefully among evergreen oaks.

There are walking, trekking, hunting and fishing opportunities in the regional and national parks. You may glimpse the swoop of golden eagles, spot a wild boar or even catch sight of the timid lynx or brown bear; both have returned to the Sibillini Mountains. There are *sagres* (food festivals) dedicated to many foods, including the *lumaca* (snail) the *vincisgrassi* (local lasagne), the *tartuffo bianco* (white truffle).

"the lusty Etruscans ruled here before the rise of Rome"

Porchetta, the whole roast baby suckling pig, is a regional speciality. The local Verdicchio or Bianchello wines go well with seafood, Rosso Conero with meat.

Pesaro, the birthplace of Rossini, holds an international festival of his music every year in August. Macerata's renowned neo-classical Sferisterio, a columned semi-circular outdoor arena, holds 7,000 spectators for the opera season in July and August. Urbino, the Renaissance capital, stages a festival of ancient music in front of the Palazzo Ducale, one of Italy's finest.

The Piazza del Popolo, the elegant main square of the medieval city of Ascoli Piceno, is an animated place for an *aperitivo* and *olive ascolane* (stuffed and deep fried) while watching the locals. The town, like so many others, has wonderful gothic buildings, fascinating galleries and good shopping.

Umbria is at the heart of the Italian peninsula. Its gentle landscape of fertile hills, forests, fortified hilltop towns and mountains has 30 bike trails though a mystic, spiritual and leafy land. The Marmore Falls are staggering and provide enough hydroelectricity to power the region's steel industry.

You can, if you are a rambler or aspiring saint, follow in the footsteps of Saint Francis, *il poverello d'Assisi.* Take the path he trod in 1207 from Assisi to Gubbio and walk though a living Renaissance fresco of soft colors and dramatic backdrops, stopping off to enjoy the sacred architecture and paintings.

Perugia is the home of the famous university for foreign students and hosts the Euro Chocolate Fair in October; the town has the lovely Palazzo Priori and Fontana Maggiore at its center.

This land, dotted with ancient castles, has a deep farming culture; wheat, olives, sunflowers and grapes thrive. A black truffle fair is held in Norcia every February; lentils are grown around nearby Castelluccio, an ancient village in spectacular mountains.

The lively, walled 14th-century town of Montefalco, the "balcony of Umbria," has panoramic views across the region and a wine festival in September to show off the locally made Sagrantino di Montefalco. Città della Pieve parades in August, in Renaissance costume inspired by Perugino's paintings; Todi hosts an arts festival and Foligno a jousting tournament.

Lazio is somewhat overshadowed by Rome yet holds many treasures; you can go "archeo-trekking" around the ancient sites of the Etruscan cities of Vulci, Tarquinia, Veio and Cervetri and visit il Lago di Bolsena and Sutri with its magnificent amphitheatre.

Go to Rome in January and you will tussle with the locals at the winter sales. Culture and fun comes cut-price, too: entry to museums and galleries, concert hall tickets and river trips are all discounted.

Sunsets in Rome can be spectacular. Go to Piazza Campidglio to admire the Roman Emperor Marco Aurelio on horseback, climb the elegant double stairway and look down on the symmetry of the square laid out by Michelangelo. Then walk behind the palazzo and take in the whole of the Roman Forum that stretches out before you in the dying sun.

There are ways of escaping the bustle. Take off for the peace of Villa Adriana where you can lose yourself among the shady ruins. This is Hadrian's (of wall fame) vast architectural playground, his country residence in the foothills of the Tiburtino mountains. Nemi, an enchanting hill-top town overlooking a volcanic lake of the same name, is famous for its perfumed wild strawberries. In June it is decked in flowers during the Fragola Profumata festival.

Lindy Wildsmith

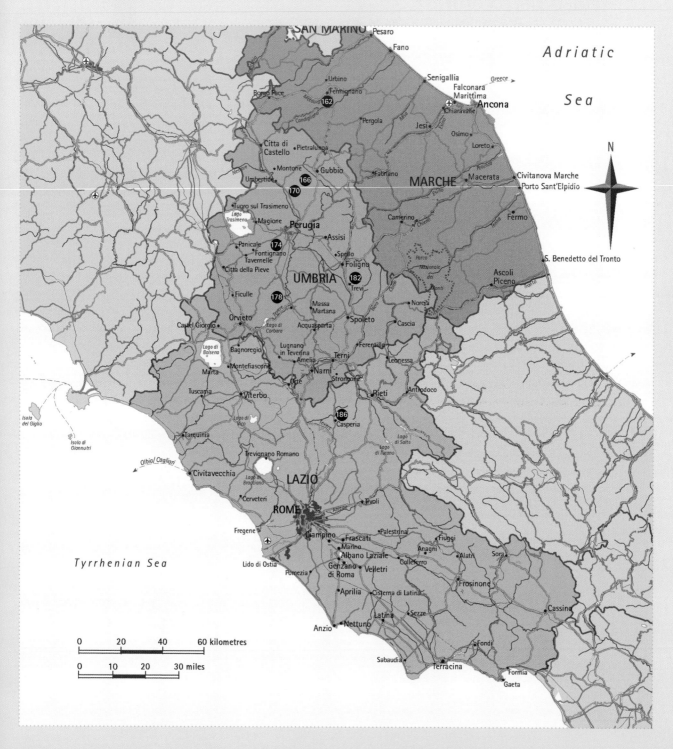

Adriatic

Sea

N

SAN MARINO

Pesaro

Fano

Urbino

Senigallia

Borgo Pace

Fermignano

Falconara
Marittima

Greece

162

Chiaravalle

Ancona

Metauro

Candigliano

Pergola

Jesi

Osimo

Citta di
Castello

Pietralunga

Loreto

Montone

Gubbio

Fabriano

MARCHE

Macerata

Nera

Civitanova Marche

Porto Sant'Elpidio

Umbertide

166

170

Nestore

Camerino

Chienti

Tuoro sul Trasimeno

Lago
Trasimeno

Magione

Perugia

Assisi

Fermo

Tenna

Panicale

174

Fontignano
Tavernelle

Spello

Foligno

Parco

Nazionale

S. Benedetto del Tronto

Citta della Pieve

UMBRIA

182

Trevi

dei

Ascoli
Piceno

Ficulle

178

Massa
Martana

Nera

Monti

Tronto

Orvieto

Acquasparta

Norcia

Castel Giorgio

Lago di
Corbara

Spoleto

Cascia

Tevere

Ferentillo

Bagnoregio

Lugnano
in Teverina

Leonessa

Lago di
Bolsena

Amelia

Terni

Montefiascone

Orte

Narni

Stroncone

Marta

Antrodoco

Tuscania

Viterbo

Rieti

Lago di
Vico

186

Casperia

Tarquinia

Tevere

Lago
di Salto

Trevignano Romano

Lago
di Turano

Olbia/Cagliari

Isola
del Giglio

Civitavecchia

Lago di
Bracciano

LAZIO

Isola di
Giannutri

Cerveteri

ROME

Tivoli

Fregene

Ciampino

Frascati

Palestrina

Fiuggi

Aniene

Marino

Anagni

Lido di Ostia

Albano Laziale

Colleferro

Alatri

Sora

Tyrrhenian Sea

Pomezia

Genzano
di Roma

Velletri

Frosinone

Aprilia

Cisterna di Latina

Sezze

Cassino

Latina

Anzio

Nettuno

Fondi

Sabaudia

Terracina

Formia

Gaeta

0   20   40   60 kilometres

0   10   20   30 miles

Special places to stay

Le Marche

162   Locanda della Valle Nuova

Umbria

166   Locanda del Gallo

170   Casa San Gabriel

174   Villa Aureli

178   La Palazzetta del Vescovo

182   I Mandorli Agriturismo

Lazio

186   La Torretta

Locanda della Valle Nuova

LE MARCHE

The Savinis' commitment to organic farming and to the environment is almost unequaled—even in this book. For 27 years they have been breaking new ground and, while realizing their ambition of creating a modern sustainable farm, they have shared their passions with their neighbors and their guests.

Giulia learned of the merits of organic farming from her parents—city-architect-turned-farmer father Augusto and her mother Adriana. In 1980, while living in Milan and running a tiny farm in Piedmont, Augusto and Adriana decided they should search for a bigger farm further into the countryside in Le Marche.

Northern Le Marche then was some way behind much of the rest of Italy and that attracted the Savinis. That the farm was within sight of Urbino delighted them, for being close to the city would add a cultural dimension to their new life.

"In the early 80s certified organic farming was in its infancy. Our beginning was not easy," says Giulia. "We lived in Milan while trying to oversee

the creation of a modern sustainable farm and of course the work and planning took a long time. Luckily Le Marche was some way ahead of the rest of Italy in organic farming although organic beef, that we planned to produce, was not easy to sell.

"We arrived with a deep respect for the soil—we didn't want to break the surface more than we had to—and we were regarded as townies who were nuts! The new machines we brought with us were seen as clear indications of our madness."

Undeterred they pressed on and are now respected for the dynamic farm they have created.

The Locanda stands among ancient, protected, oak trees. Its 1920s frame has grown into an unusual, unexpectedly modern, small hotel. The bigger rooms with the views are worth asking for.

During the renovation they double-insulated walls and roof, installed solar panels for heating water and have a wood-fired boiler that is fuelled with their own coppiced wood from their 185 acres of land. Toilets have dual flushes, all light bulbs are low energy and bed linen is 100%

natural fiber to reduce allergens. Bathrooms have dispensers for soap and shampoos, which cuts down on packaging waste.

Giulia sits on the board of Associazione Marchigiana Agricoltura Biologica, one of the oldest associations in Italy supporting organic farmers. On their farm they keep pure-bred Marchigiana cattle that graze on the organic grass

> "We produce over 70% of the fresh food that we serve in the restaurant and the rest we buy from nearby farms, most of them organic"

and home-produced barley mixed with small quantities of protein-containing seeds.

"It is a pleasure to share our story with guests. We want them to understand real Italian food and to know where the food that we serve comes from. We tell them about the food industry in this area and introduce them to a different way of producing, eating and living.

"Agriculture should be ruled by the rhythms of nature. Over the last century, however, farming experienced uncontrolled growth to meet an insatiable and increasingly diverse demand. This has culminated in the excessive and indiscriminate use of fertilizers, pesticides and weedkillers. Now there are such high levels of contamination in underground water tables, rivers and seas, that pesticide residues exist in almost every stage of the food chain."

For 25 years the Savinis have practiced agriculture "cleanly." They fertilize their land with manure, thus enriching the terrain with humus and establishing an ecological balance that eradicates the need for chemicals and weedkillers. Their farm has been certified as organic by the Istituto Mediterraneo di Certificazione since 1983.

"We produce over 70% of the fresh food that we serve in the restaurant and the rest we buy from nearby farms, most of them organic. An added benefit of our sourcing is that we have a minimum of packaging waste."

There are DOP cheeses, lamb, their own beef, prize-winning extra virgin olive oil, excellent salamis and a "heavenly" pancetta. All are paired perfectly with local wines: Sangiovese from their own grapes, or maybe a Bianchello, Rosso Piceno or the Visner dessert wine made from red wine and morello cherries.

They make bread, pasta, cakes, pastries, salamis, jams and jellies and grow many herbs for the kitchen and for homemade liqueurs. They mill their own grain and forage for nuts and, in autumn, for white truffles.

They are a dynamic threesome: Augusto with his knowledge of architecture, urbanism, local history and culture, Adriana with her love of gardening, cooking, plants and herbalism and Giulia with her gift for communication. Her knowledge of the organic movement and best ecological practices mean that you should leave enriched and full of inspiration.

Giulia Savini

Locanda della Valle Nuova,
La Cappella 14, 61033 Sagrata di Fermignano
- 5 doubles, 1 twin. €110. Half-board €84 p.p.
  2 apartments for 2, €680 per week.
- Dinner €30. Wine from €9.
- +39 0722 330303
- www.vallenuova.it
- Train station: Fano

Locanda del Gallo

UMBRIA

Carved roosters protect the doorways; indeed, they pop up everywhere. According to Balinese tradition, the rooster—*gallo*—wards off evil spirits; numerous happy guests reckon he is doing a good job. Many of the models, in stone, papier-mâché, wood and steel have been given to Paola by guests as a token of appreciation for the peace and serenity they enjoyed during their stay. Her guest book bubbles over with thanks for the calm that emanates from this castle.

The castle is huge, its history is long and its battle scars many. High on a hill 'twixt the historically warring factions of Perugia and Gubbio, it could hardly escape. Paola, from Milan, and Irish, from Germany, have been here since 1997. A well-travelled cultured pair, they have injected a refreshing colonial mood into the old bones of the place. They have created seven exceptionally comfortable and stylish bedrooms with limewashed walls, carved bedsteads, four-posters and marble bathrooms. There are heavy wooden reclaimed doors, friezes from Bali, carved mirrors, screens from India and Sri Lanka. Outside —there are grounds of 28 hectares—Indonesian furniture lines the verandas, teak and canvas loungers loll about on the lawn, a wooden swing hangs from a tree.

Umbria is known as the green heart of Italy and the urge to explore it is not resistible. There are medieval hilltop towns as in its bejewelled neighbor, Tuscany, and Assisi, Orvieto, Gubbio, Perugia and Spello are all among Italy's most beautiful. The main squares in Todi and Assisi, like the squares in so many Umbrian towns, stand on the site of Roman forums.

Their churches are often as rich in art as museums and many towns have remarkably well preserved Etruscan tombs. The lush Tiber valley

cuts through the province and, although there is no coastline, there are hugely popular lakes and lake "beaches" for swimming.

Yogurt cake

3 cups yogurt
3 cups plain flour
1 cup sugar
3 eggs
1 cup sunflower oil
3-1/2 teaspoons baking powder

• Mix all the ingredients together.
• Grease a medium saverin cake tin (this is a doughnut-shaped tin with a hole in the center so that you end up with a ring of cake).
• Cook at 180°C for 40 minutes.
• Turn out, then dust with icing sugar to finish.

Gubbio holds an annual Palio; unlike the furious horse race in Siena, this Palio is for runners only. Three teams devoted to Saints Ubaldo, Giorgio and Antonio set off around the cobbled streets in white trousers and red neckties. If you want to join in with the festival spirit, come on May 15. Spoleto's famous music festival, the Festival of Two Worlds, takes place annually during July.

Umbria's attractions and seductiveness may be enormous, but one is easily drawn back to the Locanda and its excellent restaurant (for guests only). The chef, Jimmy, is from Sri Lanka and for 14 years he has cooked imaginatively and with impressive flair, using vegetables and herbs from the garden. That he has been with the couple for so long—his wife, Kamani, is now part of the team, too—speaks volumes for the special atmosphere generated by Paola and Irish.

One of Paola's greatest pleasures is coming into contact with so many small local producers.

"There is no menu and we decide on the day what we will cook. Jimmy does the main meals and I look after the breads and cakes. We use as much of our own fresh produce as possible. The garden was wild when we came but Irish has carefully nurtured it. The land here is very dry but we choose plants that thrive in these conditions to minimize our need to water it—things such as rosemary and lavender and almond and olive trees.

"We enjoy creating dishes around the crops. For us a major part of Slow is about respecting foods available to us and, then, taking time to enjoy the finished dishes. Eating without stress is very important."

There are many courses held at the Locanda and there is a large and airy studio for dance or yoga. On request there is ayurvedic massage and, at a house nearby, Paola's friend Renza can teach guests the art of making pasta. "She is from Bologna and so very good!" (Note from Alastair: "Not unlikely: I ate my best lasagna ever in Bologna, though it was in 1968 I still remember it.") Renza, pictured at her loom, teaches weaving and natural dye, too.

Paola, a Milanese, is content in her adopted Umbria. "People have a good way of life here. It is unhurried and attention is given to food and sociability. I genuinely enjoy providing a place for people to unwind. Many of my guests lead stressful lives and I like to think that my work restores wellness."

Paola Moro & Irish Breuer

Locanda del Gallo,
loc. Santa Cristina, 06020 Gubbio
- 6 doubles, €120–€140. 3 suites for 4, €200–€240.
  Half-board €75–€90 p.p.
- Dinner €28. Lunch €12.
- +39 0759 229912
- www.locandadelgallo.it
- Train station: Perugia

Casa San Gabriel

UMBRIA

The seclusion, so high, will clear your head; the valley setting and the feeling of space create a deep sense of peace.

Neighboring towns, such as Perugia, Gubbio, Cortona and Assisi, have the sort of multi-layered history that can startle the unwary. They tell you in Tuscany that Gubbio was one of the first five towns to be founded after the Flood.

"There is not a building, a stream, a tree, an odd-looking hillock or a strangely shaped field that was not the scene of some story." Thus wrote H.V. Morton. "The moment a peasant leaves his cottage he steps into a library of fiction for which a weekly newspaper seems a poor substitute."

From the house you can see the Basilica di San Francesco at Assisi perched at the bottom of Mount Subasio. But if the tranquility of Casa San Gabriel gets to you, you may want nothing but the simple pleasures of gathering a lettuce from the vegetable patch for lunch, watching the hoopoes foraging for their young, and snoozing under a tree.

Christina and David bought the Umbrian farm buildings in November 2002, began work the next February, got married

in August and opened, albeit in a low-key way, in October, less than a year after setting eyes on the ruin.

"We came here for peace and beauty, spurred on by our love of the Italian countryside and of the Italian people. Our lives here couldn't be more different: in London I was an accountant in a city firm, away from home 12 hours a day. I met David when I was working in Australia—he comes from Victoria—and decided that if we had a family I didn't want to do what I was doing; I would hardly have seen my children. We both wanted to carve out a life that put family at the center."

Their two girls, Lucia and Elisabetta, are well-integrated—happily attending the little local school and nursery. Says Christina: "One of the things I relish is the introduction they have had to mealtimes as being happy, unrushed, shared occasions. Eli has a three-course lunch with her classmates and teachers. Everything served will be the sort of food that the cooks prepare for their families. It costs €4 a day; I think that is good value." Compare that to the budget given for English school lunches—52p. What could better demonstrate the different approach to food taken by English and Italian governments.

The property is built on a 13th-century road and the main house dates back to the 16th century. It is said that Hannibal's army camped at the bottom of the valley next to the River Tiber that flows on from here and weaves its way right into Rome.

Wild Asparagus Risotto

500 g (1 lb) wild asparagus tips
2 onions/large shallots
olive oil
1 bottle Umbrian Grechetto or other dry white wine
2.5 cups risotto rice
vegetable stock
parmesan, freshly grated
handful chopped parsley

• Trim asparagus keeping only juicy bits. Add to boiling water and cook until tips are tender. Reserve drained liquid.
• Heat veg stock. Sauté onions in oil until soft. Add rice and stir until shiny. Add 2 glasses of wine and stir until liquid has been absorbed. Add one ladleful of the hot asparagus water. Stir until absorbed.
• Continue, adding small amounts of liquid each time. Add veg stock in same way. There is about 20 minutes of stirring to pour yourself a glass of wine. The rice is ready when it is cooked but still has bite.
• Add the asparagus right at the end and sprinkle with parmesan and parsley to serve.

They inflicted the worst defeat suffered by the Roman Empire at Lake Trasimeno, where they lured the Roman army into a narrow defile, so tight that the Romans couldn't properly wield their weapons, and slaughtered them. But Lake Trasimeno is beautiful, a vast watery oasis beside, and upon, which you can shake off the dust of a hot Umbrian summer.

Three farm buildings were converted for self-catering holidays and each has its own terrace. You feel part of something yet have privacy, too. David and Christina cook for guests on Tuesdays and on request can deliver three-course meals to each apartment for private suppers; on Thursday nights you can create your own pizza using the original bread oven and eat with everyone else in the garden. "David shops in Pierantonio for seasonal stuff; we pick wild asparagus and make good risottos and he will always pick up local wine for guests to try."

There is a small, cozy library with soft seats, and lots of books on travel and cookery and a table on the garden terrace for a group of friends to use. Magnificent views are at their best from the pool at the top of their land next to the little vineyard. You look down and may spot the girls pottering among the lettuces, David attempting to tame nature in the garden, Christina chatting with guests. The densely wooded valley seems to throw a cloak of silence around Casa San Gabriel.

"For us the beauty of a Slow life is having choice. We work hard but if we want to take the children to the lake for a sunny afternoon we can, and will maybe work in the evening instead. The children stay up late to join in with village life, festivals and fairs. 'How do they cope?' people always ask us. A siesta does the trick. We are always together," says Christina. "We do miss seeing friends and family regularly but I do know that we will never leave."

Christina Todd & David Lang

Casa San Gabriel, Vocablo Cal Zolari,
loc. Santa Giuliana 114, 06015 Pierantonio
- 3 apartments: 1 for 2, 1 for 2–4, 1 for 4.
  B&B: €85. Self-catering: €400–€1,025 per week.
- Dinner €25 (Tues); pizza €15 (Thurs).
- +39 0759 414219
- www.casasangabriel.com
- Train station: Perugia Pierantonio

Villa Aureli

UMBRIA

"Time has stood still here since 1700. There are plants, fine architecture, decoration, art and furniture from that period and many generations of our family have cared for Aureli."

Count Sperello di Serègo Alighieri's family arrived in 1874. Its members were doughty guardians who protected the estate and the wider community. Sperello's father saw off plans to build a motorway and to extend the village of Castel del Piano. During the war the house was occupied by Nazis, then by American, Australian and British troops but, thanks to the quick reaction of the faithful gardener Adolfo Guelfi who hid valuable possessions away behind false walls, remarkably little damage was done.

"Each generation has protected the house and the ecosystem and we take pleasure in uniting our guests with our history," says Sperello. "We have installed photovoltaic panels to minimize energy usage, we illuminate gently and use much of our own produce."

Cleverly, water and energy usage have been cut without compromising on aesthetics. The small pool sits in the old rainwater reservoir and now

rainwater is harvested from the roofs and is used, along with water from the well, for the kitchen garden, the orangery and the fountain. The photovoltaic panels supply enough energy to air condition two external apartments.

It is a productive estate and olive, lemon and orange trees are all nurtured without chemicals. The vegetable garden yields much produce and cook Adriana can create traditional Umbrian dishes for al fresco meals. The views are pretty enough to distract even the hungriest diner.

Within the formal gardens sit lemon trees in enormous 18th-century terracotta pots; the trees over-winter in the *arancera* and, come spring, are taken to the garden by tractor. Sperello's father, Leonardo, remembered when it took 16 men to hoist them onto frames to transport them into position among the box and yews.

The 18th-century Italian color schemes remain vivid and a special light permeates the villa. The proportions of the rooms are impressive yet the grandeur is not overpowering.

In the second half of the 18th century Sperello Aureli, an intellectual and art lover, slowly extended what had begun as a 16th-century tower; he added stucco-work and friezes and commissioned many of the fittings and much of the furniture. Sperello's grandmother, Anna Meniconi Bracceschi, whose parents bought the villa in 1874, loved this house and although she never lived here her gift was the magnificent tiling that was designed by her friend and crafted in Vietri near Naples.

There are four apartments—the two within the villa are majestic, one has four balconies and all have private access.

Sperello is an astrophysicist working at the Arcetri observatory in Florence; son Pietro, who studied philosophy, cares for things day-to-day. Pietro is a knowledgeable charming man, respectful and proud of all his family has preserved.

The jewels of Umbria are close by—the old center of Perugia can be reached via train—and some of the great grapes of the wine world thrive on the slopes of Montefalco which translates to Falcon's Mount. The tourist authorities refer to it as "*la ringhiera dell'Umbria*"—the balcony of Umbria—and the views are worthy of the hyperbole.

Discover, too, the pleasures of Castel del Piano with its food stores and bars—perfect for an aperitif in the evening sun. Children will find contentment splashing in the pool, hiding in the garden or visiting the sheep, hens, cat and dog.

If you need to stay in touch, you can at least do it Italian style in the garden under the "internet tree" in the company of the bees and the birds.

Sperello di Serègo Alighieri

Villa Aureli,
via Luigi Cirenei 70, 06132 Castel del Piano
- 4 apartments: 1 for 4, 1 for 4–8, 1 for 6, 1 for 5. €700–€1,500 per week.
- Occasional dinner with wine, €36. Restaurant 2km.
- +39 340 6459061
- www.villaaureli.it
- Train station: Perugia

La Palazzetta del Vescovo

UMBRIA

Polished perfection and professionalism run through the veins of La Palazzetta. Its owners are a delightful couple that fled the strains of their careers in marketing to reconnect with people—and to gather a little serenity.

They brought considerable skills from their former life—not least their languages: French, English and Spanish—and gently transplanted them to great effect here in Umbria. The house is beautiful, a magnet for visitors, and so is the food. They take huge pride in what they have done and it is fun as a visitor to be immersed in it all. "We did not move to make money," says Stefano. "We came to reclaim ourselves, to make the sort of connections with people and nature that are difficult to forge in corporate life when you are rushed and stressed." To further their aim of reducing stress in their guests, there is massage available in the old cellars, an easy-going labrador called Chiaretta, wine-tastings in the cantina and every possible inducement to slow down and relax.

Here only the bells from a nearby convent or the hum of the tractor will disturb your thoughts. The 18th-century

hilltop Palazzetta—once a summer residence for the bishops of Todi, utterly abandoned in the 1960s—was bought by Paola and Stefano in 2000.

They began the restoration in 2004 and by 2006 had created four cool, elegant sitting rooms and nine lovely bedrooms in subtle, muted colors. Some have muslin-draped four-posters, some have antiques gathered from Naples, some hand-painted cupboards and bedside tables. They are all beautifully furnished but unpretentious—not an unusual Italian achievement. Even the fabrics are delightful: handmade covers on the beds, fluffy towels and bathrobes, and Quagliotti linen sheets.

Everything about the house seems generous. To add to all this, each room has a head-clearing view over steeply falling vineyards and the Tiber valley. Stupendous! On a clear day you can see as far as Perugia. The newly-planted gardens, the terrace and the infinity pool give you those same, ineffable, views.

Paola's mother is Umbrian and family connections drew them here, as did the authenticity (their word) of the region. "Umbria is not geared

around tourists in the way that Tuscany can be. No
doubt Tuscany is beautiful but sometimes it can feel
too busy, busy with tourists who make little
connection with real rural activity," says Stefano.

Paola is a patron chef with considerable flair,
taking organic, local ingredients and traditional
recipes then adding her own twist with unexpected
flavors and combinations of ingredients. She and
Stefano, a sommelier, respect the Slow Food
movement for protecting artisan food producers
who hold out against EU hygiene regulations. "Take
Lardo di Colonnata. It has been made for centuries
in northern Tuscany by putting the pork belly fat in
a marble sink with salt and spices and leaving it
for six months. It is part of Italy's culture and
identity," asserts Stefano, "but suddenly it was not
going to be allowed because of health fears. The
Slow Food movement awarded it a Presidio status
and has saved it from being banned."

Stefano and Paola have done a lot to reduce
the environmental impact of their business. There
are automatic light sensors, rainwater tanks,
careful policy on laundering towels, and they have
not only reused old materials in the renovation but
have used furnishings made with natural fibers.

The time they have clawed back for themselves
has, then, been put to a greater good. "We take
time over important things and being with people
is our greatest reward. We spend time with people
in their best moments and a big part of our salary
is the sheer fun."

Paola Maria & Stefano Zocchi

La Palazzetta del Vescovo,
via Clausura 17, Fr. Spineta, 06054 Fratta Todina
• 9 doubles, €180–€260. Singles €125–€180.
• Lunch, on request, €15–€25, . Dinner, 4 courses, €40.
• +39 0758 745183
• www.lapalazzettadelvescovo.com
• Train station: Marsciano

I Mandorli Agriturismo

UMBRIA

Wanda, mother and grandmother, is the overseer of this 45-hectare estate. With her three daughters, Maria, Alessandra and Sara, and their daughters, you have the privilege of seeing Italian family life in action.

I Mandorli is a higgledy-piggledy house with little steps here and there leading to rooms and apartments, outhouses, lofts, old olive mills. Flowers tumble from pots, capers scale stone walls and fruit and cypress trees give shade in the garden. Bedrooms are sweet, simple affairs with new wrought-iron beds and pale homemade patchwork quilts; the small bathrooms are spotless.

The vineyard is managed organically; vegetables and sunflowers are grown and there is a little outlet for the estate's produce; you can buy wine, lentils, oils and jams to take home. Sara says: "Guests can relax into our lives here, wander on our land, pick herbs, help with the olive harvest, take cookery lessons, cycle, walk and go rafting. Children will love the wooden slide and seesaw, the old pathways and steps on this shallow hillside, the new pool

—wonderful to return to after outings to Assisi and Spoleto.

Umbria is rich in festivals, too, particularly in October. There are solemn processions honoring patron saints in January, a jollier San Feliciano feast day on 24 January, a San Emiliano feast day on 28 January, and in October a medieval fair in Trevi. You can visit the oldest olive tree in Umbria just across the road or go to Assisi to see Giotto's frescoes in the basilica; it is hard to know in which direction to head first.

The family understands that most guests lead lives more stressful than they would wish. Sara speaks with poetic eloquence: "For people in every corner of the world, work is characterized by stress, deadlines and daily battles. We want people to stop, to enjoy a moment of peace. It is essential to their spiritual well-being. We want to give our guests space to experience these moments.

"We are lucky that our family has been so deeply rooted in the countryside, living among the olive trees for more than three centuries. Our culture here is born from a deep respect for everything

that nature offers us. The unexpected death of our father was a great shock. When we were little we used to follow him as he worked on the farm, in the countryside and woodland. He would always stop to explain what he was doing—and why. After school we'd head for the olive groves to meet the women who harvested the fruit. They would sing and chant as they worked, and tell us stories. These beautiful memories, and many more, made us carry on with it all when he died. It is our passion and we want to continue his good work."

The whole family speaks of the bond between man and nature, the need to value the earth not just as a producer but as a creator of tradition. The idea of agritourism is to unite guests with family traditions and regional stories and history. The Zappelli Cardarellis remain faithful to the philosophy.

I Mandorli is aptly named: there's at least one almond tree outside each apartment. The blossom in February is stunning and, in summer, masses of greenery shades the old *casa padronale*.

Each daughter speaks a different foreign language, so nobody is excluded from the conviviality of the house. Guests are helped with their itineraries and the sisters promote walking and biking—even if just through the olive groves, for there are over 5,000 of them.

"We believe the pivotal thing here, in this sea of green that surrounds us, is that each person who comes can find a different way of being."

Famiglia di Zappelli Cardarelli

I Mandorli Agriturismo,
loc. Fondaccio 6, fraz. Bovara, 06039 Trevi
- 1 twin/double, 2 triples. €40–€85.
  3 apartments: 1 for 2, 2 for 4. €65–€150.
- Restaurant 800m.
- +39 0742 78669
- www.agriturismoimandorli.com
- Train station: Trevi 3km; Foligno 15km

La Torretta

LAZIO

"Slow has been the story of our lives." So says Maureen Scheda, speaking for herself and for her architect husband Roberto.

Maureen had, like many of us, a red-hot passion for Italy, its history, language and art. Unlike many of us, she moved to Italy to embrace all that she held dear. In the 60s she left Wales for Rome, met Roberto and married him in '68. But after having two children, Rome was not Slow enough and Maureen's thoughts were turning to the idea of living in a medieval hilltop village.

They gave up lucrative careers and plumped for a move to Casperia—a higgledy-piggledy joyful, vibrant village perched in the Sabine hills. Maureen opened a small craft shop where she sold wooden dolls and the woolen clothes she made on her own loom. In the workshop next door, Roberto designed and made wooden furniture. Meanwhile, their search for a family house had begun and soon after their arrival in Casperia, they found their dream home in La Torretta. The 15th-century, dilapidated palazzo was waiting to be rescued from dereliction and this talented, visionary pair were ready.

Roberto poured his heart, soul and architectural talent into its restoration. "He used skilled local labor, he made furniture and even, one sweltering summer, 20 huge solid doors," remembers Maureen. "We kept all material and work faithful to the period."

It is a stunning, lofty house with dreamy views and beautiful interior spaces, such as: a huge, ground-floor sitting room with frescoes around the cornice, a giant fireplace, modern sofas and chairs, books, paintings and piano. The upper room, where meals are taken, is a stunning, vaulted, contemporary space with an impressive kitchen of Carrara marble and views through skylights to the church tower and valley. The terrace views are spectacular.

Pasta alla Rocca

3 onions, chopped
75 g (3 oz) butter
2 large yellow peppers, puréed
1 cup water
150 g (6 oz) gorgonzola cheese, crumbled
splash of cream
small handful parmesan cheese
500 g (1 lb) Farfalle pasta
parsley, chopped, and pepper to garnish

• Melt butter in a large pan, fry onions until soft.
• Add puréed peppers, stir and cover and cook until soft and thickened for about 40 minutes. Add a little water if dry.
• Add gorgonzola and cream and leave on low heat while you cook the pasta.
• Add pasta to sauce, toss and serve topped with parmesan, parsley and pepper.

Step out and you will understand why German historian Gregorovius wrote in *Wandering in Italy* "In all my travels I've never beheld a panorama of such heroic beauty."

Maureen had, quietly, another ambition. "Our goal was that our work would help to revitalize the village. So many people were seeking work in the cities, abandoning their beautiful birthplaces for a humdrum life of commuting. We wanted to show them what treasures they had right here in Casperia, that it could be possible to live and work in the village."

Her hunch was that if the Casperia villagers embraced their birthplace then tourists looking for a "real" Italy would be drawn there.

"I wanted to do what I could to attract visitors. I worked in tourism after moving here and became a tour director. We have battled with local authorities to preserve the environment and the identity of the village. We have made progress and

Casperia now knows a little tourism. Other bed and breakfasts run by local people have opened, there

> "Our goal was that our work would help revitalize the village"

are three restaurants, a yoga retreat and an ever-growing interest in Slow food.

"We have been a member of the Slow Food movement since it started and now have our own leader in Casperia and 26 members. I did a program with the BBC's Countryfile program introducing the conviviums and their work here."

Maureen and Roberto organize walking holidays and climbing holidays, too—one of her daughters is a qualified instructor and the other runs cookery courses. Their local Slow Food expert organizes wine and olive oil tastings and they have hosted international voluntary workers

striving to keep open the local "no asphalt" walking paths.

Maureen and Roberto would get a medal from us if we had one. Expatriates are so often out of tune with their communities, bringing in alien ideas and subtly undermining traditions. But Maureen, with Roberto's support, has sailed her little ship into battle with the invading world of Fast with the vigor and determination, let alone the panache, of a whole fleet.

Roberto & Maureen Scheda

La Torretta,
via G. Mazzini 7, 02041 Casperia
- 5 doubles, €90. 1 single, €70.
  2 connecting rooms for a family, €150.
- Dinner with wine €30, by arrangement.
- +39 0765 63202
- www.latorrettabandb.com
- Train station: Poggio Mirteto

Campania
Puglia
Basilicata

Sicily & Aeolian Islands

[THE SOUTH]

THE SOUTH

Southern Italy is a country apart; it saw the flowering of the ancient Greek colonies—the Magna Grecia—and was home to great philosophers, moralists, mathematicians and scientists. Later the Romans took over, then northern European tribes. Then Islamic, Norman and Byzantine invaders came, stayed and went, each bringing their culture, their learning and their style of architecture.

From the 14th century until Italy was unified in 1860, southern Italy was known as "The Kingdom of the Two Sicilies"; the combined kingdoms of Naples and Sicily. Naples was the capital and Palermo the second city. At different times the Aragonese, Angevin, Bourbon and Bonaparte dynasties all held the strings and left their mark.

The south is not new to tourism. The English gentry on their Grand Tours loved staying in Venice, Florence and Rome but the hospitality they loved best was found in Naples and Sicily; gastronomic and cultural encounters with their hosts there were enjoyed as much as the architectural gems of the rest of the country.

Each region has its own character but shares the same palette: the gold of durum wheat, the white peaks of craggy mountains, the silver of a shimmering sea and of olive leaves, the rich hues of fertile earth burnished by the rawness of the southern sun.

Seafood, mountain lamb and goat are easy to find, and the wild herbs and vegetables grown in small-holdings are artfully used with each. The olive oil and wine are exceptional. This is a land that has known hard times and its now-famous cuisine—particularly in Puglia—has always used whatever the climate and land allowed. Homemade bread and pasta are fragrant and delicious; it seems there is a home-rolled pasta shape for every day of the year. The region's

"southern Italy is striding into the future with confidence"

cheeses—burrata, mozzarella, scamorza, manteca, provola, caciocavallo—are famous worldwide.

No one has tasted a real pizza, nor *mozzarella di bufala*, until they have been to Napoli, nor savored a tomato until they have bitten into a pomodoro San Marzano. **Campania** is the home of the people's dish, *spaghetti al pomodoro*. It is also the home of the courtly *timballo di maccheroni*, the *sartu' di riso* and the Lacryma Cristi del Vesuvio wine.

See the jewels of the Amalfi coast from a new perspective, from the "steps of the Gods". Well-signed shepherds' paths run between Amalfi, Positano and Equense, winding through lemon groves and beehives and past smallholders working the land. The classical music of the Ravello Music Festival is performed against unforgettable backdrops.

Puglia is neighbor to Campania and there are only 130 miles between the Adriatic and Tyrrhenian Seas here. The National Park of Gargano is a promontory that juts out into the Adriatic. You'll find myriad flora, a vertiginous coastline and coastal land bars that separate the lakes of Lesina and Varano from the Adriatic. The Foresta Umbra is a rare example of a prehistoric Mediterranean landscape. The area also has the Parco Eolico dell'Alberone, one of the largest alternative energy plants in Europe.

The spiritual life of the south is legendary and all saints are celebrated with extraordinary displays of devotion, parades and feasting. The **Basilicata** landscape is animated with places of worship— pagan and profound—built over the millennia. The prehistoric Sassi of Matera, now a World Heritage site, is where Benedictine and Greek monks once lived in caves and churches carved out of the rock. Genoese architect Renzo Piano, who co-designed the Pompidou Center in Paris, has designed a cathedral in local stone to honor one of the Catholic church's most recent saints, Padre Pio. Some say it is the most popular and striking pilgrimage shrine ever built.

There is a growing literary scene in Matera inspired by Isabella Morra, a poet and one of the few female voices from the Renaissance. Author Carlo Levi lived at Aliano and his home is now a museum of rural life; in his book *Christ Stopped at Eboli,* he described the tragedy of the south in the 1930s at the time of the mass migrations.

The recipes of Basilicata often include chili, goat's cheese, pork sausages dried and preserved in olive oil, and *lampascioni*, wild onions. The finest wine is Aglianico del Vulture, from grapes grown on volcanic slopes; Malvasia del Vulture is a straw-colored slightly sweet wine.

In Palermo in **Sicily**, seven days a week, you will encounter thriving markets as vibrant as any souk. Try some *panelle rici'ciri*, chickpea fritters, as you lose yourself in the maze. On Sunday take a train to its seaside satellite and lunch with the locals; crack open *ricci* (sea urchins) and taste the sea. Check out the *pasticceria* and the *gelati con panna* (they claim that ice cream was invented here).

Disappear into the mountains from Siracusa and explore the Pantalica gorge on foot or take a trek on horseback. In June, immerse yourself in the Classical Greek Theater Festival in the ruins.

The south is scattered with small towns animated by traditions and by people who respect the food they produce and who have a powerful sense of belonging. Don't be fooled into thinking that you have stepped back into another era; southern Italy is treasuring its history, yet striding into the future with confidence.

Lindy Wildsmith

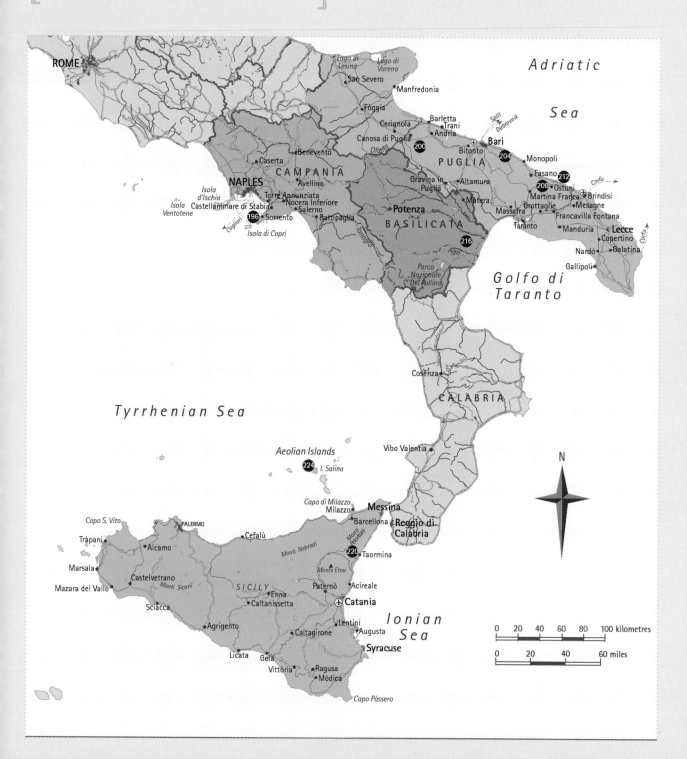

ROME

Lago di Lesina
Lago di Vareno
San Severo
Manfredonia
Fóggia
Cerignola
Barletta
Trani
Andria
Split
Dubrovnik

Adriatic

Sea

Canosa di Puglia
Ofanto
200
Bitonto
Bari
204
Monopoli

Caserta
Benevento
PUGLIA
Altamura
Fasano
212
Corfu

CAMPANIA
Avellino
Gravina in Puglia
208
Ostuni
Brindisi

NAPLES
Isola d'Ischia
Torre Annunziata
Nocera Inferiore
Matera
Martina Franca
Mesagne

Isola Ventotene
Castellammare di Stabia
Salerno
Massafra
Grottaglie
Francavilla Fontana

196
Sorrento
Battipaglia
Potenza
Taranto
Manduria
Lecce

Cogliani
Isola di Capri
Tanagro
BASILICATA
Copertino
Corfu

Agri
216
Nardó
Galatina

Parco Nazionale Del Pollino
Golfo di Taranto
Gallipoli

Tyrrhenian Sea

Cosenza

CALABRIA

Vibo Valentia

Aeolian Islands
224
I. Salina

N

Capo di Milazzo
Milazzo
Messina

Capo S. Vito
PALERMO
Cefalù
Barcellona
Reggio di Calabria

Tràpani
Alcamo
Monti Nebrodi
Monti Peloritani
220
Taormina

Marsala
Monte Etna
Acireale

Castelvetrano
Monti Sicani
SICILY
Paternò

Mazara del Vallo
Enna
Catania

Sciacca
Caltanissetta
Lentini
Ionian Sea

Agrigento
Caltagirone
Augusta

Licata
Gela
Ragusa
Syracuse

Vittòria
Módica

Capo Pássero

0 20 40 60 80 100 kilometres

0   20   40   60 miles

Special places to stay

Campania

196   Azienda Agricola Le Tore

Puglia

200   Lama di Luna – Biomasseria

204   Masseria Serra dell'Isola

208   Masseria Il Frantoio

212   Masseria Impisi

Basilicata

216   San Teodoro Nuovo Agriturismo

Sicily & Aeolian Islands

220   Hotel Villa Schuler

224   Hotel Signum

Azienda Agricola Le Tore

CAMPANIA

For over 200 years, oils and wines have flowed from Le Tore. When Vittoria took over the 18th-century farm 25 years ago she reinvigorated not only the land but, it seems, the whole community. With the help of locals she renovated buildings, planted lemon and olive groves, orchards and vegetable gardens, created a dining room from the old cantina and made generous bedrooms from high-ceilinged—Volte Sorrentine—rooms. Antonio, one of her helpers, has been with her for 26 years, tending the crops, propping up the fruit trees, putting the land to rest in autumn and managing heroically when things spring to life after winter. He manages the small weekly market, too; Le Tore has such abundant produce that they sell to local families and restaurateurs.

Vittoria is eloquent on the subject of agritourism for which Italy is famous—and for which she is qualified to speak, for she is President of the Associazione Nazionale per l'Agriturismo.

"Much of Europe has rural tourism but in Italy the association between accommodation and farming is especially close. If during your stay on an *agriturismo* you can't see farm work, you can be sure that it is happening somewhere; maybe grain is being processed off-site or grapes will have already been sent for pressing locally. Always, the owner will be connected to the land and will have a real desire to bring the guest closer to the activity of the rural community."

"Local *agriturismi* work well together, too. Among us we find everyone a bed," says Vittoria. "At certain times of year those of us who grow the same crops can't cope with B&B, so farmers who are growing different crops lend us a hand and take in guests. Then we reverse roles at their harvest time." It is a harmonious environment in which to

live, work or run a business, one in which work and pleasure are more closely intertwined than in urban areas. Working around people's talents and

> "In *agriturismi*, the owners are connected to the land and have a real desire to bring the guest closer to the rural community"

needs means that much can be achieved. "With a spirit of collaboration so much more is possible," says Vittoria wisely.

You can see, at the many festivals, the reverence given to farm produce. There is the Palm Sunday Carnival that celebrates pigs, for example, and there are fairs around the *vendemmia* (grape) and apple harvests. Many Italian farms, 15%-20%, are certified as organic and there is a high concentration of organic farms in Southern Italy.

Many of them are small-scale and have benefited from hilly sites: the breezes reduce the incidence of disease and pests. The main production on this AIAB (Italian Association for Biological Agriculture)-certified farm is olive oil and Vittoria's newest customers are the Japanese. "It's not only the oils that they like, but everything needed to make pizza and even pizza ovens. We sell 1,000 bottles of oil a year to Japan."

You can sample all these wonderful ingredients dining with other guests and taking your aperitifs together in the courtyard. Among other specialities, you are likely to have purée of broad bean with chicory, calamari salad, marinated anchovies, grilled home-grown vegetables with their own lemon, Ovale di Sorrento. Vittoria is usually there and is worth quizzing if you are planning to explore. She did a thesis on the micro-climate of the Amalfi coast so knows almost every inch, its beaches, flora, fauna and undiscovered

corners. She can point you to paths such as the CAI-marked Alta Via di Lattari that runs along the southern side of the peninsula.

Le Tore is 500 meters above sea level and on the crest of the hill of Sant'Agata sui due Golfi that divides the sunny dry gulf of Amalfi from the greener and more humid Gulf of Sorrento. You can drop down to coast level—around 15 minutes' drive, one hour's walk—for boats to Capri, Ischia and Naples; Pompeii, Ercolano and Oplonti are 45 minutes by train from Sorrento.

It is refreshing to find a place like Le Tore in an area that, down at sea level, is more known for its swish bars, its sailing fraternity, and "smart" coastline that seduces international travellers. Here you are in touch with the people who help to sustain the local economy, providing wonderful produce for many of those bars and restaurants.

Vittoria is a dynamic, busy lady who is, quite properly, more interested in agriculture than in tourism. But she takes pride in all she does, so sweeping travellers into her daily embrace is natural for her. One guest said: "What a joy to spend time at such an authentic place. Vittoria, ever kind, even gave us an Italian cooking lesson before dinner."

This passion for good food is, of course, at the heart of the Slow movement—a bright light at the end of the dark tunnel of fast and lifeless food that is doing so much to tear our communities apart. Italy, with all its Vittorias, is leading the way.

Signora Vittoria Brancaccio

Azienda Agricola Le Tore, via Pontone 43, Sant'Agata sui Due Golfi, 80064 Massa Lubrense
- 4 doubles, 1 twin, 1 family room. €90. 1 apartment for 5, €700–€1,000 per week.
- Dinner €25, by arrangement. Restaurant 5-min walk.
- +39 0818 080637
- www.letore.com
- Train station: Sorrento

Lama di Luna Biomasseria

PUGLIA

Forty-four families once lived in this substantial dwelling in Murgia, and the place still has the feel of a center for the wider community. The extended families lived around the courtyard with the bread oven in the center—an efficient way of sharing resources and bringing people together over a common activity.

When Pietro bought the place in 1990 he had no idea that his grandmother's sister had sold it out of the family in 1820, so he had, through pure and delightful chance, done the proper thing by bringing it back into the family. He immediately ousted errant sheep and began to treat the land with deep respect.

It is a most handsome and traditional farm that began in the 17th century and, after years of neglect, is going strong again. Pietro claims that it is the most perfectly integrated organic farm in Italy, and it may well be, with his passion for the environment and his respect for tradition and craftsmanship reaching into every crevice.

Shapes are rounded, there is nothing chemical in the rooms, no dyes, no bleaches; the beds are positioned north to south to ensure more peaceful sleep; each bedroom has its own fireplace—and once housed an entire family! Guests now also have a library to retreat to and a generous veranda for sunset and star-gazing.

Pietro has created his own laundry to avoid the chemicals used by outside laundries. Tiles, and even basins, are made by hand and to traditional methods; bed linen is unbleached, mattresses are of natural latex and tablecloths and curtains are of hessian; the walls have been lime-washed rather than painted, the furniture polished with linseed oil; reclaimed wood has been used for doors and the food, of course, is devotedly organic.

This is a land of sunshine, with Foggia rated as the hottest city in Italy. So it is right that 48 solar panels bring the sun's heat to the floor's underside, and the boiler is fuelled by olive nuts—in plentiful supply and otherwise wasted. Rainwater is "harvested" from the roof and taken to a vast underground tank—as all rainwater should be. It is curious how rarely this is done nowadays. Even the Georgians in England would run their roof-water into below-street vaults.

> "Shapes are rounded, there is nothing chemical in the rooms, no dyes, no bleaches; the beds are positioned north to south to ensure more peaceful sleep"

There are 190 hectares of organic farm, largely flat, surrounding the house—a serious guarantor of high-quality food. There are olives, cherries, almonds and grapes, all certified to the highest standards. Puglia is no slouch in the food department, producing a wonderful, creamy-buttery cheese called burrata—served at breakfast here with homemade cakes and jams, orchard fruits and other local cheeses—it also produces vast quantities of almonds and olive oil from trees on the vast plains of the Murgia. In September there is a cheese festival in Andria, with the *corteo storico*—a parade in medieval costume.

There are fruits and vegetables galore, wheat and wines to remember for their strength and vitality. Most of them are red, and many years ago used to be sent to Turin to make vermouth and to France to bulk out the wine harvest in thin years. The coast yields fish and seafood in prodigious quantities, with mussels and oysters from Taranto. Most of Puglia's meat comes from the very different, and slightly hilly, northern area of Foggia.

Puglia has been so little known outside Italy, to the world of tourism, that its towns and villages come as a delightful surprise to visitors. Lecce was built between 1660 and 1720, in high-baroque style and of a local golden stone. Comparisons with Florence may seem bizarre, but they are made. Martina Franca is another town of timeless beauty, with a piazza, the Piazza Roma, that some consider to be Italy's finest. Trani was a prosperous port in the Middle Ages and impressive churches, castles and Palazzo are testimony to its standing. All this magnificence has had its impact on the people too, as you will see with Pietro.

He is a lovely man, bursting with passion for his enterprise and totally—authentically—committed to using his imagination and green convictions in every aspect of it all. He is a great ally to have if you are searching for a deeper understanding of the area.

Another plus is his dry sense of humor, an essential tool for anyone who has guests to stay. I leave you with his own words: "Lama di Luna is the house where I live with my children, where I pick the fruits that nature and our work give us, among cats, dogs, goslings, geese, barn-owls and sparrows. Today everyone can share the magic sensations of this part of the Murgia."

Pietro Petroni

Lama di Luna Biomasseria,
loc. Montegrosso, 70031 Andria
- 10 twins/doubles, €140–€200.
- Dinner with wine, €25. Restaurants 2km.
- +39 0883 569505
- www.lamadiluna.com
- Train station: Barletta

Masseria Serra dell'Isola

PUGLIA

The old *masseria* (large farm) may not immediately bewitch you, but its interior and its history will. With Rita's warmth, humor, pride and gift for animatedly recounting her family's history, it will all prove impossible to resist.

"I open my home out of a love for Puglia. My great pleasure is to lead those who come to visit towards paths and scenery that are rarely seen. My descriptions, in the words of someone who has spent her life here, are my gifts to my guests. In our agricultural civilization, giving is not an indefinite and anonymous exchange of presents, it means sharing something precious. Sharing is the foundation of this society and in a world that spins around the individual, we should rediscover the genuine joy of it."

What a delightful way of articulating her way of being. It is thanks to passionate Puglians like Rita that it is such a privilege to learn more about these lesser-known areas, their customs, traditions, food and people. She and her fellow Puglians are doing a grand job: southern cuisine has a growing army of fans, as do the area's Truilli houses, coastline and archaeological riches.

Rita eloquently describes the history of the Norman, Swabian and Angevin castles in Bari, the Romanesque cathedrals and medieval villages like Polignano and Monopoli. "Outside the whitewashed walls of my *masseria* I introduce my guests to the things so easily missed by the hurried tourist."

Her 18th-century *masseria* is well worth getting to know too. Built by her ancestors in 1726 as an olive mill and summer residence, the house has an impressive library of books on history, art and cookery. Rita has hand-written recipes from her great-grandmother's kitchen,

recipes that she still uses for *rosoli* (liquors), jams, and cakes; she will happily share them with you.

The great hall has uneven stone floors and once housed the olive mill. It is, like the rest of the house, filled with portraits and antiques. The light, gracious bedrooms are named after the women who once occupied them—Donnas Angelina, Ritella, Annina—and the elegant old beds bear fine new mattresses.

Rita explains a little of her previous life: "I studied law as a student, then I became a journalist working on a daily newspaper. I reported on environmental and agricultural issues and then worked for the International Center for Advanced Mediterranean Agronomic Studies. Now I am working with Bari University, helping them with research into natural fertilizers for our land."

In 1992 she was awarded a prize for her outstanding environmental essays. "Now I dedicate myself to the study of Puglia's history," she

Cartellate (Christmas pastries)

For the dough:
330 g (13 oz) flour
70 g (2.5 oz) olive oil
half teaspoon salt

For glazing and decoration:
500 g (1 lb) honey or half liter *vincotto* (grape syrup)
1 glass of water or white wine
caster sugar
ground cinnamon

• Mix flour, oil and salt into a dough and roll out very thinly. Cut into 15-cm long finger-width strips. Curl each strip to form a rose shape (use your imagination!). Fry roses in a little olive oil.
• Warm up the honey or the vincotto then add the water/white wine. Bring to boil. Dunk the roses into the syrup, dust with sugar and cinnamon. Serve cold.

explains, "and the southern Italian identity, and I am also writing a travel guide."

Puglia, curiously, was ruled by the Byzantines for over two centuries and flowered magnificently under the Hohenstaufen Emperors. In the 13th century, under Frederic II, palaces and cathedrals were built on a grand scale, but Puglia went into a long decline thereafter and knew only rule by other foreigners, slave raids on the coast, and growing poverty. It was not until 1860, when it became part of the new Italian nation, that things began to look up. They are looking better than ever right now, with tourism giving the region a much-needed lift.

It is an honor, then, if Rita is available, to have her guide you personally through markets, historic sites, cookery lessons. Her food is all homemade, from produce mostly grown here, and accompanied by local wines. There is a real spirit of conviviality when the house is full and everyone gathers in the beautiful dining room. "I consider myself the guardian of a tradition and of a place where time and the frenetic rhythm of the metropolis are far away. The *masseria* isn't a character in search of an author or an ethereal mansion. It is a part of history and here it seems that time stopped centuries ago."

If you want to go slowly, it would be hard to begin at a better place.

Rita Guastamacchia

Masseria Serra dell'Isola,
S.P.165 Mola, Conversano n.35, 70042 Mola di Bari
- 4 doubles, 2 twins/doubles, €130.
  Whole house €3,300-€3,900 per week.
- Dinner, 3 courses, €35-€40. Wine €12-€18.
- +39 349 5311256 (mobile)
- www.masseriaserradellisola.it
- Train station: Mola di Bari, 4km

Masseria Il Frantoio

PUGLIA

"This corner of our world is rich in a deep and simple charm. The distances between villages are small; the countryside is peppered with vineyards, dry stone walls and white walled houses. It has a magic of its own."

That is Armando describing the delights of Puglia, down in the hot southern heel of Italy, and a fascinating landscape of mountains, plains, beaches and forests. Invaded and occupied numerous times, like most of Italy, it can draw upon a glittering array of cultural influences. Nearby Ostuni seems as Arabic as it is Italian. With its whitewashed houses and walls, it is known as "La Citta Bianca".

Il Frantoio is much loved for its food, especially for the eight-course meal that is a showcase for southern Italian cooking. Turn up during dinner and you may feel you have stumbled onto a film set: the courtyard twinkles with candles and sparkling glasses, music drifts from the house, Armando glides elegantly between the tables explaining the provenance and flavors of each little dish and of the wines he has chosen for you.

The *masseria* runs on well-oiled wheels, with each family member assigned a role that draws on his or her strengths. Daughter Serenella works alongside her husband Silvio and helper Giuseppe to look after the 72 hectares of olive groves and orchards; Armando looks after the staff, sources the wine and is very much "front of house;" Rosalba has worked magic within the house and the kitchens.

The farmhouse is centered on a 16th-century olive press; parts of it were built in 1544 and the 10 bedrooms are in the 19th-century part of the house. The visitors' quarter is a series of beautiful rooms, ranging from fairy tale with lace and toile to formal with antique armoires and gilt-framed

art. It is a gloriously eclectic mix. Despite the professional edge to this dynamic *masseria*, the homely touches are ever-present; linen and towels are washed in organic soap and line-dried. There is a kitchen for guests to use, sitting rooms and a library. The 16th-century citrus garden, with lemon, orange and mandarin trees and the odd peacock, is alive with colors and fragrances.

From the kitchen garden, nurtured by Abele, come vegetables, herbs and edible flowers. Rosalba

> "We conduct ourselves in a way that is at one with nature. Guests say what we are doing is special but we are simply behaving in a way that should be normal for everybody"

oversees the menus and she and her six chefs create elaborate flavors with simple ingredients; a different olive oil is used in each of the eight courses. "We reproduce centuries-old local recipes; food in the south comes from a long history of peasant dishes," explains Armando. "Specialists worldwide have recognised the diet of Puglia as a healthy one. It goes without saying that we work with seasonal produce."

They also make liquor, jams, pickles, preserves and pâtés to ensure that none of their crops go to waste; you can buy jars to take home. Armando and his helpers can guide you around the cellars and explain the workings of the impressive olive press. Rosalba's collection of antique christening robes and fabrics are on show, too. The library has over 1,500 books rescued from the cellars and each has been cleaned and restored.

The *masseria* is almost a world in itself. But it is very much part of Puglia and that special landscape. The lush Itrian Valley is rich in

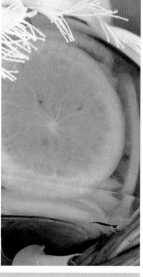

archaeological sites. Seven kilometers away are the Adriatic beaches, some lively with cafes and music and others protected nature reserves where the coastline is fringed with dunes and rich with the fragrance of herbs that grow among the wild grasses. The Oasis of Torre Guaceto is a nature reserve protected by the World Wildlife Fund.

There is a palpable sense of contentment among all who work at Frantoio. Staff are treated as if they were family, which creates a lovely atmosphere. Giuseppe is the olive expert and seems to know each tree; Thea and Lilly provide breakfast and bake the cakes; Silvana welcomes you and looks after the practicalities of your stay. The passion of the Balestrazzi couple is infectious and you cannot fail to be touched by their respect for nature, the history of the area and of the house.

Armando and Rosalba see themselves as guardians of the impressive *masseria*, judiciously mixing modern and traditional ideas. Armando refers to his olive trees as the "patrons" of the old *masseria*. "Thanks to these great veterans, some of which are the oldest and largest of their kind, we can carry on producing our exceptional extra virgin olive oil." A farmer with less sensitivity might well chop them down and replant with more "efficient" trees.

"We conduct ourselves in a way that is at one with nature. Guests say that what we are doing is special but we say that we are simply behaving in a way that should be normal for everybody."

Silvana Caramia

Masseria Il Frantoio,
SS 16km 874, 72017 Ostuni
- 3 doubles, 2 triples, 3 family rooms. €176–€220. Apartment for 2–4, €319–€350.
- Dinner with wine, €55, by arrangement.
- +39 0831 330276
- www.masseriailfrantoio.it
- Train station: Ostuni

Masseria Impisi

PUGLIA

You may know Masseria Impisi from the UK's Channel 4 Grand Designs program: Kevin McCloud came to witness its renovation by the enterprising David and Leonie and was blown away by what they had achieved. This likeable pair of artists took an abandoned olive farm, with tumble-down cattle stalls and, under the scrutiny of television cameras and on a budget of £19,000, created a Romanesque colonnaded house that is hard to resist.

On that budget David and Leonie's only choice was to do the work themselves. Their back-breaking efforts and wide-ranging artistic talents combined to create something so remarkable that they were inundated with requests from people wanting to take part in one of their "Il Collegio" holidays, or just to stay and see for themselves the finished *masseria*.

They were in danger of becoming victims—albeit happy ones—of their own success. It wasn't easy looking after as many as 14 guests, cooking three meals a day, helping them in their artwork or touring around Puglia with them was demanding.

"We were incredibly busy after the program," says David.

"We had been offering this sort of holiday for 16 years so our experience carried us through but it couldn't last. We had promised ourselves that we would run a business, not let it run us."

So, they did what we all dream of doing; they stepped back and took a long, hard look at their lives.

"We change what we do every year. Demand was still there for the courses but we wanted to punctuate the year with pauses to enjoy our home and explore new things. We wanted, too, to get back in touch with our lives as artists, to do more experimental work."

Leonie, who did the intricate mosaic work around the *masseria*, is a professional painter, was a lecturer at Falmouth College of Art and has held Artist in Residence posts. Her interest is Medieval and Early Renaissance art. David, who has made furniture and created carvings for their Italian home, graduated from Falmouth then did post-graduate studies in drawing and sculpture at the Slade School of Art. No wonder they were able to create a place of such beauty.

After much soul-searching, they decided to offer just two

or three courses a year, though artists who are happy to operate under their own steam can still use the studio facilities. People can choose to do B&B or to self-cater and David and Leonie can organize sailing, snorkeling and riding. The Via Triana Cycle Trail follows the old Roman road along the coast and you can set off on the *masseria's* free bikes. The couple's past experience of organizing art and gastronomic holidays means they have stacks of useful local advice.

They have created one apartment for two in a 15th-century gatehouse, one further apartment for two and have two more double rooms. They have hosted weddings—their olive mill room can take up to 40 people—and will take care of the legalities of marriage and help in many practical ways.

Their gardens are a lush oasis among the olive plains. They are in a tiny valley and are watered by their own well and harvested grey water. Among it all, flanked by Leonie's mosaics, is a pool hewn from the limestone rock. They are working on a little eco-dwelling to house the young students who come to help keep the grounds and the house looking so lovely.

David and Leonie are delighted that Puglia is finally being recognized: its reputation as a destination for foodies is well-earned and growing and its Slow credentials are impressive. It is largely a self-sustaining community, too, as so much produce is grown here.

The locals were helped by the European Agricultural Policy that dished out subsidies in the 60s and 70s to lift market gardens out of their moribund state. A quarter of Europe's wine is produced here and oil from the olive groves around Brindisi was among the first to be granted DOP (denomination of protected origin) status by the Italian ministry of agriculture. "Puglian farmers used to export their best produce, now they keep it here for themselves. And it is impossible to eat badly. Food is beautifully cooked and presented, and it is

great value. The number of restaurants with Slow Food status is growing apace."

Traditionally there has been a divide in Italy between Northern Italians and Southern. The south has been economically repressed while the rich north prospered on the back of big industry and cheap southern labor. But we are beginning to value natural wealth, particularly in times of economic turmoil and rising fuel prices.

"Northerners can be very rude about the Southerners. But the people here are rooted in the earth, they have used every patch of land to grow something, and the quality of their wine, oil and fresh produce is now acknowledged. Much of what is produced has been organic; they simply couldn't afford the fertilizers. The bulk of our food comes from within a 10-mile radius and the low transport costs make it far cheaper than elsewhere.

"There is an old-fashioned courtesy, too. If you ask someone directions to a restaurant, they are likely to walk you there. They feel duty-bound to look after visitors."

Ostuni has applied for World Heritage status and generally, David says, the South's self-respect is growing. It can compete on many fronts and is gathering respect worldwide. "Untangling all the threads of Puglia's history takes time," says David. "We are still discovering so much and slowing down will give us time to explore further. This area is magical."

Leonie Whitton & David Westby

Masseria Impisi,
Il Collegio, Contrada Impisi, 72017 Ostuni
- 2 twins/doubles, £50-£70 (min. stay 2 nights); 2 apartments for 2, £450-£550 per week.
- Dinner with wine, €25, by arrangement
- +39 340 360 2352
- www.ilcollegio.com
- Train station: Ostuni

San Teodoro Nuovo Agriturismo

BASILICATA

The Marchesa's sense of pride in San Teodoro Nuovo is delightfully obvious. Her openness and her enthusiasm for her old family home are palpable. She is from a land-owning family that has had estates in both Calabria and neighboring Basilicata and wears her considerable family history lightly. Her great-grandmother came to this house in 1870 when it was a hunting estate. The Duke and Duchess Marcello and Xenia Visconti di Modrone turned it into a farming estate in the early 20th century. The farm now specializes in organic citrus fruits, wheat, wine and olive oil; they produce their own vegetables, fruit, ricotta, eggs, honey and jam, too. It is best-known, though, as a producer of the best-quality organic table grapes that are sold throughout Europe. This a high-maintenance crop, especially as the grapes ripen, for even a heavy spell of rain can spoil a whole crop.

The rose-tinted house, flanked as it is with bougainvillea and majestic magnolia trees, makes up three sides of a square and is a cool haven from the southern sun. Further relief from the sun is provided by a green sea of citrus and olive groves. You can rent an apartment in a wing of the house, with family antiques and a balcony with tumbling jasmine, or choose one of four beautifully converted ones a short stroll away in the old stables where you can find the restaurant. Every room is elegantly furnished; each has a small parterre garden.

Inside and outside there is a sense of history and place. San Teodoro sits in the middle of Magna Grecia, once under Greek rule and where many majestic sites remain. The main towns of the Magna Grecia are Metaponto, Kroton and Sybaris; the Temple of Hera, just north of nearby Metaponto, is the

most complete of the ruins, with many of its Doric columns still standing.

Maria has added to the family's collection of art and almost every wall could grab your attention. "Our passion for art is fired by the Magna Grecia's rich cultural history," says Maria. "Our chapel in the grounds, in contrast with the house, however, is a simple, sacred space. We hold wedding services there and can welcome up to 100 guests; our family has used it for christenings since my great-grandmother's time. There is also a very old cemetery in the grounds that we intend to leave untouched, for to disturb it would disturb the spirit of the place."

There is another family property nearby—a 13th-century castle. Maria's grandmother owned Castello Berlingieri and Maria sometimes pops over with guests on informal visits. "Occasionally it's fun to show people around and we have a picnic in the gardens. They are always thrilled to be taken to a place not normally open to the public."

The bountiful estate produces enough to keep the kitchen staff busy. Your dinner, in the converted-stables restaurant, will be mostly organic produce from the estate or from selected local farms that sell DOP (denomination of protected origin) and IGP (indication of protected origin) produce, such as pepperoni from Senise, or beans from Sarconi. "We cook typical Basilicata dishes and we strive to work creatively, discovering new ideas for traditional recipes," explains Maria. "We are proud of our entry in the *Slow Food Italy* guide and our occasional cookery courses are popular. We explain how we grow our produce, how we prepare our dishes and we dine together. We take participants to local markets and producers, too, to introduce them to local culture."

The area is popular with artists, and particularly with ceramicists. Grottaglie, to which thousands of Albanians fled in the 15th century after the Ottomans tried to impose Islam upon them, has been the center of ceramics since the 10th century.

The streets are littered with pots and vessels to tempt tourists and it has a famous pottery school, the Instituto Statale d'Arte. Matera is fascinating, too, for its well preserved and very ancient cave dwellings—houses for peasants that were carved out of the steep rock face. The warren-like structures are not unlike Turkey's Cappadocia.

It is good to know that the future for San Teodoro is safe in the D'Oria family's hands. Of Maria's three children, one is in London and two are nearby and Maria is certain that they will, somehow, carry on. "Greeting guests personally and telling them about the history of our home is a gesture that makes a real difference. That is why people come to stay here rather than in a hotel." Indeed, once you have enjoyed San Teodoro it will be hard ever to enjoy anything less lovely.

Marchesa Maria Xenia D'Oria

San Teodoro Nuovo Agriturismo,
loc. Marconia, 75020 Marconia di Pisticci
- €120–€140 (€840–€980 per week).
  Half-board €80–€90 p.p.
- Dinner €25–€30, by arrangement.
- +39 0835 470042
- www.santeodoronuovo.com
- Train station: Metaponto

Hotel Villa Schuler

SICILY

"At the bottom, a high wall and a pink gateway... they were in a delicious garden descending a pergola of roses and grapes. Violets and freesias, geraniums and heliotropes spread in a dazzle of colour and sweetness under gnarled olives and almonds and blossoming plums; stone benches, bits of old marbles, a violet-fringed pool and a terrace leading down to a square white house, a smiling young German girl inviting them in, and then a view—dazzling even to their fatigued, dulled eyes. In front, a terrace, and then nothing but the sea, 700 feet below, the coastline melting on and off indefinitely to the right in great soft curves and upspringing mountains. They would have slept anywhere to belong to that."

The passage comes from a travel novel written in 1909, called *Seekers in Sicily*, and is a rich description of the Villa which was going strong as a Schuler family-owned hotel even then, at the time when Taormina was already a magnet for sophisticated travelers. From all over the world they came, to the sun-kissed slopes of Mount Etna and history-drenched views over the Bay of Naxos—but equally to the

artists' colony of the town that had been made famous by, among others, Goethe.

In fact Taormina had always attracted the famous—like Brahms and Wagner and, later, hordes of others, including King Edward VII, Cocteau, D.H. Lawrence and Marlene Dietrich. They still come.

Taormina has suffered a little, of course, from so much attention, and there is little green space left. What is left is the garden of the remarkable Villa Schuler, through which you may stroll up to the famous pedestrian street, the Corso Umberto. I use the word "remarkable" partly because of the touching way in which the family has managed to hang on to the house despite the appalling vicissitudes of two world wars. It was expropriated in both wars. After the first, local buyers, so pleased that Signor Schuler had returned to buy the house back, withdrew their own bids. After the second, the house was returned to the family, but in grim condition.

So the rebuilding has been painstaking and devoted. What has been recreated is a wonderfully handsome, up-to-date hotel with the charm and elegance of its own past. It is

cool, quiet, impeccably run, with tiled floors, antique furniture and stone balconies on one level and more modern rooms with large terraces at the top. In fact, they are as modern as can be, with WiFi, jacuzzis, and most of the gadgets you could possibly need.

In spite of the part-modernization, Villa Schuler can claim to be one of the greenest hotels in Italy. Gerhard seems to have thought of everything, so the following may seem like a litany of ecological achievement. But it is worth spelling out, even if briefly:

They have used traditional building methods and natural materials. The ventilation "system" cunningly uses the up-drafts from the sea. Toxic materials, blithely accepted by most, have been rigorously excluded—even electromagnetic "smog". Waste, of course, is separated and recycled to an

> "Sun heats the water, local farmers grow much of the food, natural fertilisers nourish the garden"

impressive degree. The sun heats the water, local farmers grow much of the food, natural fertilizers nourish the garden, ecological cleaners are applied to the walls and floors, clever devices will alarm and protect you in case of fire, fossil-fuels are treated with respect and water is conserved. Materials are natural (cotton towels, of course), disposables are reduced to a minimum, and all discarded furniture and equipment is donated to charity. The standards are set at the highest level and the hotel is ISO 14001 certified, which is about as good as it gets. Lastly, all the staff are involved in this commitment.

Gerhard says: "An important part of work has been helping our staff to understand our green philosophy. We encourage them to take their own green actions outside of the hotel, too."

The breakfast of regional specialities is chosen from a menu—rare in Italian places where one most often finds a buffet. Gerhard has chosen the menu option to make breakfast more relaxing—everything is brought to you—and to minimize waste and packaging; similarly they provide magazines for guests in communal rooms rather than newspapers, for there is less to recycle.

It is rare in the world of hotels to find a family so devoted to the family tradition. That, alone, is a seductive feature for those looking for Slow. But the long lazy afternoons in their garden (about which Gerhard and a horticultural expert are writing a book), the views over the sea and to Etna, the deep commitment to running a hotel with the lightest ecological touch—such things are enough to slow a person down.

And the family thrives there: Gerhard's two sons, Alessandro and Andrea, help him and Christine. "We are all totally committed," says Gerhard, "and will always strive to improve."

Christine Voss & Gerhard Schuler

Hotel Villa Schuler,
Piazzetta Bastione, via Roma, 98039 Taormina
- 21 doubles, 5 junior suites, €99–€206.
  Apartment for 2-4, €149–€390.
- Restaurants 100m (special prices for hotel guests).
- +39 0942 23481
- www.hotelvillaschuler.com
- Train station: Taormina-Giardini

Hotel Signum

AEOLIAN ISLANDS

Leave the car behind in Sicily and set off for the island of Salina by boat. The frenetic activity of the port behind you dissolves from memory as you behold the rugged beauty of the Aeolian island.

Salina, 90 minutes on the ferry from Sicily, is the second largest island in the Aeolian archipelago but only 27km across; you'll be able to borrow or hire bikes to explore. The island, a small patch of land floating in the sea between Naples to the north and Sicily to the south, can claim some fame: *Il Postino* was filmed here. The gentle storyline aroused curiosity all over the world. Nevertheless, the celebrity set and the flash yachts tend to head for the nearby islands of Lipari, Stromboli and Panarea, leaving Salina blissfully peaceful.

It is a volcanic island but the last eruption was a comforting 13,000 years ago, leaving underwater craters that still attract international divers. Naturalists are drawn to the diverse wildlife that lives among the myrtle and broom and forests of poplars and chestnuts. The coastal lake at Lingua in the south was a salt pan and sea salt was the island's main export—now replaced by capers, olives and the sweet Malvasia wine.

Salina, unlike many other small Italian communities, sees very little leakage of youth and talent to cities. Might family-run hotels be pivotal to the success of thriving communities? If so, the Signum can take some of the credit. The owners employ up to 30 staff in the summer and their philosophy of working with local fishermen, farmers and producers fuels the local economy. Clara Rametta-Caruso, Signum's owner and matriarch, feels that the island is a vibrant community and that the young have a sense of place, of belonging.

"There are only 2,500 people on the island so everybody knows everybody. The children like that, not resent it, and want to stay on the island and

work. We employ up to 40 people in summer and have more willing workers than we have jobs."

Clara and husband Michele can count on the help of their two children, too. Son Luca already knows a lot about running the hotel; daughter Matina is at Gambero Rosso's school in Rome. She is looking forward to joining her father full-time in Signum's kitchen. "Signum will always be family run," says Clara, "the children have always wanted to be involved."

Salina packs a punch for its size and there is a thriving ecotourism sector. "Six hotels have now applied for the European ecolabel and we are witnessing something of a revolution," says Clara. "I am on the tourism council and we try to preserve the island, protect it against environmental damage and set up new initiatives. We want to build a sustainable, year-round approach to tourism. Festivals such as the June Caper Festival and the Salina DOC Fest in September bring many people."

The friendly Signum has a special atmosphere that pulls people back again and again. It sits quietly at the end of a narrow lane and you'd hardly guess it was there, a promising start for a Slow destination. Dining on a terracotta terrace with chunky tile-topped tables and colorful iron and wicker chairs, you gaze out over lemon trees to the glistening sea. A winding labyrinth of paths, where plants flow and tumble, leads to simple and striking bedrooms with antiques, wrought-iron beds and starched lace fluttering at the windows. There is a beautiful infinity pool—that view again—or steps down to a quiet pebbly cove.

The Signum Spa uses one of the the island's best natural resources, geothermic waters, for restorative treatments. The waters emerge at a warming 30°C and are full of minerals said to enhance well-being. The Carusos have installed a 19th-century bathtub and a thermal stove inspired by those first used in Lipari 3,500 years ago; massages can, believe it or not, take place on a bed of rose-perfumed sea salt.

There are lemon scrubs, prickly pear and almond milk baths and orange blossom massage oils to induce further serenity. Swathes of linen fabric divide massage spaces in the tropical garden, and smiling staff further convince you that you have stumbled into a fairy tale oasis.

There is a sense of slow organic growth at Signum. They started with 16 rooms in 1988 and have increased the number to 30 by buying old properties nearby. "The feel is of a borgo—a self-contained village—rather than a hotel," says Clara.

The sense of self-sufficiency can lull you into "stasis". You need hardly step outside to experience island life, for with the lovely local staff and exceptional local food, the whole place is infused with Salina's easy-going spirit. You can arrive with a clear conscience, too: if you have no reason to come via Sicily you can just take the train to Naples then hop on a ferry.

Luca Caruso

Hotel Signum,
via Scalo 15, Malfa, 98050 Salina, Aeolian Islands
- 28 doubles, 2 singles, €130-€340.
- Dinner à la carte, €35-€45. Wine from €15.
- +39 0909 844222
- www.hotelsignum.it
- Train station: Milazzo

Italy on a bike

This book would not be complete without extolling the virtues of cycling in Italy...

"More and more people are intrigued by the charm of moving slowly in their moments of relaxation and leisure, on foot, by bicycle. In our society, invaded by engines and enslaved to speed, this is a luxury that makes us feel free, happy and relaxed; it's a way that helps re-establish a relation with oneself and with nature. Thus the trip is a moment of cultural growth, a way to move that is more careful towards the values of the territory and more respectful of its integrity, a way that helps rediscover new landscapes, forgotten and astonishing. This explains the growing interest in the so-called 'smooth mobility'. Italy has hundreds of kilometers of embankment roads and towpaths..."

Thus runs the introduction to Umbria's *Green Heart of Italy* booklet that focuses on the 60-mile long Spoleto to Assisi "Greenway."

Any attempt to change our lifestyle and go more slowly must involve forsaking cars for some of the time and learning to explore new places and new countries by other means. Fortunately, to cycle in Italy is no sacrifice—quite the opposite. The bike gives you new freedoms to explore towns and countryside. Picking up a bicycle even for just a few days will add enormously to your Italian holiday.

And you won't be alone. Wherever it is level you will find numerous everyday cyclists. In the flat lands of the Po Valley—in Mantua, in Modena, in Parma, in Cremona and countless other cities of the plains—you will find the bicycle a standard way of travelling. Ferrara has one of the highest levels of cycling in all of Europe, with a third of everyday journeys in town made by bike. Recreational trails stretch out to the Delta and the Adriatic.

It is usually easy to hire bikes in Italy, and your hotel or the local tourist office should be able to help. For me there is no better way to see a town than to drop off my luggage, jump on a bike and wander freely around the squares and streets. The bicycle gives you range and freedom, is so much less tiring than walking and is an efficient way of carrying things. You also quickly become integrated into the place.

One thing that strikes me about cycling in Italy is how much time I spend just standing around in piazzas, leaning on my bike, talking to people and absorbing the atmosphere. Another remarkable thing is the number of women cycling: women shopping, with children, elderly women too, and even women in extraordinary furs. Compare that to the more macho cycling culture in Britain.

In some towns you will find a sophisticated system of bike hire from stands scattered around different areas, and most operate on nominal rates for the first hour or so. You can make a journey from one place to the other, walk around the museum, church or park and then pick up another bike for your onward journey. Parma has a fine example of this scheme. It also has a system for trading in motorbikes for electric bikes, which, of course, helps to reduce noise and pollution in the city.

As well as enabling you to get around towns, a bike can take you further afield. In Italy you will find quiet roads and, amazingly, drivers far more courteous than those in the UK. Traffic-free routes are often beautiful as well as interesting. From Lecco along canal towpaths and riverbanks to Milan you use works engineered by Leonardo;

from Peschiera di Garda the floodbank paths take you through the remains of the lakes guarding Mantua. The railway cycle path from Calalzo to Cortina through the Dolomites to Dobbiaco is one of the most memorable off-road routes in Europe. If you are fond of tunnels then the magnificent route from Spoleto toward Norcia will be hard to beat when it is finished, especially as its numerous *galleria*, spiralling inside the mountain, will remain unlit to preserve the atmosphere of the line!

Taking your bike on public transport is relatively easy, too and the use of a bus or train to take you up some of the bigger mountains is wise. For example, if you take public transport from Verona to Brixen, you can reach the wonderful and largely downhill route from the Brenner Pass all the way back down to Lake Garda. There, you can join one of the northernmost sections of the Ciclopista del Sole, Italy's national route that stretches all the way to Calabria and then carries on to Sicily.

You can usually find good information about each cycling route locally. Tourist information offices should be able to give you maps and details of bike hire centers. A few Italian websites do give cycle route information, notably www.ediciclo.it (for Emilia-Romagna in bicicletta— Touring Club Italiano); www.turismo.pesarourbino.it (for Pesaro and Urbino cycle tour itineraries); www. bicitalia.org; and, best of all, www.vasentiero.it (for numerous detailed guides, some in English, by Albano Marcarini who covers walking and cycling routes with equal knowledge and enthusiasm).

John Grimshaw, CBE, President of Sustrans

Italy by train

If you're sick of being herded around airports and have half a conscience about your carbon footprint, travelling around Italy by train is for you. It is not always cheaper, but if you regard the getting there as part of the holiday you'll add a new dimension to your break.

Trips from Turin

Head to Levanto and the coastal towns of the Cinque Terre. It's an exhilarating destination for families as there are beaches, restaurants next to the sea, high and low coast paths for walking and boat and train trips from one town to the other.

Culture vultures could head down the west coast line, then hop to Arezzo, Siena, Pisa or Florence. Journeys are cheap and if you've tried to drive around the hinterlands of these cities, you'll appreciate that this is the stress-free option.

Trips from Venice

Head round the coast to Trieste passing the glistening Castello di Miramare, built by Maximilian for his young bride Carlotta. Jan Morris's exquisite book, *Trieste and the Meaning of Nowhere*, should be your companion. When there you can hop on bike, boat or funicular railway. On your return journey to Venice, stop off at Treviso, Castel Franco Veneto, Vicenza, Padua and Verona for shopping and art.

Trips from Parma

Mantua, Cremona, Ferrara, Faenza and Bologna line the Po Valley and all have a rich heritage of producing quintessential Italian produce: Parma ham, balsamic vinegar, parmesan. "Eurostar Italia" (not the Eurostar), "Intercity" and "Regionale" are

the trains you will need; Regionale is cheap and most open to accommodating bikes.

Trips from Sulmona

Reach Sulmona, the center of Italy's rail network, via Turin or Rome. Both routes reward you with a magnificent entrance into the mountainous Abruzzo. From Sulmona you can reach mountain walks by taking a bus to Scanno. Foodies should take the bus from Sulmona to Pacentro for lunch at Caldoro, one of Italy's most celebrated Slow restaurants. It's a pleasant 1.5-hour amble back to Sulmona through green lanes, fig groves and allotments.

The Terni line speeds you up to Umbria. Villages before L'Aquila, along the Aterno valley, are worth alighting for: Raiano for the San Venanzo Gullies, Fagnano-Campana for the Stiffe caves. Follow the steps of St. Francis by walking between the stations of Contigliano and Gréccio.

Trips from Perugia

If you are staying near Trevi or Spello, take the Umbrian Regional branch line from Perugia's Ponte S Giovanni station to Piero della Francesca's hometown of Sansepolcro to see his earliest known work, an altarpiece. Fit in a brief stop at Città di Castello to climb the campanile then take an espresso in the buzzy bar below. Also worthwhile is the walk over the hills from Asissi back to Spello; buy a bus ticket at Asissi station's newspaper shop for the short trip up to the start point.

Trips from Rome

Head south from Rome's Termini station to reach Naples within 2 hours; skip the queues by buying tickets in advance. From Naples, avoiding the hawkers and card tricksters within the station, change onto the independent Sorrento railway for Pompeii, Herculaneum, Vesuvius and Capri. Best of all, you avoid the heavily trafficked peninsular road. Or you can go direct to Palermo in Sicily and get an eyeful of beautiful Calabrian beaches before your train shuffles on to the ferry at Italy's toe and you cross the Straits of Messina.

Useful info

Get your hands on a European Rail Timetable, available in UK bookshops, and a printed version of the Trenitalia timetable from Italy's main stations. Tourist offices have bus and train timetables and info on walks and bike hire. www.raileurope.co.uk is the place to book train tickets to Italy; or to book tickets after discussion call + 44 (0)844 8485848. www.trenitalia.com is the place to book trains within Italy. The website www.seat61.com is popular with many travellers.

Sue Learner

Place index

Andria
200   Lama di Luna Biomasseria
Arezzo
116   Agriturismo Rendola Riding
Bibbona
144   Podere le Mezzelune
Borgo San Lorenzo
88   Casa Palmira
Bovara di Trevi
182   I Mandorli Agriturismo
Buonconvento
136   Podere Salicotto
Carpineti
50   B & B Valferrara
Casperia
186   La Torretta
Castel del Piano
174   Villa Aureli
Castellina in Chianti
128   Fattoria Tregole
Castiglion Fiorentino
120   Relais San Pietro in Polvano
Colle di Buggiano
72   Antica Casa 'Le Rondini'
Faédis
46   Casa del Grivò
Figline Valdarno
108   Locanda Casanuova
Fratta Todina
178   La Palazzetta del Vescovo
Greve in Chianti
104   Fattoria Viticcio Agriturismo
Gubbio
166   Locanda del Gallo
Isola del Giglio
152   Il Pardini's Hermitage
Levanto
58   La Sosta di Ottone III
Loro Ciuffenna
112   Odina Agriturismo
Marconia di Pisticci
216   San Teodoro Nuovo Agriturismo
Massa Lubrense
196   Azienda Agricola Le Tore
Mola di Bari
204   Masseria Serra dell'Isola

Montaione
92   Fattoria Barbialla Nuova
Montefiridolfi
100   Azienda Agricola Il Borghetto
Ostuni
208   Masseria Il Frantoio
212   Masseria Impisi
Pierantonio
170   Casa San Gabriel
Pistoia
76   Tenuta di Pieve a Celle
Radda in Chianti
124   La Locanda
Rocca di Roffeno
54   La Piana dei Castagni Agriturismo
Roccatederighi
148   Pieve di Caminino
Sagrata di Fermignano
162   Locanda della Valle Nuova
Salina, Aeolian Islands
224   Hotel Signum
San Quirico d'Orcia
140   Il Rigo
Siena
132   Frances' Lodge
Stazzano
26   La Traversina Agriturismo
Taormina
220   Hotel Villa Schuler
Tavarnelle Val di Pesa
96   Sovigliano
Tortona
30   Agriturismo Cascina Folletto
Toscolano Maderno
34   Agriturismo Cervano B & B
Udine
42   Agriturismo La Faula
Verona
38   Ca' del Rocolo
Vicchio del Mugello
80   Le Due Volpi
84   Villa Campestri
Vorno
68   Villa Michaela